The Ballplayer's Son

About the Author

Dell Franklin, always a practicing athlete, tended bar most of his life, with occasional cab driving, a stint as a riverboat storekeeper, and futile stabs at waiting tables, sales and construction. At one time he published the *Rogue Voice*, a monthly literary journal. He has written for *Easy Reader*, *New Times*, *Coldtype*, and currently pens a biweekly column for *Cal Coast News* in San Luis Obispo county in California. His book, "Life on the Mississippi, 1969," was published in 2021. Dell lives in Cayucos, California.

Cover photo: Hollywood Stars' Ted Beard slides spikes-high into Murray Franklin of the Los Angeles Angels on August 2, 1953, triggering perhaps the biggest brawl in professional baseball history. (David Eskenazi Collection)

The Ballplayer's Son

Following the Footsteps and Escaping the Shadow of Big Moe Franklin

Dell Franklin

SUMMER
GAME
BOOKS

ISBN: 978-1-955398-08-4 (print)

ISBN: 978-1-955398-09-1 (ebook)

For information about permission, bulk purchases, or additional distribution, write to

Summer Game Books
P. O. Box 818
South Orange, NJ 07079

or contact the publisher at www.summergamebooks.com

*For John Willingham, literary guru, and
Texas-tough drinking buddy.*

Introduction

My mother always urged me to write about my father, and when I asked her why, she said, "Because he is different than most men, and he is especially different from the other players he played with in his career. Oh, his teammates loved him, and he fit in, because he always managed to find something good in just about everybody, and he is the kind of man people trust without knowing why."

I always felt I was different, too. How many other children at the age of seven got to stay up past bedtime to watch their father come to bat on an old black and white TV? How many kids had children hanging out in front of their home hoping to see and maybe meet and get an autograph on a program or baseball from a man who played in the Pacific Coast League? It was the early 1950s, when the Major Leagues were far away and the brand of ball in the PCL was so sound and entertaining and spirited that their fans were as crazed as those in New York or any other big-league town.

And very few kids ever got to meet let alone be shaped by Great Depression/WWII-era baseball players in the professional baseball clubhouse, dugout and ball field. When you are a child, you are a sponge, and since professional baseball players at every level, from the lowest bushes to the big leagues, are the worst gossips in the world, you hear it all and remember just about everything you hear.

This was a time when the NBA was largely unknown to most sports fans, the NFL was just emerging, and baseball and boxing prevailed. Our heroes were Mickey Mantle, Ted Williams, and Sugar Ray Robinson. And to me, anybody who played baseball was somebody I wanted to know about, and since Dad was a riotously funny raconteur of baseball stories, I begged him to tell me stories over and over and over until I could mimic his voice, vernacular and sense of detail.

Part of this book is in his voice. The other part is the result of being embedded in baseball so deeply, so mindlessly, so obsessively from age 7 on that nothing else was allowed to enter, as I, in a sense, tried to be my father all over again.

But that is only part of the story. My father, though a happy, thriving man, was profoundly frustrated about his baseball career, which lasted from 1937 until 1953. As much as he loved baseball, by which I mean the game itself, which he loved "like the most beautiful woman in the world who never loves you back," he despised the powers-that-be that ran organizations, felt he should have been in the Big Leagues sooner, felt without making excuses that being a Jew worked against him, and in retirement had no use for the game, could barely watch it; his only involvement was coaching the local American Legion team to championships that had always escaped them before he arrived.

My dad was a fearsome man, a hard and demanding coach, yet his players worshipped and would go to hell and back for him. He was a successful businessman after his retirement, a family man, a man whom so many men called when they were in trouble or broke or on the verge of tragedy. Yet through it all he carried a certain bitterness toward baseball because it had been so important to him, so all-consuming and life-possessing, so indispensable to his pride and ego. What could have been, but was not, always gnawed at him.

So this is his story, a baseball story, and my story, a writer's story, the ballplayer's son.

Dell Franklin, May 2023

The Ballplayer's Son

Sitting with Dad on the bench with the Hollywood Stars.

Playing Pepper with the Pros

Gilmore Field, Hollywood, California. I sit with my mother a few feet behind the screen and the field and we are surrounded by the wives and children of my father's teammates—the Gene Handley's, the Mike Sandlock's, Chuck Stevens', Jack Salveson's. We are an intimate island unto ourselves, an extension of the royalty spotlighted on the lush green field below. Murray 'Big Moe' Franklin, my dad, walks up to the plate and spreads his legs, digging his rear right foot into the dirt. He pumps his bat twice before settling it on his right shoulder, staring at the pitcher. There is a sense he is relaxed and sure of himself, and yet he is coiled when the pitcher goes into his elongated windup. He lifts his front foot slightly and steps forward as the pitcher unleashes a ball that spits past Dad with a violent hiss that makes me cringe and crashes into the catcher's mitt and the umpire raises his right hand and bellows "STEE-RIKE!" I hear voices from the stands:

"Hey Franklin you take the good ones and swing at the bad ones! No wonder you ain't hittin' yer weight! YER A BUM!"

"You ain't got a hit in two weeks FRANKLIN—YER WASHED UP!"

That is my first memory of baseball, and it is as if that was my first day alive in this world. Everything bright technicolor as if I'd just hatched from an egg or emerged from a cocoon. I knew nothing else at the time. I did not understand that my dad was in a terrible slump and local sports writers were excoriating his performance as well as the Hollywood Stars front office and manager Fred Haney, who'd gone out on a limb to sign him to the roster for a stretch drive in chase of a pennant. Dad had been injured and suspended from baseball for a year for jumping the big leagues in 1946 to play in Mexico. He'd been just recently reinstated and, at thirty-five, he was not and would never be the ballplayer he'd been before the war.

Dad wasn't one to stay in shape when out of the game. Trying to make ends meet after moving into a tract home in Compton, he worked sparingly for coolie wages at JC Penny's in the sporting goods department, and his college degree in Physical Education allowed him to substitute coach in grammar schools. But our family survived mainly on what was left of his Mexican League bonus, most of which went to the house.

In time, Dad took me to the clubhouse, a private sanctum suspicious of outsiders, where acceptance had to be earned, even by me, a seven-year-old. Grown men ambled about half naked, revealing pale legs and torsos, only the necks, forearms and faces baked dark by the sun. They were not heavily muscled, though strong in the arms and legs – men who moved with a graceful assurance uncommon among men on the streets. Smells of liniment wafted from the cramped trainer's room and neutralized individual odors of sweat, flatus and sour feet.

Big Moe, second row, second from the right, with his Mexican League team in 1946.

I came to feel a part of the clubhouse. Dad gave me an old glove and the clubhouse attendant, a Japanese man named Nobe, restrung it with rawhide, oiled and placed it on my hand, a large swatch of flimsy leather into which I worked my tiny fingers, flapping the glove like a duck flapping its wings, then pounding the pocket with my fist and then a beat-up practice ball. Soon I was bouncing the ball on the concrete floor and catching it, then firing it against the cement walls, snaring bouncers as players dodged out of the way, until Dad ordered me to quit tearing up the goddam clubhouse and scaring the hell out of everybody.

Johnny O'Neill and Gene Handley sort of adopted me and gave me the nickname of 'Little Meat.' They tossed balls across the clubhouse floor for me – and I was a fetching dog pouncing for his masters, imaginary tail wagging.

The oldest player on the Stars, a rotund relief pitcher with lim-itless patience and a passel of kids, the beloved 'Kewpie' Barrett, taught me to tie my shoe laces, an assignment handed him by my father after his own effort failed. "Your daddy makes you a little nervous," he said. Barrett spent a batting practice in the dugout making me tie my laces over and over until I got it down. When I took time off from that exercise it was for a trek to the drinking fountain, which proved an obstacle course of players spurting tobacco juice at me. They sat on the bench working on large chaws, aiming and arching their salvos of dirty brown spit, building puddles beneath them on the cement floor littered with Beechnut wrappers, gum wrappers, wadded gum, regular spit, cigarette butts, clods of red clay, old line-up cards, pages from *The Sporting News*...

"Hey Meat, wanna plugga tobacky? Grow hair on yer chest."

Dad warned me that if I chewed tobacco my teeth would fall out and I'd be ugly like the tobacco chewers on the Stars. He flashed his pearly whites in a smug grin and showed me his pack of Spearmint. "Keeps the mouth clean and wet."

"Now ya can kiss the girls like a lover boy, Little Meat," a player goaded.

When the stars donned shorty uniforms, Dad had the club make me one. He showed me how to roll my long sanitary socks to keep them from slipping to my ankles (which looks bush), without using a garter, which Dad claimed cuts off circulation in your feet. Over and over Dad rolled his own sanitary socks into his stirrups and then did the same for me. I had skinny legs, and when I rolled my own socks they immediately drooped to my ankles. Dad grew impatient with my ineptitude; and finally outfielder Herb Gorman slipped me heavy rubber bands when Dad wasn't looking.

After weeks of begging Dad to coax management into allowing me onto the field during batting practice, Haney agreed, providing I stayed deep in center field with infielders Handley, O'Neill, Buddy Hicks, Jim Baxes, and Dad. Here they played pepper, which involved one man hitting the ball back to team-mates who stood perhaps ten yards away, fielding each ball they tossed to the hitter, who placed the ball firmly, going from play-er to player. Each player got to hit – all exercising precise con-trol of the bat. The fielding and throwing were of a particular rhythm that picked up speed and acrobatic flourish as the game gained momentum.

They were doggedly competitive, bantering, goading, gambling for sodas and beers. From time to time, to break up the magi-cal domination of an exceptionally adept hitter, they lobbed a ball wide or zoomed it low, and the hitter was always prepared. They were like magician jugglers. Flipping balls behind their backs with uncanny accuracy. Faking throws. Handing off. They laughed and joshed and spat, and while doing these things they groomed me to field, and only field, instructing me to stay low and keep on the balls of my feet and make sure my ass was down, glove open and out in front, throwing hand perched above the glove in case I needed to bare-hand a bad hop or a boot. At first they slapped me soft grounders and made a fuss over my snares. But soon they recognized my intensity and hit balls harder, putting a little spin on them, and then it became a challenge for me to flag down every ball, wanting more and more.

One day Dad instructed me to choke up on a smaller bat and hit pepper. "Don't try and place the ball like we do. Just watch the ball into your bat and meet it, like a bunt, but hit it a little harder than a bunt." His teammates encouraged me. So I stood against the fence and eagle-eyed each ball lobbed to me and met it with the barrel and heard the clean sweet knock and watched the ball jump in a straight line or bounce in front of the fielders who snatched the ball and showed it to me before flipping it overhand on a slow arc so I could adjust and knock it back. I grew more confidant with each pitch. They were elat-ed with my progress, my father beaming. I became more and more adept at the bat, now trying to place each pitch to a new player, going down the line just like my mentors, who seemed to be accepting me unconditionally into their established domain.

Walking off the field after pepper, Dad placed his arm around me as we approached the dugout, which was mobbed by kids hanging over nearby railings wielding fifteen-cent scorecards for autographs. Their eyes suddenly switched to me, hawk-like, curious, unforgiving. Dad and my mentors signed the kids' cards, asking them if they wanted to be ballplayers when they grew up, patting their heads fondly when they exclaimed that they did. Then the players headed for the batting cage or their positions on the field, and I found myself eye to eye with the knothole kids. A hot sinking feeling flashed through my stomach. I nodded at them. None of them nodded back.

"Who's that?" one kid grumbled, eyes black agates.

"Ain't he cute in his little shorties."

"You a sissy boy?"

"He ain't no ballplayer."

"Fuck I ain't," I replied.

BIG MOE

The 1920s—A Fighting Jew

I grew up in Chicago, northwest side. Walking down those streets, every kid gave you the dirty look like he wanted to take a poke at you. After a while you had no choice but to fight. I found out I could scrap, but I was outnumbered because our neighborhood was almost all Poles and Germans, and I was the only Jew. The Poles and Germans were terrible haters, and that's what I grew up with every single day of my youth. They jumped me on the way to school, spit on my sisters, called them sheenies and kikes and Jew bitches. And I was Jew boy. So I went after them and I took some beatings because some of those kids were bigger and older than me, and when that happened I got mean, and I guess I've been that way all my life, the kind of guy not to take anything lying down and has to get his revenge. The kind of guy your mother says has a chip on his shoulder twenty-four hours a day. Your mother is nothing like my mother. My mother was a fighter. She was the oldest and her father wanted a boy and treated her like a boy, put her to work before she was nine years old, because that's what they did in those days, and she never stopped hustling and working her whole life.

At first my mother was angry and half crazy when I came home beat up and bloody, my clothes torn up. She wanted me to stay home, but I couldn't stay home because I wanted to play ball in the sandlots and I didn't want anybody telling me where I could and could not go. And after a while, those Polish and German mothers were dragging their kids up to our doorstep and showing my mother the bloody noses and knocked out teeth and gouged eyes. My mother stood on the porch and told them if they didn't want their kids getting the hell beaten out of them to stop calling me a Jew boy and a kike. You have to understand those times. The Jew baiting and hating in Chicago was very bad, and there was this belief that Jews wouldn't fight back, that we were bookworms and pussies, and to a certain extent the few Jewish kids I knew didn't want to fight, but I did, and I was a target. I developed a certain look that let people know I was ready to fight at the slightest provocation. I waited for those kids who were the worst bullies and bigots and went after them and gave them vicious beatings they'd never forget. I established myself as a fighting Jew.

The Clubhouse and the Dugout

"Make sure to wear yer cup, Meat. Gotta protect the family jewels."

"You a lover boy, Meat? Got a girlfriend?"

"I ain't got no girlfriend."

"Heard you like to kiss the girls, Meat."

"Bullshit. I ain't kissin' no girls."

"You will, Meat. Hey, kid, you a lover or a fighter?"

"A fighter!"

I sat at Dad's stall. The Hollywood clubhouse was spacious, clean, bright, as good as most big league clubhouses according to Dad. There was enough room for two of us, but I preferred sitting on his traveling trunk working on his equipment while he signed autographs or played cards. There was a table where players pulled up folding chairs to play cards or sign baseballs, bats, or black-and-white glossies of themselves. Everything in the clubhouse was organized by Nobe, who was indispensable to the players, seeing to their every need. Nobe treated everyone with kindness and respect.

"How you, little Franklin? You want soda pop?"

Just off the manager's office was a big red Coca Cola cooler with beer and soft drinks chilling on blocks of ice. Nothing was free. On the wall above the cooler was a checklist of the entire roster of players and coaches, and every time one of them pulled a bottle out he checked his name. If I shoved my little paw into the painfully icy water to withdraw a Nehi or Delaware Punch, I checked Dad's name. Nobe took note, smiling.

"You smart like your daddy."

Dad was one of the few college graduates on a team where most of his teammates began their careers ahead of him by signing before or after high school and kicking around in the minors, while Dad starred at the University of Illinois. His first real year of pro ball was at Beckley, West Virginia in the Mountain State League, where he hit .439, the highest average that year in all of organized baseball, earning him a silver bat exactly like the two given to the players with the highest averages in the American and National leagues. So Dad was a phenom, quickly moving up to Beaumont in the Texas League, Detroit's toughest proving ground for the big team, where he first appeared in 1941, already twenty-seven years old.

"Hey Moe, the kid's a phee-nom!" That was dark, burly Jim Baxes, 'The Greek,' an affable jokester and member of the pepper crew, one of my favorites, along with Gene Handley who never teased me with the 'lover boy' tag or called me 'Little Moe.' Gene referred to me as 'Digger O'Dell,' a handle I liked.

A few stalls down from Dad was Jack Salveson, who, according to Dad, was a legendary drinker with few rivals in the game. "Rudy York and Jimmie Foxx, they could put it away too. When I played at Little Rock we had a catcher named Tony Rensa. After every game he went to a little bar downtown and drank close to a case of beer, then went to his room and went to bed and showed up the next day at the park bright and bushy- tailed like he hadn't had a drop."

Hollywood Stars team picture. Murray Franklin is top row, second from the right.

When thick, balding Salveson, cap low over his eyes, pitched, sweat popped from his face and streamed down his neck. No matter how cold the evening, his uniform was soaked through by the middle innings. He changed sweatshirts at least once a game. If it was a warm afternoon and Salveson pitched, he was a brutal, almost pitiful sight as he lugged around through the late innings huffing and puffing. Salveson had an elaborate yet economical windup, throwing hard sinking stuff that hitters beat into the ground; a control pitcher, he often went nine innings on less than a hundred pitches. His mechanics put very little stress on his arm. He'd pitched in nearly 100 games in the big leagues and played for nearly twenty years, a mild and gentle man who drove to the ballpark with Dad and was one of Dad's closest friends on the team.

After each game he pitched, Salveson sat at his stall in only his jockstrap and drank six beers in about thirty minutes. The first beer went down in one amazing swig. After several beers he'd trudge to the shower where he remained under the steaming hot pulverizing spray for a very long time, exposing his right shoulder to the water, returning to his stall red as a lobster, towel around his waist. Nobe would hand him another cold one. Then he and Dad and Gorman and Sandlock and Handley would gather and rehash every single play of the game. They drank beer. These were pre-war ballplayers, meat and potato eaters, older than most of their teammates, and this was their tradition: Get to the park early and discuss the opposition, play cards, joke around, and stay after the game for the rehash. They were as reluctant to leave the clubhouse as they were eager to enter it, and my mother claimed that those men were the happiest in all of America and wouldn't trade places with anyone.

I watched, listened, steeping myself in their every move and jargon until I was a cloned amalgam of every ritual, whim and habit a pro picks up in his career. Dad's habitual ritual at the plate became my ritual exactly.

"Wearin' your cup out there, Digger O'Dell?"

All pitchers and infielders wore protective steel cups in their jockstraps. I quit wearing mine because it jabbed and chafed my thighs, but then one day a pepper grounder took a wild hop and popped me in the groin and I went down writhing in pain, and merciless ballplayers had a big time riding me for being too dumb to wear my cup. When I explained to Dad that the steel cup cut my thighs, he bought me a plastic cup cushioned on the edges with foam rubber, a "pussy cup."

"You don't listen to those guys, you plenny tough," Nobe told me. And Frankie Jacobs, the trainer, nodded. Without Frankie Jacobs the Stars would have had trouble fielding a team. Dad always tipped he and Nobe a sawbuck, unlike most of the players who came from parts of the country where money was scarce and food was fought over and tipping was alien to them. Dad spent a lot of time on the rubbing table while the diminutive Jacobs kneaded his muscles, joints and limbs. Being in the war, and playing so many years, his shoulders and knees were rickety. Often his knee swelled to the size of cantaloupe. He pulled muscles, and he played, Jacobs wrapping the discolored areas tightly with Ace bandages. Most unsightly were Dad's variety of 'strawberries' from hard slides; along his hips, buttocks and upper thighs were ugly abrasions, red jelly welts scabbed over and torn open again each time he slid. Frankie treated them with ointments to keep down the hot pain, covering them with compresses held tightly with white adhesive tape, and he played, and after each game Frankie ripped the compresses off his hairy skin and Dad never made a face. Both men winked at me, sharing secret pride in the endurance of pain.

"Gotta be tough if you wanna be a ballplayer, kid," Jacobs said. "Your dad, he's as tough as they come. You grow up half as tough as Big Moe, you'll be a helluva man and a ballplayer."

Dad laughed. "Dell's tough, Frankie. He eats nails for breakfast."

I managed to worm my way into the dugout during games, claiming I couldn't stand sitting with a bunch of "yakkety women." Management felt I was too young to be a bat boy, but as long as I behaved myself I could sit in the dugout. There, I felt part of the action. I wore my Hollywood Stars uniform. After the game I showered with the players. They all had individual methods of lathering up and toweling off. They spent a lot of time primping. They whipped soap brushes into cups of lather and carefully applied it, then scraped their faces smooth with Gillette blades advertised on TV boxing matches. They smacked on aftershave lotion and cologne, dabbed on deodorant. They were natty dressers and experts at folding neckties. Each player seemed to regard himself as cock of the walk, and especially Dad, who was once voted by the local press as the 'best dressed player in town.'

Gorman was a persnickety groomer. He was Dad's young Jewish protégé and roomy on the road (they wore bow ties), and engaged to a knockout named Rosalie, who sat with my mother and the other wives during games. Gorman always invited me to sit with him at his stall. He smelled strongly of liniment, and was forever advising me.

"You can be a fighter and a lover, Dell, just like your dad."

"Dad's no lover boy."

"Sure he is. Like me. You will be too when you meet the right gal." He watched me bone the bat. "Push down hard on the meat of the barrel, Dell. See where the wood is loose and dented? That's from hitting the ball solid." Gorman had two good years in a row, hitting over .300, driving in 100 runs. "We call that the sweet spot. You know you're getting good when you keep hitting the sweet spot. I've gone two months without breaking that lucky bat." He rapped his knuckles on the side of the wooden stall. "That's why I choke up an inch or two, so I won't bust the handle. When I finally break this bat I'll nail and tape it up and give it to you cuz you've done such a fine job of boning it. Okay, that's enough. Let's go to work on my glove."

Like Dad and most players, Herb Gorman used a broken-in, flabby glove during games, and broke in a backup glove during practice. Dad always shoved an old ball into a new glove, bound it with twine and tossed it into a tub of water and let it soak a couple days to soften the leather and take the stiffness out of it. Then he rubbed it with a lot of neatsfoot oil. I'd become an expert oiler of gloves and boner of bats, and Nobe was pleased that certain players allowed me to do these jobs from time to time, though I was not allowed to touch anybody's gear unless asked to, while Nobe was free to do what he wanted.

On the way from the clubhouse to the dugout, I walked with the players up the wood-slatted ramp below the stands in the darkness latticed with cracks of light slicing through dust motes sifting down from myriad cobwebs, rotting timbers, stale beer accumulation, dead rodents, decades of trapped cigarette smoke, leaky urinals, human vapors, and all of it combining to produce the familiar stench of a ballpark as we clack clacked toward the glimmer of daylight that was the gateway to the emerald green field shimmering beneath the bright blue sky.

I took my usual spot toward the far end of the dugout, away from the hive of activity up front by the drinking fountain and bat rack, where Fred Haney and his coaches Jo Jo White and Big John Fitzpatrick entered a world in which their faces turned into stern, beady-eyed masks as they delivered signs, whispered to each other, conferred with players, yelled at umpires and opposing players, chewed, spit, cussed, scratched, kicked at debris on the filthy floor or clapped their hands in approval of a play well done. Bench players joined the intense transformation as soon as the first ball was pitched, composing a chorus of amusing, and sometimes lethal bench jockeying.

"Hey pitch, what snake pit were you in last night? We can smell you from here! Yer eyes look like piss holes in the snow!"

Nothing encouraged a bench jockey more than a player visibly distracted by relentless carping. "Hey Rabbit Ears! Got a red ass?"

Among these men, the desire to win bordered on psychotic. Even when competing at cards in the clubhouse, they kicked over chairs when they lost. If the ball club was on a losing streak they were all sour, glum and nearly unapproachable, and I stayed away. On the bench, Dad warned me to look, listen, learn and keep my mouth shut. I was a guest. Though it was not easy to sit still and be quiet.

I couldn't help but observe differences between infielders, out-fielders and especially pitchers. Dad said pitchers were not normal and the bullpen was a world unto itself. Pitchers were his enemy, always had to be the center of attention during games, only worked four or five days, and were the worst cheaters.

"If you are a pitcher's best friend and get traded to another team and have to face him, you are the first player he will throw at. Most deplorable, they are trying to drive you out of the game and starve your family."

"Even Salveson?"

Dad nodded gravely. "Let me tell yah something, Dell: Every single man who puts on the uniform is out for himself. They want your job. You can be friends, and I've made some good friends in this game, but we're all fighting to survive, just like everybody else in this country, only we're worse."

On this Saturday afternoon both teams were on each other. The air was charged with the tension of an impending brawl. Dad and his teammates held old grudges against certain players. Everybody was on the top steps of both dugouts, hollering, ready to surge out onto the field. Finally the umpires, whom the Hollywood players had been needling and calling "Horseshit" and "Blind" throughout the game, warned both benches to put a stop to it.

This only provoked the players on the Stars to become personal and vicious in their abuse. Even a squirt like myself could see that the umpires were actually human – and turning red in the neck at the storm of insults coming from the dugout. Most of the vileness was directed at a block-jawed sourpuss first base ump whose intelligence and manhood were brutally savaged as, evidently, he'd called a horseshit game behind the plate the night before. Finally he couldn't take any more and moved several steps toward our dugout, pointed a warning finger and issued a retaliatory salvo at the bench – which only served to ignite the wronged players, who now leaped at the dugout screen like a pack of wild dogs, cursing and insulting the ump with caustic profanity.

"Who the fuck paid YOU off last night? You goddam blind Tom!" roared my father.

The ump immediately ejected him with a thumb.

Dad, whom this umpire called out the night before on a low outside pitch that Dad insisted was a foot off the plate, exploded from the dugout, ripping his cap off, and headed for the umpire at full speed, miraculously stopping inches from the ump's face and, jaw to jaw, his head bobbing so close to the ump's I feared they'd butt heads, Dad cursed him with such startling ferocity and profanity I found myself recoiling. The ump turned away, but Dad was on him, implacable. They moved in a comical circle. And then Haney was on the field wedging himself between Dad and the ump. The Stars crowd booed lustily. Haney blew a gasket and tossed his cap and kicked it and went nose to nose with the sourpuss. Then Fitzpatrick was between Haney and Dad, and the ump tossed both of them. But the rhubarb went on and on, as the other umpires came over to stand between the players and the sourpuss, and finally the three ousted penitents strode to the dugout and hurled upon the field catcher's masks, shin guards, chest protectors, bats, balls, towels – and the crowd booed and hissed while the opposing team stood calmly on the top steps of their dugout, amused, some laughing, for they had dominated the series and were eight runs up.

When order was restored, Dad, Haney and Fitzpatrick retired to the clubhouse, and a squeaky voice chirped at the umpire who stood arms folded behind first base: "Goddam blind Tom, open your eyes you fuckin red ass!" Gorman and Sandlock quickly stashed me between them.

The umpire marched to the dugout and peered in. "What the hell was THAT? A bird?" His tiny eyes roved down the bench in a severe squint. Nobody said a word. Then he spotted me. "Who's that goddam kid?"

"It's Franklin's kid," Sandlock piped. He took my cap off and placed it on his head like a beanie and pulled his own cap down over my ears. "He's a criminal – like his old man."

"Get him OUT-A here! No kids in the dugout!" He jerked his thumb at me, "You. Out of the goddam game. Get that little mouse in the clubhouse, or so help me God I'll run the whole goddam team."

The players hustled me out of the dugout and down into the clubhouse, all of them laughing and roughing my head. When Dad found out I'd been kicked out of the dugout for cussing the umpire, he growled and told me I was finished sitting in the dugout, and if I continued to be a pain in the ass he'd take away my clubhouse privileges and make me sit with the women, in the stands. He was still tongue-lashing me when one of the pitchers, stocky Pete Mondorff, a quiet ex-football player, walked by and patted my ass. "Little Meat," he said, "Don't take any guff from those umps."

Later, John Lindell exclaimed, "Kill the umpire, Meat!"

And Handley: "There he is, Digger O'Dell, chip off the old block."

A Mother's Warning

My mother felt I was becoming too "one-dimensional," and in an effort to see if I might be interested in things other than baseball, attempted to get me to take up a musical instrument. After two lessons I was kicked out of accordion school. I suffered through the Cub Scouts, wanting no part of going to the mountains where there was no baseball. Next was Hebrew school, where I was again kicked out by an outraged rabbi who informed my parents I behaved like an anti-Semite when I pummeled studious fellow Jewish kids; they decided to put off Hebrew school indefinitely.

Mother was also alarmed at my profanity, my swaggering about, my teasing her when Dad was gone on the road, once chasing her around with a dead mouse. She slapped me for the first time and cried when I used the word "nigger." She washed my mouth out with soap, explained to me the ugly sin of using that word, and made me promise to never use it again. She related the history of our country treating Black people as slaves, of humiliating them, stealing their pride and spirit.

Mother worried that I wouldn't be well-rounded. Already a teacher had recommended I see a child psychiatrist because I disrupted class and craved attention. I was too aggressively competitive. She took me to a lady shrink who had me draw whatever came into my mind. I drew two baseball players, one a giant of a man, the other a small child.

My mother and father quarreled over his influence on me. She tried to convince him to keep me out of the clubhouse and away from the crude ballplayers. But Dad insisted I was just like him when he was a kid and he'd turned out okay, and besides, Dad added, taking me away from the ballpark would break my heart.

Fourth grade at Emerson Elementary School, 1952. I'm second row, third from the left, probably thinking about baseball.

I got my way. I'd sort of become the Hollywood Stars mascot. Over the winter Dad hired Handley, a carpenter, Maltzburger, an electrician, and Sandlock, a roofer, to build a den connecting the garage to the master bedroom of our house in Compton. All three of those men had their individual trades but could do anything when it came to building a home, and since Dad was starting a small shoe findings supply business in the garage, they were all occupied, though Dad was not allowed to help build the den because he was so inept they referred to him as 'Six Fingers McFiddick' and sent him on runs to the hardware store and lumber yard with a prepared list so he wouldn't come back with the wrong supplies.

Dad claimed no team he'd ever played for was as close as the Stars. They held team parties. Big John Lindell had the biggest, best parties.

Lindell was the size of a coke machine and as irresistibly engaging as he was big. "Hey, Little Meat, come on over here and say hello to Big John." It was almost as if I'd hurt his feelings if I didn't come over. He scooped me up in hands you could sit in, held me eye level and chucked my chin. His clutch hitting and .500 average in the 1947 World Series for the Yankees was a feat nobody on the club had come close to achieving. Still, Dad reminded me that Lindell had his best years during the war "while the best players were away fighting for the country." Lindell walked, talked and carried himself with a swagger. A similar swagger illuminated all professional baseball players as special beings placed on pedestals to be admired, like famous generals and statesmen. Yet among them was an undeclared pecking order, and since Lindell was such a big man with a huge outgoing personality and he'd had those big years with the gloried Yankees and was a World Series hero among that exalted realm, he was on a loftier level, like a war hero. A magnificent athlete, Lindell was in the process of working his way back into the big leagues as a pitcher after falling on hard times as an offensive weapon with the Yanks. He was hoping to catch on with the Pittsburgh Pirates, possibly the worst team in all of the big leagues, a team so bad that Dad said "they'd be lucky to finish in the middle of the pack in the Pacific Coast League. They got a bunch of raw bonus kids and war time players still hanging on after stinking up the field."

Lindell thrived in the Hollywood atmosphere, doing commercials, winning a lot of games and becoming a draw. The Stars and Angels were the biggest draws in town, bigger than the LA Rams football team. Gilmore Field games were attended by show business names like Bob Hope, Jack Benny, Milton Berle, and starlets like Kim Novak and Anne Bancroft, all of them sitting in box seats above the Stars dugout.

So if the team had a star it was John Lindell. Big John was so well known that his son, a few years older than me and, like his dad, a gifted athlete, became the target of mean-spirited antagonists at Little League games. His mother, who sat with my mother at games, told Mom that kids and their parents jeered Lindell's son, forever comparing him to his father in a demeaning way. They were jealous when he dominated games, and gloated when he screwed up. Finally, at thirteen, Lindell's son quit playing schoolboy baseball because he no longer wished to endure the abuse, and his mom warned my mom I would soon face the same treatment. Worse than the kids were the parents, whose behavior toward young Lindell was so cruel and vicious that he could not force himself to step onto a ball field. Mother said Lindell, like my dad, wanted his son to experience the game that had been his life and his love; and his son being deprived of a game Lindell loved so much that he hung on in the minor leagues after his talent as a big leaguer had deteriorated, had to be a crushing blow. Big John seemed to love every aspect of the game: playing, batting practice betting and kidding, clubhouse camaraderie, road trips, signing autographs, giving interviews to writers, the adulation and perks—and now his immensely talented son was so disillusioned that the great national pastime had turned sour in his mouth.

If Lindell, a resilient presence who had withstood the highs and hard knocks of the game was a "big fish in a small pond," my dad was a smaller fish. Dad sometimes had his picture in the paper, his name in the headlines of the sports page. For a pittance he did a newspaper ad for vitamins. He was accorded a long feature article in the *Long Beach Press Telegram* hailing his career exploits. There were pictures of Dad in his Detroit uniform and of our family sitting on the davenport while Dad stood above us wielding his silver bat—the caption below stating dad was giving me "pointers on hitting."

Everybody in our neighborhood and beyond knew about the article, and already several kids had told me in nasty terms that I would never be as good a ballplayer as my dad, and was a bum. Mother was already leery of my playing Little League.

"I don't want our son ending up like John Lindell's son, Murray."

"Every kid's different, Rose. Dell's not Lindell's kid. Maybe John's kid doesn't love baseball like Dell does. I loved the game so much nothing could keep me off the field. He's the same way. He lives, eats and breathes baseball. He goes to bed with his glove. He's already playing with kids bigger and older and holding his own. He wants to test himself. He's a competitor. He's not like your family. He's like me. He's gonna play ball whether you like it or not."

BIG MOE

Sandlot Ball

I was nine, I think, maybe younger, the first time I passed a sandlot and saw a bunch of kids playing baseball. I watched those kids, some my age, others older, kids of all ages, and I thought: I can play that game. I can hit that ball.

Hitting the ball, that's what hooked me. I didn't have a glove. The kids had little gardener-type gloves, flimsy leather or cloth, the fingers separate, no webbing, but I went out there with no glove and caught balls bare handed. Right off, a bigger kid, maybe a teenager, told me I had "good hands." He let me use his glove to shag in the outfield. I watched the other players. I knew I could do what they were doing. Some of them could hit the ball, others struggled. I saw where they struggled. They swung too hard or swung up on the ball or they looked away when they swung and missed, or stepped away from the ball because they were a little scared, or they held the bat wrong with their hands, didn't have their knuckles lined up right, or just didn't have a knack for hitting.

The first time I swung a bat I cracked a line drive. Just happened. But everybody took notice. The big kid watched me hit a few more, and said: You're a natural, kid, you got good whip in your swing. You got wrist action. You're gonna be a ballplayer. You're gonna play on my team, kid.

I rode my bike into another neighborhood to get away from the goddam Poles and Germans, and I saw right away that if I could play baseball, well, I'd be accepted anywhere. I had a free pass. Here I was, from another neighborhood clear across town, in alien territory during a time in Chicago when people seldom strayed from their home turf, and because it looked like I might become a decent ball-player.

This kid Kelly, who ran the neighborhood, wanted me on his team, took me under his wing. He told me to get myself a glove, and that's what I did. I found a gardener's glove to keep the ball from stinging my hand. When you start out with a glove like that you have to make sure to watch every ball into your hand and use your free hand to corral the ball, and it ends up making you a better fielder down the line when it's time to get a bigger, better glove.

Now, everything changed in my life. Baseball took precedence over everything, including school. All I thought about in school was getting on my bike and sailing the few miles to the sandlot to play baseball with the Irish kids. They didn't care if I was a Jew or a monkey with a tail, as long as I could play ball. Hell, I could run and I could throw, talents you can't learn. Even at a young age I could outrun most of the kids, and I realized also that I had exceptional reflexes and reactions to balls hit and pitched to me. When summer came, I played morning, noon and evening, came home late for dinner every night and received a beating from my father, who warned me he'd beat me with the strap every time I was late, but already I loved baseball so much that getting to play an extra hour was worth the beating. My mother, she didn't like the strapping every night. But my father was the ruler of the household, and though they fought over the nightly strapping, he got his way.

Lefty O'Doul and the San Diego Padres

I woke up in the wee hours and found Dad swinging his bat in the living room after another game where he'd taken the collar, going 0-4. He was thirty-eight, and told me he'd been fouling off pitches he used to hit for "blue darters." He didn't know whether to switch to a lighter bat or choke up more. My father, who always had the answers, was totally befuddled and said, "I'm not going to bow out as a Punch and Judy hitter."

The next day he was traded to the San Diego Padres along with Herb Gorman. Dad was reluctant to go south because he wouldn't be home much or be able to stay in touch with the shoemakers who bought from him, but Padres manager Lefty O'Doul, and his coach, Jimmy Reese, urged Dad to come down and play second base and work with a young shortstop prospect named Al Richter. Dad considered O'Doul a prince of a man, and Reese, a fellow Jew, talked him into playing for the Padres.

He found a small apartment near the water, in Mission Beach, not far from Lane Field where the Padres played. Mother drove my sister and me the three hours down Highway 1 to Mission Beach on a weekend, and Dad took me to the park where O'Doul, a stately man, winked at me and said I could take grounders from Reese, who immediately took me under his wing and hit me grounders before the players took the field. Reese used a strange looking fungo bat with the barrel shaved flat on one side and taped. Dad said nobody in all of baseball could handle and control a fungo bat like Reese, who consistently lifted fly balls a foot from the fence and made every grounder do any trick he wanted. He had me lunging and staggering with wild bouncers, skidders and short hops.

Dad yelled at me to stay low, stay on my toes, and adjust!

I had to get used to a new bunch of players, and they had to get used to me. Every organization was different when it came to kids hanging around the clubhouse, and Dad warned me not to rampage through the new one like I did at Gilmore, pestering players. This clubhouse was more cramped, older, moldier, smellier, and missing the intimacy and family atmosphere of Gilmore, which was a unique situation. So I hung out with Gorman and Salveson, whom the Padres had also picked up.

Right off, I found a nemesis in Jackie Tobin, a lean and fleet outfielder who liked snapping his towel at my fanny and testing my toughness. "You a fighter, Meat, or a lover boy?" he sneered. He pulled my cap down over my eyes and squeezed my bicep so hard it hurt, grinning meanly. Tobin, a left handed hitter, exploded out of the batter's box on grounders and picked up momentum down the line, his legs pumping like pistons as he leaned forward to hit the bag on throws to first. He was an adept bunter, always a threat to drag one down either line. He was a world class needler and agitator.

Dad warned me, "Don't get on the bad side of Tobin, he's meaner than a rattlesnake and not like the guys on the Stars—he hates kids."

Dad's expression was grim as a few players nodded at me, just as grim.

"Why's he hate kids, Dad?"

Dead serious, Dad nodded toward Tobin who was fooling around at his locker across the way, and said, "Look at Tobin. If you looked like that you'd hate kids too. You'd hate everybody. You'd hate life. He's funny looking. Look at those ears and that schnozz. Teeth full of tobacco. Tobin's captain of the all-ugly team."

Every player within earshot nodded in agreement.

Dad nudged me. "Thank your lucky stars, Dell, you're gonna be a handsome man, like your pappy, and not ugly like Tobin, and have to go through life hating everybody, and everybody hating you. Poor Tobin, he's never had a girlfriend. He's no lover boy."

Tobin, needing a shave, leered crookedly in my direction. His long, humped nose seemed to start from his forehead. His ears jutted out from the sides of his long, narrow face, like an elephant's.

Salveson said, "Meat, go ask Tobin if he can fly away on those Dumbo ears."

Dad, nodding, said, "Go ahead. Just because he's ugly and acts mean doesn't mean he's tough."

I walked toward Tobin who was looking away. A yard or so from him I uttered, "Hey Dumbo, you're on the all ugly team..." And before I could continue, Tobin was chasing me through the clubhouse snapping his towel, staying just far enough behind to keep me skidding and dodging among chairs and trunks and tables as players jumped out of our way.

"Gonna get yah, MEAT!" Tobin shouted. "I HATE KIDS!"

Lefty O'Doul, who paced the dugout during games with his hands tucked under his belt to keep them warm, used Dad like a coach on the field. O'Doul was no taskmaster, didn't over-manage or dress down his players unless they were young and stupid, and then he was fatherly. O'Doul preferred experienced players he could trust and leave alone. His name alone was a draw at Lane Field, for he'd been a PCL star, as well as a man who hit .398 in the big leagues and owned a .349 lifetime average—a legend.

The Padres were the oldest team in the league, a bunch of "old cockers," according to Dad. The infield, comprised of Dad, Lou Stringer (who'd also come over from Hollywood and had a pretty daughter on whom I had a secret crush but, of course, couldn't mention), Jack Graham, who'd had big PCL years as a first baseman but hit poorly in the majors, and Al Richter, all in their late thirties, except young Richter.

Early on, the Padres played inspired, intelligent, nearly flawless baseball and led the league for almost two months. Dad, though still struggling at the plate, hit in the clutch--his trademark. The old cockers were confrontational, aggressive, underhanded cheaters hell bent on winning at any cost. Every game was a crusade, and O'Doul allowed the team to pretty much run by itself.

Jimmy Reese was always clapping his hands and encouraging players, loved baseball players, had no aspirations to ever manage, was too nice a man to rule a bunch of ballplayers who saw him as a beloved icon and uncle figure. Dad claimed Reese was as fine a person who ever existed in this world. He was the first man to enter the clubhouse and the last to leave. He didn't drive a car. Somebody on the team, Gorman, Dad, Salveson, would pick him up at his apartment and drive him to the ballpark, or he took a bus. He framed pictures of ballplayers who'd played with and for him, and in his life there was no other alternative to baseball. He regarded every day at the ballpark a great day, never complained and he was always positive and cheerful. I pumped him about Babe Ruth, his roomy on the 1931 Yankees.

"What was he like?"

"Well, The Babe could consume half a dozen hot dogs and half a dozen Cokes before a game and still hit two homers and party all night, and come right back and do the same thing the next day." Reese, a "clean liver," couldn't keep up with him, was supposed to be a good influence on him, but nobody else on the team could keep up with The Babe or temper his huge appetites for fun and pleasure.

"But what was he LIKE?"

"He'd like you, Dell. Babe Ruth loved kids more than anybody I've ever known. He had a big heart. He was just a big kid who never grew up. That was the beauty of The Babe. There will never be another like him. He was a sweetheart."

When I asked Dad about The Babe, he always said the same thing. "He wasn't just a power hitter, he was sneaky fast in the outfield, a good baserunner, a hell of a pitcher, a great instinctive ballplayer."

Dad fit in with the Padres. Gorman was his roomy on the road, but he was also fond of Al Richter, a Maryland transplant who lived downtown in the San Diego Hotel, where a photo of Al was displayed in the big lobby window beside the front entrance. Dad didn't think this was a wise thing for Richter.

"Hell of a nice kid and a pretty fair shortstop," Dad said. "But I don't know if he has the stamina. Short's a tough position and he already looks pooped after two months. When I played short for Beaumont in the Texas League I was leading the league in hitting half the season, but after a while the hot humid weather and the traveling and the doubleheaders wore me down, and I ended up hitting .298 after hitting around .330 most of the year. I started out the season weighing around 180 and ended up at 165."

"What's that got to do with Richter's picture in the window, Dad?"

"Well, I think that goddam picture's getting Al too much snaff and boogair."

"Snaff and boogair? What's that?"

"You'll find out some day. Richter's got some pretty hot snappers hanging around in the hotel."

"Snappers...? What are snappers, Dad?"

"You'll find out. You gotta watch out for the hot snappers. They're the ones make you crazy, get you in a slump. Richter looks like he's gassed half the time. I've seen the strongest guys in baseball fade in August because of snaff and boogair and the hot snappers."

"What about you, Dad? Do you stay away from the snaff and boogair and hot snappers? That why you been in a slump?"

"Dell, I've played every inning of every game for two months and I'm thirty-eight years old, and I'm not half as tired as Richter. What does that tell you?"

"You aint been messin' with the snaff and boogair and hot snappers."

Dad nodded.

"What about Gorman and Salveson and Tobin and Earl Rapp and Graham and Stringer, Dad? Do they stay away from the hot snappers?"

"Uh...that's enough on that subject. Let's go play pepper."

The team started fading, and then went down quick, dying. And sure enough, the bachelor Richter, a lean man with a crew cut and handsome mug, looked sluggish in the field and his bat went to sleep. Dad, who'd started to regain his batting form during the Padre rise to first place, was out of gas too, his bat in a worse tailspin than Richter's. The clubhouse went from a happy place full of humorous horseplay to a glum collection of players cursing, punching lockers, kicking over chairs and tossing gloves after each loss.

The Padres ended up slumping to fifth place. When the season ended on that dismal note, Dad and Mom had a serious discussion on whether he should continue his career "hurting all over" and with a .227 average, a humiliating embarrassment and by far the lowest average of his career—he, a man who had been the gem of the Detroit minor league system and in 1938 had led the world in hitting with one of the highest averages in baseball history.

The last two months of the season Les Cook, the trainer known as "Cookie," a bit of a grump, spent half an hour before and after games trying to keep Dad whole. Dad wanted to hang on and atone for his rotten second half of the season—"a Goddam disgrace." He believed he could still produce, if he could stay healthy. And he did need the money to get his business going. And O'Doul wanted him back.

But watching him play, and go downhill, and listening to the fans boo him and yell at him to hang it up, cut me to the core.

Hitting .000

Little League tryouts were on the other end of Compton at Colin Kelly Park. I refused my mother's offer to drive me and rode my bike across town, my glove hanging from the handlebars, bat on shoulder, steering with one hand—a hotshot. There were hundreds of kids warming up, a lot of fathers. Nobody knew me. I was nine and the smallest, youngest kid on the field. I sized up my competition and felt I belonged. There were to be six minor league teams, which took on big league names—Yankees, Indians, etc.—and four major league teams sponsored by the Lions, Rotary, Kiwanis and UCT.

One of the coaches looked me over and commented on how small I was and asked my age. And when I lied and said ten, he told me he was going to try me out with a minor league team. I told him I was going out for the majors like everybody else. He smiled and told me I'd have to grow and earn my way to the majors, just like pro ball. "I oughta know," he said. "I played some ball."

A dozen or so kids tried out for each position and the best players were at shortstop, and so was I. We lined up behind each other for our chances at ground balls. They tried the 11- and 12-year-olds first, then us smaller kids. I charged my first grounder, snared an easy hopper in my crouch and snapped a sidearm throw to first. When they hit me one to deep short, I planted my back foot, fielded and threw overhand in one motion, hitting my target. A bunch of coaches clustered at home plate looked at each other, nodding.

One of the coaches along third base asked another coach, "Who's the peewee with the good glove? Kid's slick." I refused to look at or talk to the other kids trying out for shortstop. Dad had explained to me that when he went to Spring Training with the Tigers there were dozens of players fighting for that position in the farm system, working their ways up to the big leagues, and it was dog-eat-dog, and "somebody trying to beat you out was trying to take food off your plate. They were the enemy."

The coach with the fungo, who'd played some ball, tried and failed to hit a ball through or past me. My throws were on target. When I stepped into the batting cage to take my three cuts, I turned to bunt as I'd been instructed by Johnny O'Neill, deadening the ball, dropping a dead fish on the third base line. Then I choked up and smacked three knockers between third and short, into left field. The coach who'd been hitting grounders stopped me when I finished. "I don't know who you are or where you're from, Peewee, but you're a ballplayer, a natural. We're gonna find a spot for you somewhere."

When I got home I tossed my bike down in the yard, busted into the house and told mother I thought I'd made the majors. And if I didn't, well, they could jam it. She made a long-suffering face. Then she looked into my eyes, smiled and roughed my hair. "You're my little brown nut. I'm sure you'll make the majors. You're a chip off your father's block. He'll be so proud of you."

Next day, Mr. Roark, coach of Kiwanis, called and welcomed me aboard. I was going to be his shortstop.

* * *

Dad was overjoyed I'd made the majors as the youngest kid, but disappointed he was not able to see me play because he was starting a new season in San Diego.

The Lions and UCT had the best, oldest players, and the Lions' coach was the son of the league president. Kiwanis and Rotary were allotted kids who were better than those in the minors but nowhere near as good as the Lions and UCT players, including Jim Rooker, an obvious star. Our first baseman, the 12-year-old coach's son, looked like he belonged on the last place team in the minors. He could hardly catch the ball. Coach Roark was a kindly man, but knew nothing about baseball and depended on his stocky assistant, Mr. Fletcher, who claimed he played semi-pro ball and had a tryout with the Chicago Cubs. He and I took an instant dislike to each other when I refused to alter my hitting style at his urging.

"Who the hell are you that you know so much?" he wanted to know.

"My dad's Murray Franklin. He played for the Hollywood Stars and the Detroit Tigers and now he plays for the San Diego Padres, and he knows more about baseball than you'll ever know," I told him.

His dislike turned to hatred and he grumbled to Mr. Roark that I should be moved to second base, but Roark refused.

We all hated Fletcher and our team played badly. UCT skunked us our first game. We were inept clowns. I was furious and felt helpless. I hated losing and was already a bad sport at any game on the playground. When Dad came home when the Padres played Hollywood, I told him how awful we were, but he didn't seem to want to get involved. In a way, I was disappointed, yet also relieved, for kids at school and on the playgrounds and in Little League were telling me that their dads were saying my dad stunk as a ballplayer and so did I, because my dad was not playing well again this year. "Yer dad's a bum." I was getting in fights.

The Lions skunked us, too. Though Rotary was little better than us, they had a good coach and edged us out. When UCT skunked us again we were a laughingstock. So far, at bat, I had walked a lot because I was short and Fletcher urged me to take pitches until they threw me a strike. His base signs were un-baseball like. I was hitless. We were all flailing hitless wonders. And while UCT, Lions and even Rotary and minor league teams went out with parents after games to Foster's Freeze or A&W Root Beer for burgers and shakes, we straggled home, tails between our legs, whupped dogs without treats.

The Kelly Field stands extended from behind both dugouts and climbed to a small press occupied by a man who announced the names of each hitter and always mentioned I was Murray Franklin's son when I came up—"Murray Franklin, formerly of the Detroit Tigers and Hollywood Stars and now with the San Diego Padres." I felt like a giant searchlight was singling me out. A roaring like the ocean filled my head and I chewed gum furiously and pumped my bat repeatedly like I was not supposed to, and I ground my teeth and felt humiliated when the son of Murray Franklin dribbled or struck out—as if I, like Dad, was playing on television.

One night the umpire called me out on strikes. Next time up he continued to call strikes on balls just over my shoe tops. The second time he called me out the ocean roar in my head was so loud I panicked and found myself, bat discarded, pushing the umpire in the chest protector. His eyes widened in shock as I pounded on his chest and called him "a fucking blind Tom." Mr. Roark was on the field pulling me away. Mother was in the stands and hurried down to the dugout in tears and dragged me to the car—the crowd eerily quiet and still. We drove home in silence, and then she began to weep as we pulled up in front of the house.

"I don't want you playing Little League," she said firmly.

That night, Dad called from Seattle and mother railed at him on the phone, sobbing, then she put me on the line.

Dad wanted to know why I hit the umpire. I complained he was cheating me. Mother grabbed the phone and railed at Dad some more, claiming I was imitating him by going after umpires. "He sees you do it, so he does it. But Murray, you've never touched an umpire, and never would. Your son punched an umpire tonight! I don't think he should be playing. He feels too much pressure to do well and be like you, and he's so young and so much smaller than the other kids. I'm just sick, honey. I can't eat. I just want to throw up." And she sobbed.

I was suspended for a game. When Dad came home he sat me down and explained that from now on I was never to question an umpire, no matter how bad he was. These umpires were not professionals. And from now on I was NOT to listen to or look at anything going on in the stands or anywhere else, but concentrate only on what I was doing on the field, if I wanted to be a ballplayer and not a "busher."

"You can't get the rabbit ears, Dell. You're going to have to listen to a lot of ugly garbage because of who you are. Mostly they're just jealous because you're a good player and I'm a professional. From now on, don't worry about anything except playing the game. The game's for you."

Mother still wanted me off the team, insisting it would not hurt me a bit to wait another year, especially since I had three more years of Little League.

"Rose, sooner or later the kid's going to have to face what he's facing now. He has to start working things out on his own or he never will. He needs to play, not be coddled."

I was feeling really down. For the first time, I didn't want to go to the ballpark with Dad, because I knew his teammates would want to know how I was doing, and I couldn't bear to face them when we'd lost every game and the son of Murray Franklin was hitting .000.

BIG MOE

A Philosophy of Hitting

I didn't have baseball idols when I grew up, and I didn't pattern myself after any of the Cubs players when my dad took me to Wrigley Field. My father was from the old country in Russia and didn't know a thing about baseball and didn't care about sports. Sports were something that interfered with business. In those days, the Irish kids idolized the Irish players and it was the same with the Poles and Italians and Germans. All I had was Moe Berg, and he played across town for the White Sox.

As I developed, I worked out my own techniques and simplified hitting and fielding. I didn't want to be a power hitter who hit long fly balls, because fly balls were almost always easy outs in the big parks, unless you hit one out, but most of our games were played in sandlots, and if you had power, like I did, they played you a hundred miles away and allowed you singles and doubles. I practiced a level swing that was slightly down on the ball, my right wrist on top, so I hit everything with a topspin and made ground balls hop and skid and take wild bounces so it was tough for outfielders to stay with the ball. When I hit the ball on the meat of the bat and pulled it, the ball curved toward the line, and because of my short compact swing, I stood close to the plate and pulled the ball while protecting the outside of the plate. I learned to hit down on the low ball and drive it on a low rise or a high bounce. And I tomahawked the high pitch and hit sinking liners. When I played pepper I choked up on the bat about six inches and made sure as I followed through with my swing that the knob of the bat passed between my wrists and forearms, which automatically kept my right shoulder level. This way I never dipped my shoulder or hitched. This little exercise developed strength in my wrists and shoulders and quickened my bat, and the quicker my bat became the more confident I was I could hit anybody, no matter how hard they threw. Even at a young age, I was developing what you call a "philosophy of hitting." I adopted a style that fit my physical abilities. I was an infielder, and infielders didn't hit for power. Just hit line drives and drive everybody nuts. Be a tough out. Choke up on the bat an inch or two with two strikes and don't strike out. Wear the pitcher down, discourage him by fighting off his best stuff until you get a fat one you like and drill it.

One afternoon at Wrigley Field I saw the greatest right-handed hitter of all time, Rogers Hornsby, and watching him gave me another piece to add to my philosophy of hitting. He stood deep in the box in a closed stance and hit every ball where it was pitched, and his style was like a "second coming" to me, a revelation, like some people get religion. He hit the

outside pitch down the right field line, in the gap between right and center and up the middle. He sent
the pitch up the middle anywhere he wanted to.
He took the inside pitch down the line or between
third and short or into the alley in left-center—blue
darters. His hitting was like poetry and the next day
I went to the sandlots and kept my old stance and
mechanics but instilled some of the things I'd seen
watching Hornsby. I became a terror. Everybody
wanted me on their team. I felt strong and unbeat-
able on the field. I had my own style. Walking down
the streets of Chicago, or riding my bike five, ten,
fifteen miles across town looking for a bigger, better
game, I had a sense of who I was—a hitter. A ballplayer. People waved to me on the streets and asked
about my game. At synagogue, all the Jewish kids
and their parents treated me like a crown jewel, because already I had a reputation as a good ballplayer
going places.

I'd found my calling.

Big Trouble in Little League

When Dad pulled a muscle and went on the disabled list, I asked him to please help our team. We still hadn't won and were desperate and I was walking around like my whole world was falling apart. So Dad called Mr. Roark, who said he'd be thrilled to have Dad come out and "shore up the team."

When Dad arrived at the practice field there was an atmosphere of excitement. He shook Roark's hand and then Fletcher's, then picked up a bat and swung it like a golf club and addressed us kids. "I hear we've got a lot of aardvarks and goony birds on this team," he grinned. "Any of you kids know what an aardvark and goony bird is?"

Nobody knew.

"Aardvarks and goony birds are somebody who can't win at anything. They've always got excuses. Their feet hurt. They didn't get enough sleep last night. The ump's make bad calls," Dad recited in a namby-pamby voice." That's what we call an Alibi Ike. Any of you kids Alibi Ike's?"

"NO!" came the chorus.

"Okay, you bunch of aardvarks, get your gloves and pair off and warm up those hoses, and then we're gonna hit pepper.

Any of you clowns know what pepper is? My kid—the umpire beater—thinks he knows. Let's hope he's no Alibi Ike."

Everybody gawked at each other. Then we warmed up. Dad strode along, fungo bat in hand, watching us. When warm, he separated us into groups of four and showed us how to hit pepper. Right off he told us all to cease cocking the elbow up. He told us we were looking good, that we weren't aardvarks and goony birds after all. He gave every kid individual pointers. He said we were going to make UCT and the Lions and Rotary look like a bunch of donkeys.

"Pepper covers all aspects of the game—hitting, fielding, throwing, footwork. Before every game, before you hit, play pepper, so you sharpen your skills. Thattaway, boys. Keep your eyes on the ball. Watch the ball into your bat. Watch the ball into your glove. Make good, accurate throws. It's a simple game. You aardvarks are a lot better than you think you are."

Instead of our usual infield practice, he put us all at shortstop and slashed us grounders. After watching us muff just about everything, he grabbed a glove, strode out and demonstrated the correct way to field a grounder—ass low, on the balls of your feet, legs spread, knees bent, glove down. "I don't care where you play, you gotta be able to field a ground ball."

Roark retrieved balls while Fletcher moped on the sidelines. "Remember, asses down, like ducks. Arms low and loose like monkeys. Let's hear you quack! Quack, quack, quack, come on you goony birds, get those spindly asses down and charge everything!"

We responded, quacking, skittering like monkeys, gobbling Dad's grounders. He hit a few pop-ups to see who could shag, then assigned positions, changing everybody but myself at short. Denny Long, now known as "Whitey," was moved from second to catcher. Roark was stuck in right field. Our third baseman,

Kenny Lighthouse, became our pitcher. After Dad settled everybody at their positions and hit us grounders and fly balls, he worked with Lighthouse, teaching him a straight change-up. Then we had batting practice. He taught everybody to swing level and slightly down on the ball, and had us choking up on the bat an inch or two, and delivered a pep talk about being "battlers at the plate."

"You kids are gonna rip shots and dehorn people. They're gonna boot your grounders. They're gonna be scared of you and then you're gonna run those bases like wild Indians."

Next evening we played the Lions. Dad stood behind our dugout as we faced the biggest, most terrifying pitcher in the league, Lindy Kurt, a lefty who popped the catcher's mitt. Dad told us to "chip away at him." Meanwhile, Dad kept subtle eye contact with Denny Long and frequently signaled him to throw the change-up to their biggest, hardest swinging hitters. The Lions hitters lunged and popped up and struck out; and we made the plays in the field as Dad clapped his hands and encouraged us. Mr. Roark was smacking us on the butt while Fletcher sat silently on the end of the bench.

As instructed by Dad, I fouled off one after another of Kurt's pitches then hit a line drive over their first baseman and tore to third for a triple. Everybody on our team choked up on the bat and met the ball. We kept hitting grounders that produced dropped balls and wild throws and indeed we ran the bases like wild Indians as our dugout and rooters in the stands went crazy. We ended up beating them, 9-1. Afterwards, Denny Long ran over and hugged Dad.

"That Lighthouse kid's a natural," Dad told me later. "A dummy can see it. The kid's loosey-goosey and he's got a lotta guts."

The Lions were in shock. Their manager, Kurt's father, a tall, red-faced man, stormed off. We were jubilant, celebrating our first win, and my first two hits. Our parents came down to hug us. Then we piled into cars and in a caravan drove to Foster's Freeze.

When we got home, Dad roughed my head. "Attaway to rack that pea, Meat. You took that big kid down and the whole team followed. That's being a leader. That's my boy."

Next game we edged the powerhouse UCT. Dad came to both games and stood behind our dugout conferring with Mr. Roark and giving signals to Denny behind the plate. He'd taught Lighthouse a sidearm delivery that had right-handed hitters "stepping into the bucket." Dad's strategy bred confusion that led to panic and finally a loss of confidence in our opponents.

As my confidence grew, I developed a feel for the game, sensed where to play hitters, anticipating where they were going to hit the ball. Dad noticed this and after games he warned me not to anticipate too much and gamble, but that he saw I had "baseball in my blood, an instinct that is rare." He was so pleased with me he bragged to his teammates on the Padres, and when I entered the clubhouse with a swelled head they patted my ass and roughed my head and called me Slasher and Scoop and Scooter. Dad even bragged of my getting kicked out of the game and somehow a reporter for the San Diego paper mentioned it in his column.

When a player asked me my average, and I told him, he grinned and said, "Thatta boy. Any ballplayer says he doesn't know his average is fulla shit."

* * *

On a rematch with the Lions, Dad in his Padres windbreaker, was pacing and agitated with the proceedings. He began badgering the umpire, a kid around sixteen who nobody had seen before. He called me out on high pitches and did the same with our other hitters. Then he called the same kind of pitches Lighthouse threw for balls, loading the bases. We fell behind. The Lions whooped it up and their crowd rooted them on.

Dad started talking softly to the ump from behind the backstop. "I know what you're up to, kid. Don't for a minute think I'm not wise to you. Who the hell got to you?"

The ump stayed mum.

"Who's paying you off, son?" And then, after another pitch, Dad, irritated, barked, "You call that a strike? Shame on you! Cheating little kids! You're a disgrace! Turn around. Turn around. Look at me!"

The umpire took off his mask and turned to face Dad.

"How the hell can you go home and look yourself in the mirror?" Dad demanded to know, the vein in his neck pulsing, his bald head turning red.

The ump turned around, refit his mask.

"I thought I'd seen it all, but in thirty years of baseball this is the lowest, rottenest thing I've seen..."

A booming voice from the stands interrupted what had been stunned silence of the crowd as Dad berated the umpire. "Shut your big mouth, Franklin! Pick on a man, not a boy!" The voice thundered.

Dad turned and searched the packed crowd for the face belonging to the voice. "Who told me to shut my mouth?" Dad growled, the vein in his neck pulsing. "Show your face if you're gonna challenge me," he called up to the stands.

A man bigger than Lindell, wearing a bulky black tanker jacket and owning a tough, meaty mug stood up, halfway up the stands beneath the press box. "I told you to shut your mouth, Franklin," he growled back. "You don't belong here!"

Dad walked over to Mother, who was scrunched up in the first row behind our dugout, peeled off and flipped her his watch, then returned to the area behind the screen and, a mad grin on his face, pointed a finger at the man. "You wanna shut my mouth, come on down here!"

I felt myself shrivel in fear at the immensity of the menacing figure in the stands. But then the menacing scowl on his face began to wither.

"I know who you are, Franklin," said the man, softening his tone.

"You told me to shut my mouth, so you better get down here and do it, buster."

The man began to shrink. "I know about you...yer a ballplayer... yer in shape...yer a boxer..." He was blubbering.

A group of fans surrounded and stood before the man, making a show of restraining him from coming down after Dad, who motioned him to come on down.

"Let's go behind the barn and fight like men!" Dad yelled up at him. "You're the one asked for it, get your ass down here, buster!"

The man made a half-assed attempt to break through the shield of men, but he said nothing. Mother by this time had Dad by the arm and warned him he was a professional ballplayer in the spotlight and could not get into fights. I was beside him and he ordered me to fetch my gear. The look in his eye was terrifying. He issued the big man one last look of disgust and mother led us to the car.

During the ride home he was bristling with anger and claimed the Little League officials were a "pack of gutless cowards who'd bribed the umpire."

At home, Mr. Roark called to explain that Dad was banned from coming to our practices and games because it was "unfair to other teams to have to compete against a Kiwanis team with the advantage of an ex-big leaguer and current professional coaching them."

"It's never about the kids, huh?" Dad said. "What horseshit."

Mr. Roark felt terrible because the kids on our team were having such a great time, improving their play, loving the game, loving Dad. Dad told Roark to stress the points he'd been making—but from that day on our practices were lifeless and we went into a tailspin losing again to everybody. The man who challenged Dad turned out to be the nephew of the league president, a truck driver, and both were related to the Lions coach. Dad healed and went back to the Padres, and the rest of our season was no fun without him. He'd made things exciting, made us all laugh, made us like ourselves and the game to such joy that we showed up a half hour early for practices, eager puppy dogs ready to play.

BIG MOE

Golden Gloves

My mother had no idea I was boxing in a gym across town. Where the most important thing I learned was how to throw a left hook. Short and crisp. Torquing my hips and shoulder and planting one in the ribs where you can tear cartilage or paralyze a guy with a shot to the liver, or to the side of the jaw so you can snap a guy's neck. When you hit somebody on the side of the jaw all the gray matter slides over to the other side of the brain and the lights go out. I was blessed to be light on my feet and moved well laterally, side to side, and had good footwork. I had quick hands and developed a pretty good jab. I found that the right hand was not that important, especially in the streets where kids were always trying to sucker punch you with a big right hand. Nobody looked for the left. I pumped that hook into the heavy bag over and over and learned how to set up the left hook and straight right with my left jab, and later I set up opponents for a counter-punch by teasing him into a punch I anticipated. I liked the cat-and-mouse aspect of boxing, where you looked for a weakness and capitalized and were always competing, trying to outsmart the other guy.

Everybody at the gym told me I had a natural punch, what we called "the heavy hands." They urged me to get into the Golden Gloves, so I took an Irish name and started my amateur career. I had a killer instinct and started beating people up pretty good. I liked it. I had a lot of anger. I had a shock-absorbing neck, long arms and a knack for moving my head and slipping punches. And my balance kept me from lunging and getting nailed in the kisser coming in, like a hitter lunging off his front foot instead of staying back. After I won a few fights I decided to go after some of the oldest, worst bigots in the neighborhood. They'd forgotten, but not me. I hung in the park, and when I caught those bastards alone I beat the living hell out of them, broke their noses, knocked out their teeth. The Gorski brothers were the worst sadists. I got one of them in the lavatory at the high school and when I got through beating him bloody I shoved his face in the urinal and told him if any of his brothers and Polish friends wanted to mess with me or my sisters I'd make them eat shit the next time. I ended up getting all the Gorski brothers. Word got around. I had a reputation.

Not everybody can fight, has the heart or attitude or the physical tools for it, but I did. My parents had no idea I was boxing in the ring and never would have allowed it. I made up lies during bouts. Told them I was visiting friends, doing homework at the library. The more I boxed, the more I learned, the more I appreciated the art of it, the strategy. The great Barney Ross worked out in our gym, and just watching him you could learn all there was to know—how to neutralize power, cut off the ring, set a guy up for a punch, make a guy miss. He was a master. You couldn't hit him, yet he could hit you all day. He was somebody to admire, a fighting Jew. Those were different times than today. You had to do what you had to do to survive. Survival of the fittest. I found out one thing: Everybody looks up to a guy who can and will fight to the end. The guy in the street can smell it a mile away.

Family Acrimony

"You're Franklin's kid, ain't ya?" said Mike Laken, a high school senior who ran South Park and the surrounding neighborhood. "We got a park team here, we play kids from other parks in town. Sometimes we go to their park, sometimes they come to our park." Mike was big, with black hair and a tough, chiseled face. His Nemesis was Jack Reinholtz, who had his own South Park team. Jack was a bully, but Mike could kick his ass. They both went to Compton High. They were not really good athletes, but organizers. Both planned to join the Marines after graduation. Mike, the toughest guy in the area, grinned down at me. "You're playing for me, little Franklin, and not that asshole Reinholtz, right?"

I liked playing park games, competing against older kids. I yearned to hang around the older guys, picking up their jargon, their swagger. Laken became my neighborhood idol. The kids I hung out with were close to junior high age, and I adopted their cynical attitude and disparaging talk about girls. I acquired a smart-ass persona that was probably insufferable to my parents and teachers. So be it. I played in the parks and streets. Mother never worried about me even if I was always late for dinner. We were a pack, on bikes or afoot, and above all, we were up and coming athletes of the type only a tough, blue-collar town like Compton produced.

* * *

When the 1953 season started, Richter, Salveson, Graham, Stringer and Tobin were gone. Of my old buddies on the Padres, only Gorman remained, and he was coming off a disappointing year that had probably dashed any hopes of his making the big leagues. And Dad's decline continued. His batting average hovered at .220. One game, when the starting catcher was pinch-hitting for an ejected backup, Dad volunteered to catch and ended up with a busted finger on a foul tip. Cookie came onto the field, jerked the mangled digit back into its joint and taped it to another finger, and Dad gripped the bat with the finger extended. For the first time, I saw my father visibly depressed and even demoralized. He was in a constant pain. No longer was baseball any fun.

After a series at Gilmore, where the Padres took a thumping from the Stars, the club was slated for a home stand. Mondays were always a PCL off day and the team gave Dad permission to drive our family down to the apartment in Mission Beach. We left early in the morning. Mom and Dad had a heated argument the night before, and Dad was edgy and morose behind the wheel, because Mother was giving him the silent treatment. Her face was wounded, persecuted, unforgiving. As we passed out of Long Beach on highway 1, Mother sat as far as possible from him in the front seat, her body and face turned away gazing out the window. Dad chewed furiously at his fingernails. One of the reasons for their fight was my roguish attitude and foul behavior. Mother blamed Dad's influence for it; that, and my teasing and torturing Susie, my younger sister. We were riding in the back seat. I burped in her face, which prompted her to cry hysterically and climb over the seat to cuddle against Mother. Dad eyed me balefully in the rear view mirror and barked that if I continued teasing my sister he'd ban me from the ballpark!

"I'll pull over right now and so help me God I'll break you into a thousand bloody pieces! Goddammit I'm in no mood!"

I went silent, and we drove on down the coast. Peering at Dad's mug in the mirror, I sensed his frustration and anger, the rapid darting of his eyes indicating a frantic search for a strategy to get mother to cease her brutal silence. The air between them was so tense that any look or word from either would spark a full-scale war. I knew without a doubt that Dad could not in a lifetime win an argument against her. And he knew it, and it galled him because he couldn't stand to lose at anything, let alone to Mother, who had his number and knew she was punishing him with each passing moment of her loaded silence.

Finally, Dad couldn't take it anymore. "Yeah, it's always me. Always my fault. I'm always the villain. One hundred per cent wrong, hey? Guess I'm just a terrible person. You can always find a better man out there," he said, bitter, sarcastic.

Mother made a face indicating his statement and perhaps his very presence left her nauseous.

Dad went on: "Yeah, I get blamed for everything. In thirteen years of marriage I've never been right about anything. I've been wrong a thousand times and you've been right a thousand times. I'm oh for a thousand. If it's dark out, and you say it's light, you're right, because you've never been wrong once in your life! You're perfect! Just like your family! You're all geniuses! World beaters! Beauties! Too good for me and MY family. Even if your old man did desert the family during the Depression and you're the biggest bunch of goddam freeloaders in the world!"

"Pull over," Mother snapped, her lips compressed to a tight line. "I want out of this car right now!"

Dad wrenched the wheel, jerking everybody around, bounced over a shoulder and skidded onto the dirt beside the beach. "Go on, get out," he snarled. "Goddam fishwife, lousy carping fork-tongued shrew, rotten gutter whore! Go find a man! You're on your own!"

Mother, petite, uncommonly beautiful and feminine, proud virgin before marriage, calm though her eyes brimmed with tears, said, "Murray Franklin, YOU are an ugly man. I no longer love you." She calmly stepped out of the car and commenced marching down the dirt shoulder, heading south.

Dad gunned the engine and veered toward her, and I feared he was going to run her over, but he veered away at the last moment as she jumped away, her eyes frozen in disbelief as Dad aimed the Pontiac onto the highway drawing honks from drivers. I looked back through the rear window—Mother marching on, head high, wearing jeans, a white turtleneck sweater, blue denim jacket and Dad's old sailor cap. Susie was sobbing and hysterical, yelling "MOMMY! MOMMY!"

Dad slowed down. "This is the last straw. Alright I'll leave. That's what she wants. She doesn't love me. She can go live with her family of deadbeats and parasites and starve! I've always been a good husband, a good father, a good provider. Who you think bankrolled her family's move out here from Wisconsin? Me! I did! They're lucky they got a pot to piss in. Well, now they can have their precious daughter back. Let her test the waters and see what kind of man she finds."

I tried to imagine a life without mother and felt immediate panic. "Dad, she could go back to nursing and find a doctor. All kinds of rich Jewish doctors wanted to marry her before you met her."

He bit savagely at his upper lip, glaring at me in the mirror.

"I want Mommy!" Susie wailed. "Please Daddy, I want Mommy!" She was sobbing.

Dad made a U-turn, again peeving honking drivers. "Okay, for you, honey," Dad said. A mile or so down the road we spotted mother, who refused to look at Dad, who made another U-turn, again drawing honks and shouts, and crept alongside Mother, who continued marching. He leaned across the seat, rolled down the window and while steering with one hand implored her to get back in the car "for the good of the kids" even if she hated him and no longer loved him. Mother increased her marching pace. Dad kept alongside her, and she whirled on him, "You tried to run me over! If I hadn't moved you would have run me over! How dare you!"

"Rose, goddammit, if I'd wanted to run you over I would have." She turned and marched on as Dad continued steering with one hand.

"Dad, you better go get her," I said.

He stopped, turned the engine off, sat there a moment, sighed, then got out and loped after her. She saw him coming and tried to scurry away, but he caught up and blocked her path, pleading, gesturing. Mother, hands on hips, looked away as he talked, remaining stiff, unresponsive. Dad looked like the most miserable human on the planet.

Finally, she turned to face him, and he had to listen while she let him have it. Head hanging, he nodded in accord with her tongue lashing. When she eventually stopped, he put a hug on her. Her arms went around him. He kissed her on the forehead, the cheeks, and they held each other for a long time. She was no longer crying as they returned to the car holding hands. It was obvious they had both been crying. They got into the car and sat close together like sweethearts.

Dad drove off, Susie curled up against Mother. Their faces in the mirror were serene, content. Dad caught my eyes. I grimaced in disgust and silently mouthed the words: "Real corn." He looked sheepish. But I was relieved. Nothing could be worse than not having Dad around to tell me about facing Feller and playing against DiMaggio and Williams when I pumped him for stories.

As we drove on, they chirped and discussed pulling over at one of the little beach towns for a picnic. It had been foggy all morning, but now the sun shone. We pulled off the highway, found a corner grocery store, drove a couple blocks to a spacious park. Mom spread a blanket. We had ham sandwiches, sodas. Dad mentioned how the picnic reminded him of when they'd done the same in parks in Havana. Real mush. I finished quickly and excused myself to go to the bathroom, when in truth I was drawn to the distant sounds of a baseball game.

Not far away, I found a diamond where a game was being played by a bunch of kids older than me. I decided I was easily the equal of these players, walked up and announced I wanted to play. A kid who seemed in charge flashed me the stink eye and said I couldn't play. I told him I was better than any of them and would prove it if they let me play. The big kid puffed out his chest and said I couldn't play and if I didn't like it I could do something about it. So I slugged him, knocking him down, and then I jumped on his chest and pummeled him. He tried to throw me off, but I was crazed and crying, and now the kid was crying because I'd bloodied his nose. He quit struggling and all the kids around us were pulling and screaming for me to stop, but that only inspired me to continue hitting him—with a sadistic viciousness that was new to me. I was flailing away when I was snatched off the kid and held in the air swinging wildly, crying—and it was Dad, carrying me away, his eyes wide and concerned as he urged me to cool off, asking me what was wrong and why was I fighting strange kids? I wiggled free and ran toward the blanket, where Mother sat with her face in her hands. She looked up. We were both crying.

"Oh God, what have we done," she wailed.

"For Christ Sake. Why were you fighting with that kid?" Dad wanted to know.

"He wouldn't let me play ball."

"Oh God," Mother cried, and started collecting the picnic items.

* * *

"There he is! Slasher!"

"Hear yah got in a brawl, Meat."

"Meat ain't no lover boy, he's a fighter."

I was a clubhouse hero, disappointed Tobin was gone because he'd been proud of me. But Herb Gorman wasn't. He gave me a long look and told me to sit beside him at his stall. He was one of the few players who read the front page of the local newspaper. He gave me a stick of gum. Dad had confided to me

Roomies in the San Diego clubhouse during a rain delay, spring 1953.

that Gorman's chances of making the majors were pretty much over. At twenty-eight, without much speed or power, he'd have to resign himself to a career as a solid AAA player, which meant in a year or two he would get his release and have to find something else to do in life. Dad said that Herb had an "old body" and was already past his peak.

Herb patted my knee and smiled. "Dell, your father is my best friend in this world, and there is nobody I like more, along with your wonderful mother. But you are not your dad. You are yourself. You don't need to fight to impress your dad or me or anybody else in here. You understand?"

I shrugged. He grinned, roughing my head. "You know, if I ever have a boy, I want him to be just like you."

We walked out onto the field together and started playing pepper. Herb tapped balls to my right and left, moving me around, an expert with the bat; and when I hit he changed speeds and even threw me a knuckle ball. After pepper I sat in the dugout watching batting practice. Later I joined the team in the clubhouse, installing myself beside Gorman at his locker, polishing his spikes with a can of black wax Dad had given him from his shoe supply business. He promised to share his ham sandwich with me between games of the coming Sunday doubleheader. Before I left he snagged my arm. "No fighting," he said, dead serious. Then he laughed and smacked my ass when I walked off.

The first game of the doubleheader, Dad was at third, Gorman in left. I watched part of the game, at their urging, with mother and Rosalee, Herb's twenty-year-old fiancée who was beautiful and smiled at me in a manner that disarmed my tough guy act and melted me into blushing. I couldn't take any more of it and started out toward the left field bleachers where I planned to sit with an old retiree who wore a straw hat and was a regular at the ballpark. We'd meet and talk baseball.

He was from Cleveland and saw Dad play for Detroit before the war, and was thrilled to have me join him. He always ate a hot dog with everything on it and insisted on buying me one and smoked stogies. We sat together anticipating bunts, hit-and-runs, steals, plotting strategy, so immersed in the game that people sought us out for our predictions. He never missed a game, never failed to mark a play in his program scorecard, read *The Sporting News* religiously and knew about every baseball player in every league in the country and never left the ballpark until the last out no matter what the score. His name was Mullins and he said, "Every day is a good day at the ballpark, I don't care if it's snowing, kid."

I was almost to where Mullins sat when there came a long, low sigh from the crowd, and then everybody stood up. The stadium went dead. Herb Gorman was sprawled in left field, not moving. Somebody said: "He just toppled over." Dad and the shortstop, along with the center fielder, sprinted over to him. They checked him briefly and then together hoisted him on their shoulders and ran to the dugout with him. The entire Padres team followed.

I pushed my way back to our box, where mother was holding Rosalee. Her eyes were wild as she clung to mother. I tore down to the area under the stadium leading past concession stands to the clubhouse, where I pounded on a big heavy door. A cop there tried to restrain me. A Padres official opened the door and told me I couldn't come in, but I broke free from the cop and dashed by him, and when he saw me run to my dad and hug him, he didn't intervene. There was a crowd of ballplayers in the training room and I heard players weeping. Dad knelt down, his face wet. His voice was strained and hoarse as he whispered in my ear that I had to leave the clubhouse; then he took me by the hand and led me to the door. "Go to your mother. Tell her I'll see her as soon as I can. You can't be in here."

Mother stood with a crowd of newspapermen and ballplayer's wives and kids at the door. I watched, helpless, as Rosalee screamed and collapsed while my mother held her. Mother's eyes met mine and they were so sad I could not look at them. Rosalee's wails echoed throughout the stadium. Everything blurred when the announcer's voice thundered over the confines of Lane Field that the doubleheader was canceled out of respect for left fielder Herb Gorman, who had passed away.

Mother collected Susie and I and drove to the apartment. We sat around crying and holding each other. Dad came home later, and said to mother that he thought that Gorman had died of a heart attack. Dad said that as he helped carry Herb off the field he heard him grunt and shudder and then his grip went limp and Dad knew Herb was gone.

Later that night, he came into the living room and sat on the sofa and put his arm around me "We lost our dear friend today, Dell. I was looking forward to having him as a friend for the rest of my life. We have to be thankful for the short time we had with Herb." He sighed and shook his head. His eyes were raw. "He was twenty-eight-years old, had a beautiful fiancée... sometimes life just isn't fair, and there's not a damn thing you can do about it."

BIG MOE

Facing Satchel Paige

I took a football scholarship to the University of Illinois so I could play baseball. They didn't give baseball scholarships in those days. Wally Roettger was my baseball coach. He'd just finished a big league career and knew the game—refined me. Believe it or not he had Lou Boudreau, a future hall of fame shortstop, at third and me at second. Even as a kid Boudreau knew where to play the hitters and where everybody should be playing. He understood the subtleties of the game. He was a gifted schmoozer and a good psychologist and a natural politician. But he was also a guy who knew when to be tough and demanding. Lou and I worked as a double play combination when we barnstormed against Negro League teams for side money, and the one weekend I came down sick as a dog and couldn't make it, Lou got caught taking money and had to leave college. He was already prepared for the big leagues. Nobody could bunt or control a bat like Lou. He became a playing manager at Cleveland at 24 and devised the Williams shift.

If you were considered an outstanding prospect, you got to play against the great Negro League players of

Dad starred at the University of Illinois.

that time and that's where I got to face Satchel Paige. Probably around 1935. Satchel was in his prime, and to this day, after facing Feller, Grove, and those great Yankees, Satchel was the toughest. He had a high leg kick that hid the ball and pin-point control. Without ever seeing you before, he could size you up right away and know how and where to pitch you.

Josh Gibson was behind the plate, a powerful man with shoulders like a damn bull, he could sit on his haunches, and without rising, peg a ball to second on a straight line. An arm like a rocket. He swung hard and he swung big, and he swung quick. You thought the ball was by him, but his bat was so quick he picked the ball up before it passed and rifled it. Gibson had a big arc on his swing and the balls he

Great pitcher, great sport: Satchel Paige.

hit climbed like golf shots, getting incredible distance. Everybody stood still when he hit batting practice, like Ruth in his day, and Mantle now.

Well, I was a tough out. I knew Satchel liked that. He liked to toy with kids who thought they were great hitters and teach them a lesson, and at the same time, let them know Paige was the best in the business. Unhittable. He was a man with a lot to prove when Negro players were barred from the big leagues and organized ball. I battled him all afternoon, and he started talking to me, and he got me out, but he couldn't strike me out. He broke my bat once. Got me lunging, made me look bad. But he couldn't strike me out and he knew I was up there with one thing on my mind: Not strike out. If a blind squirrel could find an acorn, I could manage to get a hit off him.

Sure enough, the last inning, he knew when I'd be coming up. There were two outs and three batters ahead of me. Satch walked all three and then waved his team off the field except Gibson. He's on the mound staring me down with this sneaky sliver of a grin when I come up to the plate. Well, now he's really coming after me. He tells me he's been using his "back yard stuff" and now he's going to use his "good stuff." He threw one right by me. Up and in. Then he nicked a corner. Strike two. Then I started battling. I fouled off a bunch of pitches, inside high, low and outside. I'm on top of the plate and he brushes me back. I worked the count two and two. I'm up on the bat a couple inches and the last two foul balls I hit were just off the right field line. I was beginning to time him. His ball ran in, and moved out. I knew he was stubborn and too proud to throw me a hook. He was gonna blow one by me one way or the other—and he came in just a little fat with a waist-high fastball and I got decent wood on it and laced it right past his ear into center field and hightailed it down the first base line. I was so excited that, for the first time, I took my cap off as I rounded first. As I started for second, Satchel was running alongside me. He followed me around second and was still with me at third, and the whole time he's talking to me—"You hit Satchel, kid. Way to hit that ball. Tell your kids some day. You hit the great Satchel Paige."

When I crossed home plate he smacked me on the ass and everybody in the dugout went crazy and even the Black players were laughing and having a big time of it. I'd just gotten a legitimate hit off the greatest goddam pitcher in the world, a living legend.

Boo Birds, and Then Good-Bye

The fans at Lane Field had been booing Dad. He and Mom were having a lot of whispering conversations out of my earshot. He looked worried all the time, fearing the inevitable unconditional release every ballplayer receives when he is no longer able to produce and is cast into the real world of dog-eat-dog survival.

While home during a series against the Angels at Wrigley Field, an old friend named Jules, who'd played against Dad in the Mountain State League in 1938, came to the house. Small and wiry, with a bald dome and a severely hooked nose, Jules admired Dad as a fellow Jew and kept an eye on his career. He dressed in slacks and sport coat and an open-collared shirt and wingtip shoes with white toes. Dad told me Jules was a little left-handed "junkballer" who got no higher than A Ball and eventually became a player/coach on low minor league teams. Finally he tired of the hard life of grimy buses and fleabag hotels in the Midwest and Appalachia, and became a "bird-dog."

Jules was an exuberant, jovial man who solemnly informed me that I was the "spitting image" of my father. He told me what a great ballplayer my Dad was and how he got the "royal shaft" from Detroit. Jules stayed for dinner, raving over mother's cooking. Afterwards he gravitated to the living room where he picked up Dad's silver bat from the mantle above the fireplace and respectfully inspected it, admiring the mirror sheen from my weekly polishing.

"I don't care where you play. To hit .439 is one of the wonders of the world. I hated facing your father. I never saw a player like him. Powerful man. Playing shortstop and hitting ropes all over the field. And run? Fastest man in the league. He should have been up with Detroit the next year. Musial went right up. Boudreau went right up. Your dad was good enough to play right then."

After he left, Dad told me Jules knew he'd been playing badly, and since he was in the area scouting, wanted to "lift his spirits." He also explained that Jules couldn't sign a prospect, but scouted high school players and reported what he'd seen to a head scout, who is the only one can sign a kid. "Most scouts try and play down the talent of a kid and steal him, sign him up as cheaply as possible. Scouts are not to be trusted."

"Not Even Jules?"

Dad shrugged. "Jules is a fine, honorable man. He's one of those guys in love with the game. Even more than me. It's like being in love with a beautiful woman who never loves you back, but you keep loving her all your life. That's Jules. The game's everything to him. He's what we call in the business a "lifer."

I asked Dad why Jules thought Detroit gave him a raw deal. He explained that the owner of the Tigers, Spike Briggs, was a Catholic and played favorites. He'd actually handed rosary beads around in the clubhouse and he'd find them in his locker. Dad said they played Charley Gehringer, a Hall of Fame legend, when he was "so far over the hill he was finished, useless," while he sat. But he never said a word, swallowed his pride, even when Mother, who knew little about baseball, could see he was getting the shaft and urged him to demand to play or be traded. But Dad said that no amount of demanding would've made a difference because "they owned you."

"What'd you do with the rosary beads?"

"Gave 'em back and kept my mouth shut."

"What about Hank Greenberg? He's a Jew."

"Hank was already established, a legend like Gehringer. But he put up with his share of Jew-baiting. He outworked the bastards and shoved it down their throats." He paused, looked at me. "Sometimes, Dell, you have no control over the events in your life. You have to eat a little crow, and sometimes a lot of crow, and you gotta make the best of it because there's no other choice. It's no different in baseball than in life."

* * *

Dad and I drove to San Diego while Mom and Susie stayed home. We talked baseball all the way down, at my insistence; relentlessly quizzing him about everybody he played against, especially the great ones like Williams and DiMaggio. I had a shoe box full of baseball cards and shocked my parents by memorizing the batting average of every player in the Sunday sports page statistics. I also wanted to know about Earl Rapp, the Padres star player, one of the best in the PCL, an outfielder who carried himself with quiet dignity. Rapp was graceful on the field, fluid at the plate, a fine left-handed hitter. Rapp had all the tools—a pretty good arm, some speed, good fielder, decent power.

"I think the front offices of most teams get it in their heads that Earl can't hit lefties. I think he can. But after a while, if THEY think that way, well, YOU start thinking that way too. Earl goes up to the big leagues, and time after time, he stops doing the things he does in the PCL. I think it's a mental thing." Dad pointed to his head. "And he's an outfielder. An outfielder has to hit or it's no dice. A great infielder, like, say, Eddie Miller, even if he can't hit, he'll find a place in the big leagues."

"Rapp's tearing up the league. Will he get another chance?"

"Not now. He's over thirty. Too late."

* * *

Dad remained mired in the most brutal slump of his career. The best part of his game had always been his hitting—his trademark as a ballplayer. But now he couldn't buy a hit, and I wondered if he was ever going to hit again. I sat with Mullins and listened to the fans boo and accuse Dad of being over-the-hill and ready to be "put out to pasture" and replaced by somebody who could produce. "He's barely hitting his weight," I told Mullins. "He always said he'd quit when the day came he couldn't hit his weight."

"He'll hit," Mullins reassured me, adjusting his glasses, showing me his tobacco-stained teeth. "Besides, your daddy's the kind of player don't always need to hit to help the team. He does everything right. Some day you'll understand that."

But Dad had a miserable game, booting a routine play at second, hitting into a double play, getting called out on strikes with the bases loaded. The boos rained down. Later, he was pulled for a pinch hitter. The next day I sat with Mullins again, and Dad was on the bench, but pinch-hit in the ninth with the winning run at second, and connected on a pitch that sent the left fielder sprinting to the fence. At the crack of the bat it sounded like a home run. Mullins and I and everybody around us stood as the left fielder punched his glove and caught the ball eye level, his back against the fence. Dad kicked dirt as he rounded first, then chugged off the field, head down.

"Snake bit," Mullins muttered.

After the game we stopped at a diner for burgers, and he told me about a game in the Texas League where he hit nine line drives in a doubleheader and went 0 for 9, either hitting one right at somebody or getting robbed. "Next game I dragged a bunt for a single my first time up, then hit a ball off the plate that bounced so high I was on first before it came down, then broke my bat blooping one into right field for another single. My last time up I hit seeing-eye-dog single up the middle, went 4 for 4 and never hit the ball hard. So what that tells you is, if you're a good hitter

69

everything evens out. I'm not sure I'm a good hitter anymore. It's hard to keep your confidence up when your body no longer responds."

Back at the apartment, Dad put me to bed and phoned Mother, and they talked for a long time. I couldn't sleep. Dad came into the room and sat on the bed. "I quit baseball tonight, Dell. I called O'Doul and told him I'm done. I don't have it anymore. Right now I'm hurting the ball club. I'm embarrassing myself. I always told myself that when it came to this I'd hang it up. Thing is, it's a helluva a lot harder to do than I thought it'd be." It felt like somebody died. Dad said it was okay. He was okay. He'd prepared. He'd had enough.

"I gave it everything I had, every play, for damn near twenty years. I never cheated the game or anybody I played for. I earned every cent they paid me. That's the way I played the game. All in all, your old man had a pretty good career and lived a life few men experience." He managed a smile, smacked my shoulder. "Now it's your turn."

BIG MOE

Hitting .439

I signed with Detroit for $100 a month and they sent me to Beckley, West Virginia in the Mountain State League. I took a train from Chicago and got off in the middle of the night at a tiny deserted depot outside of a town called Prince. Pitch dark outside. Only sound the crickets and frogs. I sat there on a bench for hours, wondering how long they were going to leave me out there until an old guy in a beat up truck came for me. Had about three teeth in his head. Hillbilly. But he was in a suit. Right off he welcomed me to Beckley and the team and all he talked about all the way to the boarding house where I'd live was the ball club.

In those days, before television, it seemed every little town in the country had a ball club affiliated with a big league team. *The Sporting News* was thick as a book, covered every minor league, and each big league team had around 15 to 20 farm teams, so that when you went to Spring Training there were at least 20 players trying out for your position.

These mountain people loved their baseball and loved their players. They'd do just about anything for you if you were a ballplayer. If you played well you got little

Dad shaking hands with his father, Louis, at the Silver Bat ceremony in Beaumont in 1939.

rewards, like a free haircut or a dinner at one of the diners. These were poor people. The country was poor even before the Depression hit, so now they had nothing, and when they came to the ballpark to watch us play it was something very, very special for them. I saw right off that we, as players, the way we played, meant a lot to them, raised their spirits, and you learned that the little things you gave to them meant a hell of a lot in the long run. It was a damn good lesson on life, and humility, to never get too big for your britches.

Going away to play ball as a professional and getting paid for it made me appreciate how good I had it. Most of these folks would never have the opportunity to get an education or make a lot of money or get taken care of health-wise. They had bad teeth, bad posture and joints from going down in those mines, a place I'd never go, and so you didn't bitch at your own living conditions, or going from town to town to places like Huntington and Bluefield in an old jalopy of a team bus through those treacherous mountains on bad roads. On those hairpin turns the fog was so bad that sometimes I'd sit on the front fender and yell directions back at the driver.

But it was fun, just to play ball and be part of that life, and see the look on the faces of these people when you talked to them at the ballpark or in the streets and gave them an autograph. It was all you needed to go out there and play your ass off.

I hit .439 in 1938, led all of the baseball leagues in America, and won the only silver bat handed out to the player with the highest average, along with the top hitters in the American and National Leagues. It was a magical year. Everything I hit felt solid. I was close to reaching my physical maturity and I ran the bases like a wild man, turning singles into doubles and doubles into triples, and in the local papers they called me "Grease Lightning." I was on top of the world, the luckiest guy alive, because I'd met Rose the year before and she was the girl of my dreams, and we wrote every day and talked on the phone while she went to nursing school in Chicago. My father, who'd never cared a hoot about baseball, and along with my mother wanted me to study medicine or law or business like most Jewish kids in college, was so proud of me that he took the train to be with me when they presented me the silver bat.

That year I felt like nobody, nobody in organized baseball could get me out.

A Call from the Angels

Dad, a little grouchy from retirement and trying to get his business going in our garage, laid down the law to me: "I know you've been going against my rules the minute I'm away on a road trip. I know you disobey your mother and tease the hell out of your sister and come and go like a free agent, but your corking-off days are over as of this minute, now that I'm here full time." He was also irate with me because I'd been kicked out of two Hebrew schools where a Rabbi had tried, along with other serious Jewish kids, to tutor me toward a Bar Mitzvah, when all I wanted to do was play ball with my gentile friends, and now this sacred Jewish rite seemed out of the question, a situation that further infuriated him because he'd been forced as a kid to make his Bar Mitzvah and was hell-bent on steam-rolling me into making mine. At this point, no Hebrew teacher would have me.

So, I was overjoyed when Dad received a call from Stan Hack, manager of the LA Angels of the PCL, asking him to come out of retirement and play for him the last two months of the season. Hack, a stellar third baseman for the Chicago Cubs for years, was now managing their top farm team. He told Dad that if the Angels finished near the top of the division he'd land the Cubs job in 1954, and he needed a veteran to play an all-around utility role.

The "other" Wrigley Field, home of the Los Angeles Angels and other PCL teams.

Dad hung up the phone smiling. "Stan thinks I can still do it. I'm going to play out the season for him. I wouldn't do it for anybody else. Stan's one of the good guys in the game, Dell."

The entire time Dad played for the Stars, the Angels were their crosstown rival, and since that time, the rivalry had grown heated and bitter; stony grudges existed among players on both teams, what Dad called "bad blood." Dad, who was familiar with almost all the Angels players, still harbored animosity toward the Stars, not only because they traded him, but especially since they hired Bobby Bragan as their catcher-manager and signed a bunch of young players and good prospects, making the Stars the premiere team in the PCL. Bragan possessed nearly every fault Dad despised in a ballplayer: He made his bones in the big leagues during the war, he was a pop-off, a showboat, an instigator, a clubhouse lawyer, a front office politician and stooge. That Stan Hack felt the same way about Bragan pleased Dad no end. But still, the Stars had a few players who'd been Dad's teammates, and he'd always been on good terms with Handley, Maltzburger, burly, quiet Frank "Mouse" Kelleher, feisty catcher Eddie Malone and Chuck Stevens.

The Angels played at Wrigley Field, a near clone of the stadium in Chicago, holding twice as many fans as Gilmore Field. Dad took me with him to the ballpark and everybody came over to shake his hand and welcome him aboard.

Right off, I made a friend—Dixie Upright, a reserve left-handed hitting outfielder with a southern drawl; a balding, square-shouldered man who wore colorful sport coats and shoes, a "dandy," according to Dad. Upright was like Gorman in that he invited me to sit at his locker and bone his bats.

The Angels clubhouse, compared to Gilmore's, was a pit. No fan had any idea that this beautiful ballpark with ivy-covered walls housed a rank, dank grotto of a clubhouse as second rate as some bush league locker rooms. But Dad didn't care, he was happy to be playing again. A couple of weeks off had allowed him time to rest and heal. He liked Hack's coach, Jackie Warner. He'd played Navy ball with catcher Al Evans. He liked Joe Hattan, a tough lefty pitcher. Dad said there was a good "feel" to the team.

"Some guys, you just look at them, something about their faces, you know they're good guys, but other guys, they got the kind-a faces you'd like to hit." That's how he felt about Hollywood outfielder and notorious base stealer, Carlos Bernier. "The little rooster likes to show people up. He slid hard into me down in San Diego, stealing second, and I 'accidentally' (he winked) fell on top of him and kneed the little showboat in the balls. He got the point."

Dad didn't seem to like any of the new players on the Hollywood Stars, and said: "I'll force myself to dislike the ones I like, because it's just like raiding a whorehouse, the good ones go with the bad."

Throughout the year a slowly burning fuse had simmered between the Stars and Angels. By midsummer of the long PCL season—one hundred and eighty games—the feud had turned ugly. Even Stan Hack, a man of perennial sunny disposition and known as 'Smiling Stan,' was spoiling for a reason to bait Bragan into a fight. A lot of grudges had developed. Also, since the Stars led the league, they carried themselves with a swagger, serving to irritate the Angels all the more. Every inning of every Stars-Angels game was heated and spiced with knockdowns and bruising take-out slides at second base; and the bench jockeying was personal and vicious. There were constant rhubarbs with umpires; the fans, always into the fray and yelling down at the field. And the situation was further heated by sportswriters in the local papers. Every baseball zealot in the L.A. basin felt a brawl coming on. Stan Hack must have had a nugget of wisdom filed away in his brain when he invited Murray Franklin, a renowned brawler, into this incendiary mulch.

Joe Hattan lived near us, and he and Dad drove to the ballpark together, while I sat in the back seat. Hattan had pitched well for Brooklyn and was in a World Series. Now, at thirty-seven, he'd lost movement and velocity on his fastball and had become what Dad termed "a junker." There were more than a few junkers in the PCL—pitchers who once threw hard but lost it and learned to use various delivery angles, curves, change-ups, palm-balls, knucklers and scroogies that somehow set up a mediocre fastball to come in like a shot from a bazooka—like the master junker in the big leagues, the Yankee's Eddie Lopat, whom Dad described as really tough to hit after facing fireballers like Allie Reynolds and Vic Raschi. San Diego had a lefty named Bob Kerrigan who threw a bunch of incredibly slow, bobbing, sinking, bending pitches that tied hitters into knots. "The sonofabitch could hit you between the eyes and never hurt you—but he gets people out," Dad said.

Hattan was a large, pale, lanky man with a deeply creased face and light, spiky hair. On the way to the ballpark he and Dad talked about certain players, the game that night, and what they planned to do after their retirement, which was soon. But the moment they entered the clubhouse, everything changed.

Normal people, with no affiliation to baseball, tried mostly to be gracious and civil to one another, shying away from confrontation and competition. But ballplayers in the clubhouse challenged each other to bets in cards and golf, constantly taunted and teased each other. In the clubhouse, any unfortunate physical defect could earn you a name: Fatso, Banana Nose, Prune Face, Slew Foot, Piano Legs, Chicken Legs, Butcher, Fiddler, Hog Jaw, Liver Lips...Nothing was sacred, nobody above exposure and ridicule; and that included Dad, and me. And right off on a tip from my Dad, I got the "Lover Boy" treatment from the Angels, and was coming right back at my new idols.

One of Dad's new teammates was Calvin Coolidge Julius Caesar Tuskahoma McLish, a strapping, thick-chested, right-handed pitcher from Oklahoma, an Indian owning a deadpan sense of humor and a sly twinkle in his eyes. Dad said McLish was a natural athlete, "one of those quiet guys you don't want to mess with." Dad regarded Indian athletes as "game, skillful fighters."

Rudy York, an Indian player out of Georgia who had monster years with Detroit and Boston, was Dad's roommate when he was with the Tigers. Unlike McLish, York was a boozer who became unmanageable when he drank, yet had the ability to recover from terrible hangovers and perform well every day. Prodigiously strong, York did everything in his power to help Dad, and was one of the best sign stealers in the game, once getting picked off second base while trying to signal Dad at the plate, for a curve ball. Dad never wanted to know what was coming, unlike York who was a brilliant 'guess hitter.'

Rudy York drove in more than 100 runs in a season six times in the majors.

"Rudy could guess right, and when he did he hit it a mile. He was so broad he had to turn sideways to get through a doorway. He hit seventeen home runs in a month one year. He got in a fight with a teammate once when he was drunk and it took five of us to pull him off before he killed the guy. He had him dangling out of a fire escape ten stories up."

One night York came in late in a despondent state, woke Dad up mumbling over and over, "Murray, I got no plume, I got no plume, Murray, you got a plume." It took a while for Dad to figure out that York meant a college diploma, which he revered. Mother said that York worshiped Dad because "he looked down on nobody" even though he was educated.

McLish and Dad talked a lot, though as usual Dad hung out with the infielders. The Angels had a feisty, undersized second baseman named Frankie DePrima and a slick shortstop in Gene Baker, quiet, polite, the team's best player and only Negro; and a bulldog third baseman named Bud Hardin. Dad was to relieve these players and get some action platooning with Upright in left field, while future big leaguers Bob Talbot, a fleet, blond center fielder, and Bob Usher, a thickset right-fielder who wore his pants low to his ankles like Mantle, played full time.

Right off, Dad began scalding the ball, and the team seemed inspired as Dad gave them a lift. His body english regained its old bounce. One evening he made a diving game-saving somersault catch in left field after charging a line drive, and the entire team came out of the dugout to smack his ass and pound his back while the crowd gave him an ovation. The team started winning. Dad's batting average, below .230 when he quit, began climbing steadily as he hit over .300. He was no longer arguing with mother or getting on my ass for bad behavior.

"Your old man, he's not through yet. Rackin' that pea pretty good. I feel strong as an ox, seeing everything big. You never know about this game."

The Brawl Heard Round the World

The Angels rose to third place and were playing a week-long series against the Stars. Every night game that week was hotly disputed and the vendettas, instigated by Bragan, had grown dangerous. Dad drove to Gilmore Field with Hattan and took me and a friend, Richard Poplar, a huge 12-year-old, a brute, a Little League all star and one of the top kids at South Park. Awaiting us was a Sunday doubleheader.

Since the games were sold out and no seats available, Ron and I ended up behind the rope in right field, among a bunch of Hollywood Stars knothole kids who hated the Angels, and automatically hated Ron and me. By the second inning we were having words with them as we defended Angels players. Ropes winding from both foul lines in the outfield were set up for the jam-packed overflow.

Early in the first game, in retaliation for some fireworks the day before, Hattan planted one of his infrequent fastballs in Frank Kelleher's ribs. Kelleher, my Dad's friend, whom Dad said was one of the good guys, had been on a hitting tear that was demolishing the Angels pitching staff, and he rushed to the mound and decked Hattan, who jumped up to do battle. Players from both benches and bullpens instantly swarmed onto the field and a skirmish started near the mound as umpires and peacemakers eventually managed to quiet things down. Kelleher was ejected.

While order was being restored, several nearby kids realized my father was Murray Franklin and began razzing me, claiming my Dad would get his ass kicked by the Stars, and several grown-ups and an usher got between us.

Then short, wiry Teddy Beard ran for Kelleher and stole second. When he tried to steal third the Angels had him by five feet, and as Dad, straddling the bag, caught the ball, Beard started his slide too close and flew into him thigh-high, spiking him on the forearms and knee. Dad's cap flew off, his bald head glinted in the sun, and then his fists were working in a blur. Both dugouts and bullpens charged onto the diamond and skirmishes whirled like spinning tops. A mountain of bodies piled up near the mound, new bodies entering while others flew out or charged back in; smaller skirmishes, moving, squirming, flailing, broke out all over the infield like a runaway saloon brawl from the movies. Certain players squared off, while others flitted around swinging wildly. While Dad was pummeling Beard, Gordy Maltzburger, coaching third, trying to be peacemaker, pulled Dad off Beard from behind, leaving him open for Beard to punch. Dad ducked the punch and shrugged off Maltzburger, who was being pulled off by Stan Hack. That was when McLish, on a full-tilt sprint from the bullpen, leveled Beard with a vicious punch and then proceeded, as Dad described it, "to pinch the little bastard's head off." Then Dad and McLish, like roving commandos, went head-hunting, which meant trying to inflict as much pain and damage as possible on anybody in a home uniform, be they peacemakers, friends or not. The umpires were helpless to stop it.

Richard and I lost track of Dad and suddenly we were engaged with the knothole kids, pummeling, kicking, rolling around on the grass outside the ropes, until an usher and some adults broke it up.

The donnybrook went on and on, showed no signs of abating until, eventually, a stream of fifty LAPD cops surged onto the field to restore order. Richard and I ducked under the rope, dodged an usher or two and sprinted across the grass toward the action, veering into the box section of the ballpark. By this time the melee was slowing down as cops separated brawling players. Uniforms were torn and filthy, caps lost. Ballplayers cursed and pointed fingers at each other as they were led to their dugouts. The last thing we saw before ducking into a tunnel was Dad pointing a finger and barking at the Stars players as two understanding cops led him away with half smiles.

The cop at the clubhouse door knew me and allowed us to enter the room full of cursing, pacing, grumbling, torn-up players vowing retaliation. Most of them refused medical treatment. Dad was sitting on the table in the training room, the trainer rubbing antiseptic on deep spike wounds on his knee and forearm. He'd refused stitches until after the second game of the doubleheader, which he intended to play. When he spotted me he grinned. "There's my boy!" I told him Rich and I fought the knothole gang from Hollywood and he told his teammates, "Them's fighting Compton boys!"

First baseman Fuzz Richards, who'd taken the worst punishment from blindside fists and was gouged and spiked when trapped beneath the mountainous pile-up, was getting sewn up by a doctor—over twenty stitches in his backside. He was furious. Bud Hardin sported a shiner and stalked the clubhouse holding an ice pack to his eye and vowing to get revenge on Dale Long. Dad began ranting about Bragan, whom he blamed for inciting the brawl by sending Beard after him. "I don't even know Beard, but he came in spikes high going for my balls. Now he's got a broken leg and two closed eyes, and that's what you get when you're a dirty ballplayer—he's finished."

Dad's face had no nicks, though his knuckles on both hands were bruised and cut and swelling. Stan Hack, who had spent most of

A high slide into Big Moe at third set off the brawl to end all brawls.

Fight instigator Ted Beard flails and misses at Big Moe. By the end of the fight, Beard has two closed eyes, a broken leg, and is done for the season. (David Eskenazi Collection)

his time looking for Bragan, who he claimed hid in the dugout, approached Dad at the training table. "Moe, Bragan's slated to catch the second game. I'm starting you and leading you off, and I want you to call out that yellowbelly. If they run you I'll pay the fine. I'll have Hardin waiting to come in for you."

Dad grinned. "Skip, I'll go after him, but Bragan won't fight— he's all mouth and no guts."

McLish, bat perched on shoulder (he was a decent hitter who sometimes pinch-hit), standing behind Dad, nodded, then rubbed Dad's head as if it was Holy, and winked at me.

For the second game, Rich and I were not about to return to the ropes in right field, instead stationed ourselves in the aisle a few rows up from the seats above home plate, ignoring and avoiding ushers who tried to move us along. Cops were posted like sentries at both clubhouse doors, in front of both dugouts, down both foul lines and bullpens and along the ropes.

When Dad came to bat, every Angel was on his feet in the dugout. Dad stood there looking down on Bragan, spewing profanity and insults, kicking dirt on the plate, on Bragan's spikes, while the ump stared out toward the field. Dad's head bobbed as he chewed on Bragan, who picked at clods of dirt, tossing them around. Finally Dad stepped into the box, pounded his bat hard on the plate and stared at the pitcher, Red Munger, who proceeded to walk Dad on four pitches.

Dad said afterwards, "I called Bragan every name in the book. I've never seen a man take more shit and hunker down like a gutless coward. He tried to blame the umpires. The ump, he was enjoying every minute—grinning like a shark. Told me he wouldn't run me under any circumstances. I told Bragan we were ON if Munger came anywhere near me—or Hack. Munger's an old hand, he knew what was going on. He threw me four straight pitches a foot outside. Bragan's a yellow cur."

The second game was uneventful. The next day, LA sports pages quoted Bragan blaming the umpires for the brawl. Sportswriters reported the bloodiest, most prolonged brawl perhaps in baseball history. The front pages were full of photos, as were the back pages; the most prominent in all the papers and later in *Life* magazine was one of Beard flying at Dad with his spikes high, like swords, his face contorted like a kamikaze, while Dad waited, ball in glove. The articles were full of descriptions, quotes, commentary, and already scribes were trying to drum up a return bout in the next series between the two teams at Wrigley, where LAPD Chief William Parker vowed to preside over a legion of cops to keep the peace. Beard's season was ended with a broken ankle. Dad got stitched up and I don't think I've ever seen him happier.

"I'm not one to condone it, but dammit, sometimes fighting is a good thing. It clears out your tubes."

BIG MOE

Ed "Bear Tracks" Greer

Greer won 287 games and threw more than 4600 innings in the minors.

After my big year at Beckley, Detroit moved me up to Beaumont in the Texas League, the last stop before getting called up to the big leagues. It was a tough pitcher's league and the weather was something you couldn't get used to—ninety-plus degrees every day, humid, you never stopped sweating, there was no air conditioning, that heat sapped you and you lost weight, so you were fighting it, and there was no use bitching, everybody was in the same boat.

Fort Worth had a pitcher, a mountain of a man, Ed "Bear Tracks" Greer. He had a lantern jaw and I guess you could say he looked intimidating. They say he was crazier than Bobo Newsome, who I played with and against—a pretty crude guy—and I think Bobo hung on because he wasn't dangerous, and ended up pitching for just about every team in both leagues.

Greer had real good stuff and threw hard, but as a person he was so wild and unpredictable that even in those days they couldn't bring him up to the big club because there was no telling what he might do. Hell, he might strangle a teammate, or throw somebody off a building, or go to a bar and get stabbed by a woman or get himself beaten to death by a mob.

For some reason I had Greer's number, and I nailed him pretty good. Sometimes baseball is just that way. We had an outfielder at Detroit, Bruce Campbell, a left-handed hitter, who wore out Feller while other guys looked helpless against him. The Yankees had a tough lefty named Marius Russo, and he had hard stuff that bore in on a right-handed hitter, and he jammed the hell out of me, and I hated facing him, couldn't hit him with a paddle. But Greer, only time he got me out was when I hit one right at somebody.

One night, after I racked him around and ran the bases like a maniac, I got up to the plate and he took his time, looking me over, and I knew he was going to dust me, and he did. Okay. I got up. He stood out on the mound, peering in at me with these spooky eyes, holding the ball in his big paw, flipping it and catching it. Well, before I settled in, he quick-pitched and dusted me again and I went down in sections, my heart in my throat. The crazy bastard was trying to kill me! So I jumped up and gave him a look. By this time I'd established myself as a guy who could take care of himself and never backed down from anybody, but Greer didn't give a damn if I was King Kong, and the crazy sonofabitch was grinning at me.

Well, I started to go after him and their catcher snagged me from behind. "Don't go out there, Franklin," he said. "Bear's crazy. He's not like other people. He's from the hills. He doesn't abide by normal rules of combat.

I don't give a damn, I told him. I'm not gonna be target practice for that sonofabitch.

"Listen to me, kid," he said. "Bear knows he can't get you out. We've tried everything all year and nothing works. If he can't get you out, he doesn't want you around. That's how Bear thinks. It's not personal. He'd probably like you if he got to know you. You seem like a pretty good guy."

To hell with him. Nobody knocks me down twice without a fight.

"Kid, you go out there and Bear'll dehorn you." I looked out there. Greer was in front of the mound, still flipping the ball, grinning at me, a dark person. "You're a helluva player, got a big future with Detroit, leading the league in hitting. Don't throw it away. You go out there after Bear, he'll tee off from two feet and plant that ball right in your kisser and hair-lip you. Stay here."

I stayed. Bear dusted me two more times, one ball a yard behind me. When I walked to first he kept his eye on me, grinning, flipping that ball. Later that year I ran into Bear Tracks at an all star game. We were on the same team and he was scheduled to start the game. When I got to the clubhouse he was drunk, had a jug of whiskey, came right over and wanted me to take a slug of the moonshine.

"I like you, Franklin," he told me. "Nice college boy. I'm glad you didn't come after me, cuz I didn't wanna kill you or make you ugly. Shit, I can't get you out. What am I supposed to do? I see you up there again, I'm gonna stick one in your ear."

Tracks never made it to the mound, never made it out of the clubhouse. They tried to get that jug away from him, but they couldn't, so they waited until he passed out on the training table, and they still couldn't get that jug out of his grip.

Towering Last Blast

Dad was hitting well and making plays at three positions. On my birthday he took me to a weeknight game at Wrigley, got me a box seat behind the Angels' dugout, got 3 hits and made a great catch against the wall in left field. On the way home he said that game was dedicated to me, a birthday present. "Sometimes things don't work out the way you want, but tonight everything turned out as well as I could've asked for—might be my last time."

I never wanted much from Dad on my birthdays. He always wanted to take me shopping and buy me nice clothes, but I hated clothes, preferred to wear old rags until they disintegrated, which seemed to bother him, because the way a person dressed, according to Dad, showed one's pride. He said that part of being a father was giving kids nice things. But I told him I didn't need anything but baseballs, a glove, a bat, a football, an old radio to listen to games in my room, and nothing else except going to games with him. What else was there?

Dad kept hitting the ball well, until September, when he began tailing off. One Saturday afternoon he dropped an easy fly ball in left field, which just popped out of his glove. He displayed no anger or disgust as boos rained down. During the drive home I asked him what happened.

"I just dropped it," he said, annoyed.

"Did you lose it in the sun?"

"No. A good ballplayer knows how to shade out the sun."

"Did you lose it in the high sky?"

"That high sky bullshit is for Alibi Ikes."

"Then how could you drop an easy fly right to you, a can of corn? You never had to move!"

"Dell, you don't go a whole season without booting one. Sometimes you make a good play on a tough chance, rob a guy, and then you turn around and boot an easy one. But I will say one thing: I never make an easy play look hard."

"How many balls you dropped in the outfield, Dad?"

He winked at me. "Today was my first."

Even as the sports pages revved up the Angels-Stars rematch to a fevered pitch, the series was without incident. Before the first game, Jack Phillips of the Stars, a big man at 6' 4" and over 200 pounds, one of the easiest going guys around and perennial peacemaker, asked Dad why he clobbered him, and Dad explained, "Jeez, Jack, I was hitting anything in a home uniform, sorry about that." Cops still stood near both dugouts throughout the series. The Stars showed themselves to be the superior team, the best in the PCL, with players like Dale Long, Lee Walls, Kelleher, Phillips and Tom Saffel putting the slug on the Angels. And the last road trip of the season was the end of Dad's career. Mother, Susie and I drove up to San Francisco to meet him on a Monday evening. Right off, Dixie Upright took charge of me so Dad could join Mom and take Susie shopping and out to eat seafood on the wharf.

"Where we goin' today, Meat? Ride the cable cars? Hit the snake-pits? How about a double-dipper at the movie house? It's your day, kid. Y'all and Dixie, that's a team, boy."

Dixie treated me to bunkhouse breakfasts, hot beef sandwiches at Tommy's on Van Ness, all the coke and popcorn I could hold and, all week long, took me to shoot-em-ups and war movies. We were not about to have anything to do with dramas, musicals or romance. It was like being with another kid, only a full grown one. I told Dixie that Dad cried when they shot the dog in "Old Yeller." Don't tell nobody, but old Dixie bawled too. Ain't nothin' worse'n seein' a dog get it."

During games, Angels management allowed me in the dugout, in street clothes, for the season-ending series. The team was still fighting with Portland and San Francisco for third place. Dad was exhausted. He'd played almost every every game since coming out of retirement—but he kept plugging away, and the Angels plugged away and ended up in third place, which ensured Hack the Cub job.

"Can't happen to a nicer guy," Dad said. "But Christ, Chicago's a horseshit club. Dumb organization. Stan won't last long there and he deserves better—he's a good baseball man."

Dad's last time up in professional baseball was a clear sunny September afternoon. Tony Ponce was pitching for San Francisco. Seal Stadium, spacious, known for its fog and damp air, often deadened long fly balls and kept them in the park. But on that day the ball Dad hit exploded off his bat as if whopped by a golf club. The crack of the bat resounded throughout the ballpark and the little white pill arced to impossible height as it climbed toward and then hit the top of the light tower beyond left-center field. The Angels jumped off the bench to follow the flight of the ball as it soared and Dad rounded first base hard and then slowed to a trot refusing to smile or show any emotion as he crossed home plate, where he shook hands with the next hitter, finally smiling, then getting butt-pats and back-slaps from all his teammates, really grinning big and proud.

Later, strolling through the lobby of the downtown hotel where we stayed, Dad picked up a newspaper and found an article on the front page of the sports section claiming Mickey Mantle had hit the longest tape-measured home run ever—565 feet! He grinned at me. "Mine would've gone farther if it hadn't hit the light tower."

I browsed the paper. "The Mick hit a beer sign after clearing Griffith Stadium, Dad. They call that the airport, don't they?"

"Best ball I ever hit today. If I'm at the airport, I hit the beer sign." He clenched his fist to show off his bulging forearm. "I'm still learning. What I learned today is you don't have to take that big a hard swing to hit one out. It's like that short, compact punch that always knocks a guy out. You hardly feel it it's so light. That's how it felt today when I hit that ball off the light tower. Hot damn! It's a helluva feeling to get a hit your first time up in pro ball, and then go out the same way."

* * *

When the Angels had their after-season awards banquet, Dad and Mom dressed up in their best, taking turns at the mirror and checking each other out and making a huge deal about what to wear before finally deciding. They were brimming with happiness, and in the morning, when I woke up, they were in the kitchen, all lovey-dovey, and sitting on the kitchen nook was an ashtray with a trophy on it of a boxer, and beneath it, on a brass plate, were the words—"Puncher of the Year."

Dad grinned at me. LAPD Chief William Parker, evidently having listened to his troops describe the great battle between the Stars and Angels, presented it to Dad. I guess his teammates gave him a pretty good ovation.

A New Adversary—Dad

"Murray, he's not ready for American Legion ball," mother insisted. Dad had coached the Compton American Legion team the last two years to championships, exciting everybody in our sports fanatical town, and felt I was ready for bigger competition. "He's not fourteen yet, you're pushing him too hard!"

"Dammit, Rose, he pushes himself hard. That's the way you gotta be if you wanna be any goddam good. Let him play. He *wants* to play. I think he's ready. I wouldn't play him if I didn't think he was."

"Murray, those are men out there. Eighteen-year-olds. Did you face eighteen-year-olds when you were thirteen?"

"Damn right I did. So you stay out of this. If *I* think he's ready, and *he* thinks he's ready, he's ready. He doesn't need any mollycoddling."

All the kids in Compton wanted to play for Dad, and I knew they resented me—a thirteen year old taking their position. I heard some of them muttering that I was getting to play only because I was his son, and should be playing Colt League or Babe Ruth League with kids my age. Just a year or two ago, as an eleven and twelve-year-old, I'd been bat boy and mascot for the Legion team, and now that the older guys who'd adopted me were gone, I was this child among physically mature teenagers with cars who drank beer and talked about pussy and regarded me as an unproven punk.

All I had was baseball, and the fact that at Roosevelt junior high, I played football, basketball, baseball, and ran track. I started and succeeded in all of them to the degree I was known as an athlete already coveted by Compton High coaches as a future star. So early on, I felt exposed, on stage. A strange new urge tugged at me—to drift away from my environment of Compton and show up somewhere else where nobody knew me and I could be Dell Franklin, and not the son of Murray Franklin playing for Murray Franklin.

I was gritting my teeth a lot. And, most agonizing, I'd suddenly begun booting ordinary ground balls. If there was any part of my game that brimmed with confidence, it was my ability to gobble and snare any kind of grounder, looking slick. I loved taking infield, loved flashing my talents. It was me.

But now I was booting everything, and my teammates were snickering and nodding. Nor was Dad pleased, and he made it a point to be harder on me than anybody else, and Christ, I was so bad, so off balance, that balls were playing me instead of me playing them, and I found myself flinching. I felt shaky, my confidence shot. I couldn't sleep at night, thinking about this. I was especially ashamed when Dad, trying to show his players there was no reason to be gun shy at the plate, allowed our hardest thrower, Dave Skaugstead, who would later sign for a bonus, to nail him on the backside several times, and Dad claiming "the mosquitoes are biting early this year, ey, girls?" Later, at home, I saw his backside was purple and red with welts.

Finally, in a game, at second base, I muffed two easy ground balls and stood in the corner of the dugout on the verge of punching the wall, fighting my temper, which had been flaring up, knowing it looked bush and nothing infuriated the old man more than his kid behaving like a busher—an immediate reflection on him and a desecration of what he was proudest. Dad said nothing, he wouldn't look at me, until the drive home.

"Tomorrow," he said grimly. "Tomorrow we'll see what you're made of."

* * *

We walked across the street to the Roosevelt Junior High baseball diamond, where I'd been a star on an undefeated team. The infield, this time of year, was a neglected rock pile, as Dad described it, full of pebbles, clods and bad hops, which Dad wanted. First off, soon as we got there, he scolded me vehemently for jogging out to shortstop—"YOU WANNA PLAY THE GAME YOU DON'T SLOUCH LIKE A GODDAM SADSACK—YOU HUSTLE OUT TO YOUR PO-SITION LIKE AN EAGER BEAVER—NOTHING LOOKS AS BUSH AS A LOAFER AND THAT'S WHAT YOU ARE RIGHT NOW, A QUITTER AND A GODDAM LOAFER!" And then, before I could even get set, Dad, fungo in hand, laced a rope that short-hopped and glanced off my bicep, stinging, and I flexed it, and before I could get set again he laced me a ground-hugging top-spinner that ate me up and bounced off my shin, which ached deep in the bone. "Ha ha ha," he jeered. "Two balls, two boots!" Another rocket smacked hard off my chest. "That's three! I'm gonna get your hair-lip next. You stink! You're stinking up the game. Wanna quit? Go on, gutless, crawl off the field like a whipped cur."

I heard myself bellow, "FUCK YOU!"

The next few minutes Dad blistered me on the foot, shoulder, ankle, and finally ripped another grass-skimmer that took a wild hop and popped me directly in the balls. I went down in an agonized heap while half the kids in the neighborhood who hung out at the playground looked on as I writhed and rolled around on the ground. Then Dad was standing over me, leaning on his fungo, a gloating mean grin on his face.

"Where's your goddam cup, dummy?" Before I could tell him I forgot it, he went on, "What's the first thing I taught you as an infielder?...Now go home, put your cup on and get your ass back out here. Then we'll really find out what you're made of. Go on."

Mother cringed as I stormed into the house limping, bruised. I slammed the door of my room shut, put the cup on and sprinted back to the diamond where Dad waited, still leaning on his fungo, grinning, about ten kids surrounding him in an adoring circle, obviously having listened to his humorous stories.

"Well, kid, there's no reason to be scared any more. I've banged you up everywhere and you're still here." He glanced at the kids, who'd been retrieving balls I'd muffed, then at me. "What's happened, Dell, is you've grown like a weed overnight. You're going through what we call the 'young colt stage.' Your legs are longer. You're not as low to the ground as you used to be. You've got to get back to the basics—stay low, on the balls of your feet, charge the ball with long, smooth strides, always low, because, like I've always said, every hop's a good hop when your ass is down. Glide. Light on your feet like a boxer. Stop thinking. Nothing dumber than a ballplayer who *thinks* too much. You got the best pair of hands around, Meat. Okay? Let's go."

He hit me several easy choppers, which I charged and lobbed back, urging him to hit 'em harder. Scorch 'em he did, and I began trapping and short-hopping violent top-spinners and grass-skimmers and one-hop rockets at my feet. He hit blue-darters to my left, my right, straight at me. I found a rhythm. No matter what he hit me, I flagged it down. As I gobbled ball after ball as fast as he could hit them, I became lathered in sweat, panting like a dog and grinning like a stooge as I began quick-releasing throws to a kid at first base, and the old man, he was grinning back

"That's my boy! Way t' scoop that ball, Digger O'Dell!" He hit me about a hundred grounders before I muffed one. At that point he was worn out and flipped the bat away and walked out to me. By this time half the neighborhood was at the cyclone fence bordering the school, watching this brutal exhibition, curious about the Franklin's, that family where the husband and wife yelled at each other and sometimes the father chased the son halfway down the block, infuriated at his hotshot insolence, shaking his fist, the son taking refuge at his mother's parents a block down the street.

Now Dad had his paw on my shoulder. "You might not boot one the rest of the year. Nobody's got better hands than you. You've always had the stuffings to play this game. Every ballplayer goes through tough times. I helped you get out of it, but later, when you grow up and play a higher brand of ball, you'll have to learn to work things out on your own."

I couldn't wait for the next game, and my next ground ball, and when it came, it was like I'd never had a doubt, making it look easy.

So, for the rest of the season, into August when I turned 14, I held my own. I choked up on a Nellie Fox coke-bottle shaped model bat, standing on top of the plate like Nellie, and chipped away, not quick enough yet to pull heat but managing to whack a few shots up the middle and into right field. When I came to bat my Dad coached third base. He clapped his hands. His uniform fit him perfectly with his socks high at the knees, while I wore my uniform baggy with the socks low like Mickey Mantle. Our relationship had evolved to my working for him in his store as a means of learning the business, contributing to the family, and earning a little money, which gave me independence, and realizing I was not in agreement with everything he said and did; and thus we argued, and I was accused of being disrespectful and a wise-ass and when he snapped and snarled at me I felt myself gorged with resentment and talked back, and a new period began in our relationship: We became adversaries. It was on!

BIG MOE

Jew Baiting

Playing for Beaumont in the Texas League, we had a pitcher on our team named Stith, a stocky farm boy who belonged to a Nazi Bund. He knew I was a Jew and he started in early in the season baiting me, trying to goad me into a fight—Jew this, Jew that, kike. I decided to let it go. I didn't want the reputation as a troublemaker fighting with teammates, because it was hard enough in those days getting to the top, and I was on my way. But Stith wouldn't let up. It was 1939, and the things going on in Germany and Europe, with the anti-Semitism, were still going on in this country. Stith kept putting Nazi arm bands and literature in my locker. He taunted me. There was still the stereotype that Jews wouldn't fight back, and Stith, a bully, had no idea I could fight, and I let him and all the guys on the team who felt that way think that, played possum.

Only a pitcher and pal of mine, John Gorsica, a Jersey guy, knew, and he wanted a piece of Stith, too.

I had hurt my leg earlier in the year and was not myself, and Stith knew this, too. Our manager, Al Vincent, knew Stith had been riding me all year with the Jew baiting and Nazi bullshit, and he and his coach let it go. Every night I came home from the park and let the rage build. Then, in Tulsa, on one of the hottest days of the year, we were staying in a hotel downtown and had just finished a series and were waiting for the bus to take us to the train station. The bus that picked us up carried the visiting team that was going to play Tulsa.

Depression era hard-noses at Beaumont, 1939. L to R: Moe Franklin, Dick Korte, Pat Mullin, Jack Tighe, Al Griswald.

As I came through the swinging glass doors of the hotel with the rest of the team, Stith, waiting for me on the sidewalk, ambushed me with a wild sucker punch and knocked me down. This was what I'd been waiting for. I jumped up and squared off with him just as the bus pulled in from the train station.

Stith kept charging me, and I boxed him—jab jab jab. He was sweating and snorting like a damn pig, trying to get his hands on me, but I kept moving from side to side, hitting him with both hands until his nose and mouth were bleeding, and then

I started teeing off hitting him as hard as I could. One of his eyes was in trouble and I went after it with one straight right after another until I had him out on his feet against the building.

By this time Vincent was yelling at me, trying to pull me off Stith, and I turned on him and told him to get the hell out of my way, and then I went back to work on Stith, holding him against that building and carving out that eye, until the eye was dangling by a thread and his nose was busted flat, and I wouldn't let him go down until his face looked like mush, and then I threw the bastard across the sidewalk into the gutter where he lay with his eye dangling from the socket, and then the trainer and a few players were there, and Vincent had hold of me. I shoved him off and told him I wanted him now, because he'd condoned Stith's Jew baiting all year, he'd enjoyed it, and Vincent, seeing the look in my eye, didn't want any part of me, but I was just getting warmed up. I was soaked in blood and sweat and didn't have a mark on me. By this time some of the players were filing off the bus and it was dead quiet and I looked at my teammates and some of the players getting off the bus and told them if any of them had any problems with Jews to get it off their chests and settle it right now, because I was good and warm.

A few of the players were green around the gills at the sight of Stith. Nobody wanted any part of me, and I don't blame them, because I was as mad-dog crazy as I'd ever been. Since the beginning of my career this had built up in me.

"We've settled our differences," Vincent said. "Let's get back to baseball."

Stith, he was finished. That eye was never any good. He never played ball again. And I feel good about that. Never regretted gutting that pig, and if I'd killed the bastard I wouldn't have lost a night's sleep, because it would be a better world without Stith and his kind.

Rag Man at Compton High

I walked around with this feeling that great things awaited me, and were expected of me. I awakened every morning exhilarated by the prospect of being a great ballplayer, a big leaguer with his own baseball card who signed autographs and lived the life his father and those who reached the top experienced. I had recently turned 15 and not only held my own in American Legion ball between my freshman and sophomore years, but had discovered as I matured that I possessed what the assistant football coach and head baseball coach at Compton High, Ray Edgmon, described as the quickest acceleration of any athlete in town, including the Black kids who eventually beat me during the last few yards in the 100 yard dash in citywide track competition. I could steal bases and run between holes in football and elude tacklers—a gift that boosted my already bursting confidence.

Coach Edgmon wanted me to play football, but Dad discouraged it, and in truth I had no stomach for the barbaric grind of the game that would threaten my knees as a future baseball hero. Instead I went out for basketball and was the only white kid to make the junior varsity, and right off I felt in over my head. The Compton High basketball team, its players culled from a huge population of kids, was the best in the state, and the coach, Bill Armstrong, was establishing himself as the Johnny Wooden of high school basketball and building a dynasty. One of the stars was big Marvin Fleming, a former basketball player of the year who would go on to win four super bowl rings for legendary coaches Vince Lombardi and Don Shula as a football tight end. His cousin, Roy Jefferson, was a starting forward on the JV basketball team and would go on to be an all pro wide receiver in the NFL and, like Marvin, win a super bowl ring.

The guard I had to beat out, Freddie Goss, would go on to be the player of the year and start on a UCLA national championship for Johnny Wooden, and was already a varsity first string guard—a sophomore phenom!

The Black kids on the team, members of junior highs across town that thrashed us at Roosevelt, held a contemptuous attitude toward me, implying it was *their* game, and I didn't belong. The only kid on the team who seemed to have a friendly nature toward me was Walter Jones, who, like me, could handle the ball and shoot, but wasn't a dynamic basketball athlete. He was a junior. When the season started, Mr. Armstrong, who coached the JVs and varsity, told both of us that our JV team could beat most varsity teams in the area, and that our chances, even though he liked our games, were slim with more good players coming up through the junior high system—kids already seen as "blue chippers" for college careers.

Walter had started as JV shortstop his sophomore year and informed me *he* was going to beat out a senior for shortstop. I quickly alerted him that I, too, was a shortstop and would beat both of them out. We began joking and joshing, picking on each other. Whenever we ate lunch at the benches just off the main quad, where racial tensions were already building, I overheard some white kids I'd known for years at Roosevelt, including Richard Poplar, muttering "nigger lover" when they passed by.

When my gorge rose, Walter clamped my arm. "Pay 'em no mind, Dell. They're too ignorant to know better."

"They used to be my friends."

"Don't need them kind of friends."

Walter and I became pals, which was rare among Blacks and Whites at Compton High, where well over two thousand kids were a melting pot of Blacks and Whites and a scattering of Mexicans. In no time, he was calling me "Rag Man."

"Look here," Walter, who was always well dressed and perfectly groomed, said one day, as we sat eating lunch and I ogled some pretty girls, "No woman gonna give you the time of day wearin' them ugly rags."

So far, I'd held secret crushes on a beautiful Black girl named Jane Cook and a white girl named Rochelle, but was too shy to ask them out. In my awkwardness, I had them laughing at me, or sometimes they'd pause to smile at me, which made me immediately blush and become tongue-tied. I'd had crushes at Roosevelt, with the same result.

"I don't need fancy clothes like you wear to get a girl," I responded. "They're gonna like me for who I am, Mr. Slick."

"Shoot, you ain't gonna get no woman the way you carry on. You need new rags, them rotted out, fallin' apart tennis shoes are gross, and that dumb-ass, white-boy crew cut don't look human when it grows out; looks like God made you bald and glued up your skull and tossed a bunch-a hay on top. You need new hair, new attitude, new jumpshot..."

"Slick, I'm gonna run circles around you when we go out for shortstop. You know how good I am? I played Legion ball at thirteen. A scout from the Boston Red Sox called my Dad and wants me to play winter ball with minor league professionals and college prospects. *I'm a prospect!*"

He put down his soda pop. "You foolin' with me?"

Dell Franklin

"Nope."

"Then you best play, Mr. Rag Man. You crazy if you don't. Why you wanna play hoop when you the white flunky nobody pass to? If you're good as you say you are, you got to go find out."

"What about you? You gonna stick it out and be the Black flunky nobody passes to?"

He laughed. "Think Mr. Cool Babe Jones gonna get a head start, too, Mr. Rag Man." He clamped my forearm. "Gonna beat your sorry ass out."

Playing with the Big Boys

I was nervous about my debut against grown men in winter league ball. I was still a skinny kid of around 145 pounds and what had saved me as a coltish brat playing against fully grown teenagers was my ability to hit a fastball with the quick, level compact swing my dad had taught me and stressed over and over; a philosophy of hitting that was simplified to succeed in the hardest, most complicated endeavor in all of sports—hitting a baseball hurled at you at various speeds from various angles involving curves and drops meant to baffle and defeat you. I stood close to the plate to protect the outside corner. My bat was ready just above my shoulder, wrists cocked, elbow down. I took a short stride. I kept my back foot planted. With two strikes I choked up on the bat and "guarded the dish," determined to fight the bastard on the mound as a mortal enemy. I seldom struck out and felt almost deranged with anger when I did. To me, the batters box was my private domain. My identity was of a hitter, a "stick," even if I had not yet acquired power.

"That'll come," Dad told me. "Take your vitamins and swing the weighted bat and the line drives'll carry farther."

An ex-catcher in the Boston organization named Marco, who ran the Red Sox winter league team for Joe Stephenson, Boston's head scout on the coast, picked me up at our house in Compton. A kindly man, he looked me over and fished a Red Sox uniform out of the trunk of his car. It was at least a size too big for me, but I was awed by it. He drove to a stadium in Huntington Park, explaining I would hit batting practice, take infield, and probably get in the game around the seventh or eighth inning.

When I jogged onto the field, after meeting and shaking the hand of the large, bearish, cigar chomping ex-catcher, Joe Stephenson, who was in street clothes, I felt like a skittish ragamuffin among grown men who'd played in the low minors and were still members of the Boston farm system. They were slick and quick and had stronger arms than me, and glanced in my direction with what I felt was amusement tinged with disdain. I still wore my socks low and pants baggy. My cap fit low over my eyes. I needed a haircut. Dad sometimes mentioned that I did not take enough pride in looking like a ballplayer in my uniform, which was "bush," and perhaps a negative reflection or perhaps an embarrassment on him.

A tall skinny kid who could have been my age but did look like a ballplayer stared at me as he warmed up with a catcher. Watching him throw, it was evident he was a pitcher, and there was about him an aura of cocky confidence, like *HE* was destined for greatness. I had to step in and warm up with two infielders to get loose, neither of whom invited me. I relished the idea of being seen by fellow players as a joke; I would show them!

After watching the pros whistle line drives all over the field, and flagging down their hard grounders at second, I tried too hard in batting practice and felt embarrassed at pulling so many high bounces and foul balls. I was overanxious. Marco, pitching BP, kept urging me to relax, stop trying to kill the ball.

When the game started, I was on the bench, and sat in a far corner of the dugout away from the bat rack and the horseplay among grown men who'd played together for years. Finally, the lanky kid who'd sized me up in a superior manner sat down beside me. A left-handed hitter, and right-handed thrower, he'd hit the ball well in BP. He offered his hand, and we shook. "Jerry Stephenson," he said. "I'm Joe's kid. You're Murray Franklin's kid, huh?" When I nodded, he smiled. He had fine features and intelligent eyes and beneath his coolness a high-strung energy. "Ballplayer's son, like me. They kind of resented me at first, too," he said, nodding toward the players. "But now they're cool. Don't sweat it. You got a nice stroke at the plate, very unique. Your dad teach you that?"

I nodded. We started talking, like instant good friends. Jerry, too, played Legion ball at 14 and held his own. He said his Dad started him out as a pitcher as soon as he could walk. As we talked, we watched the game, and, as innings passed, tension rose as I anticipated my chance. In the seventh inning, Marco called us over and told Jerry to pitch and put me at second.

Jerry showed unusual poise and command of his pitches. His technique was perfection and his fastball had movement and his curveball was more a slider and had bite. Nothing was hit to me. At the plate I faced a hard throwing right-handed low minor leaguer. After timing his warm-ups, I choked up on the bat and rifled his first pitch past his ear into center field and tore down the line, rounding first and faking to go to second. Marco, coaching first, clapped his hands.

"That's the stroke, kid. You're a singles-doubles hitter."

When the game was over (I did not get up again) Marco told me to keep the uniform and he'd pick me up the following Saturday; Joe Stephenson, standing beside Jerry, puffing his cigar, meaty face inscrutable, nodded at me. Later that night, at the dinner table, I was nonchalant when I told Dad I was one for one (a rope). Ho looked at my mother and nodded, then winked at me.

"That's my boy."

* * *

The following Saturday after my debut in winter ball, Marco picked me up and drove to the ballpark at UCLA. Again I struggled in batting practice, took a snappy infield at second base, pinch hit against a minor league lefty and roped a shot into left center for a long single. The guys in the dugout jumped up and cheered me. Then, after tearing around the bases and sliding under the catcher's tag to score, they were all laughing. Marco exclaimed, "Some guys are batting practice hitters, some guys are gamers. Franklin's a gamer, the kid's hitting a grand!"

Next at bat I walked and scored again. I made plays in the field. When Marco dropped me off at home, Dad, after working all day (he was putting in close to 70 hours a week), was waiting. "Kid's doing great," Marco told him. "Takin' some good licks at the plate, like his old man."

After Marco left, Dad asked me what I hit. I told him fastball.

"They probably figured they could throw it by you, because you look like a pipsqueak. Now that they know they can't, they'll start curving you. You're hitting minor league heat. You'll tear it up in high school."

The following Saturday Marco drove us to a park in Fullerton, a spacious yard with long fences. I hit better BP and this time faced a young prospect with serious heat and chipped off several pitches before lashing a blue darter between third and short. Hightailing it down the line, I heard one of my teammates shout, "Nobody can get that child out!"

Jerry, who went to Anaheim high, pitched well, a prodigy. Joe, watching both of us, nodded at me, puffing his cigar. So far he'd said nothing to me—the man was like a Buddha.

The following Saturday we played at Blair Field in Long Beach, a beautiful facility that was the first that winter to have a clubhouse. Marco claimed it was as good as most Triple-A league ballparks. Walking into the clubhouse, I felt a keen sense of excitement, as if I was back in the Hollywood Stars clubhouse, only this time as a player. We were to play the Pittsburgh Pirate winter team.

JERRY STEPHENSON   pitcher

Jerry Stephenson started his first game in the major leagues at age 19.

"Gonna face some real heat today, Franklin," Marco told me. "Couple of their pitchers are on the Pirate roster. I'll get you in against them, see if those guys can get you out." He grinned at me.

My stomach rumbled. As always, I sat with Jerry, watching the game, talking baseball, chewing my gum furiously. The Pirate pitcher was Black, a spot starter and reliever with the Pirates.

"This guy throws harder than anybody we've seen all year," Jerry told me.

The Pittsburgh team built an early lead. The Pirate shortstop, Bob Bailey, was a local Long Beach phenom, a high school sophomore like me, but a year older than me and already fully developed and built like a grown man. He was better than his reputation as a future bonus baby and hit a towering home run to left-center and ran it out like it was no big deal. Meanwhile, the Pirate pitcher, Bennie Daniels, stayed in the game, because he was mowing people down and throwing a no-hitter. They brought me in to pinch hit in the top of the eighth. I choked up on my thick-handled bat two inches and nicked a whistling fastball at my chest. I figured he had no respect for a skinny kid with a uniform hanging on him like sack-cloth, and could blow me down with heat. I fought off several fastballs and finally sliced one foul down the right field line. My teammates rooted me on.

I was beginning to time him and worked the count full, still waiting for his big curve and excellent change-up, but he threw me

BOB BAILEY   3rd base

Bob Bailey had a long and successful big league career, collecting more than 6000 at bats and nearly 200 home runs in the 1960s and 70s.

another chest-high fastball and I tomahawked it on a vicious line over the shortstop into left field, a one bounce single. I grabbed my cap as I tore down the line and rounded first, which I'd never done before. Jerry, from the top step of the dugout, yelled, "Franklin, you're the worst looking ballplayer on the field, but nobody can get you out!" The pitcher glowered at me as he shuffled off the mound, shaking his head. Bailey stared at me from short. "Christ, the worst hitter on the team breaks up the no hitter."

The umpire at second based walked up to him. "Hey, nobody's got that kid out in a month. He's the real thing." Up in the stands, where I shouldn't have been looking on strict orders from my Dad, I spotted Dad sitting beside Joe Stephenson and Ed Hughes, a big-nosed rumpled man who was the head Pittsburgh scout. The game went into extra innings. I walked twice and scored twice. We won. Afterwards, Dad drove me home. It was the first time he'd managed to get to one of my games, because he was making a delivery to a shoemaker in Long Beach.

"I got there just as you broke up the no-hitter. When you rounded first and took off your cap, I got chills up my spine, because that's what I did when I got a hit off Satchel Paige as a twenty-year-old college hot dog. That's the only time I took off my cap. I'm still tingling. It's all in the genes. I'm a believer in that."

BIG MOE

Angering a Legendary Lefty

It was common knowledge that Lefty Grove was the meanest man in baseball. Grove's own teammates feared him, because if you booted one and cost him a game, or a shutout, he'd give you a look that killed, and there were those who said Grove hated to lose even more than he liked to win. He was the best pitcher in baseball for nearly ten years, winning 30 games one year and leading the league in strikeouts and everything else year in and year out, a "stopper" who ended up winning 300 games and was an easy Hall of Famer.

Though Grove was known for threatening teammates when they cost him a game or even a run, if you made a big play for him or got a big hit in a tight game, he'd give you a nod of approval, and that little nod meant more than all this hugging and kissing you see with these modern ballplayers. And if you were his teammate and somebody on the other team took liberties with your health, Grove was the first to retaliate, and word was—nobody messed with Grove.

The first time I faced him as a rookie in an exhibition game, Grove was an old man, around 40. He had snow-white hair, had put on weight. The Red Sox were using him mostly as a spot starter and reliever. He no longer threw hard enough to scare people, but still, he had that aura, a big vulture, and he awed you. He acted like he owned the field, owned the game, and you were some interloper, and everything he did on the mound was effortless grace, like Williams hitting. A legend.

My teammate, Schoolboy Rowe, a pitcher, told me Grove'd been washed up for years and couldn't get off the mound any more. "Get yourself a hit," he told me. "Drag a bunt."

Jim Tabor was at third, and he was slow as an ice wagon, and Jimmy Foxx was at first, looking ragged from another hangover. So I stepped in there. Lefty glared in, looking bigger than I imagined. He threw me a fastball and I dragged it down the third base line and ran like a bat out of hell down the line. As I crossed first base, Foxx never made a move toward the bag. He stood there, watching me fly past. When I got back to the bag there was a hush on the field and in the stadium. Our first base coach wouldn't look at me. Foxx sidled up, arms folded, stinking like a distillery, with those big arms, biggest in baseball. He talked to me out of the side of his mouth.

Jesus, kid, what the hell you doing?

Over at third, Tabor stood near the bag, the ball sitting untouched between home and the bag, a perfect bunt. He was staring at me, too. "Nobody bunts Grove, kid, Foxx told me. It ain't done."

Grove led the American League in ERA a record nine times.

Now I had to look at Grove. He was halfway between the mound and first, scowling right through me. He growled and turned around and took the ball from Tabor, who looked at me and shook his head, as if to say, "Boy is that stupid ass in for it." All the guys in our dugout were having a big time falling all over each other, and the guys in the Boston dugout were quiet and grim, like they were waiting for somebody to stick my head in the chopping block.

"You're hitting a thousand against Grove, Franklin," Dizzy Trout yelled from our dugout. He and Rowe jostled each other.

I kept my head down, took a small lead, while Foxx toed the bag and smacked his glove. Lefty don't forget, he said. "Better hope he's gone next time you're up, kid."

Sure enough, they left him in there and I came up again. Lefty's glaring at me when I stepped into the box. I played it meek, knowing I was going to get knocked down and deserved it for being dumb and listening to guys like Rowe and Trout, goddam pitchers. So I braced myself to take one on the backside and Grove floated a slow curve down the middle. Strike one. Well, he'll get me now, I thought, he's setting me up.

"Hey bush!" somebody yelled from the Boston dugout. "Drag another bunt!"

I got ready to duck again and he floated I another slow curve down the middle. Strike two. I got out of the box, stared out at Grove. To hell with him, I thought. I don't give a damn what he does, I'm hitting. Next pitch he comes in tight with a fastball and I whack it off the fence in left and pull into second with a double. I stand there, proud as a peacock, and Lefty's got the ball back. He steps off the mound and gives me a tiny nod, no smile.

"Thattaway to swing that bat, kid," he growled. "You don't need to bunt."

Varsity Big Shot Battling Dad

Walter and I were locker partners in the smelly, dilapidated Compton High locker room. We were practically panting with excitement for varsity tryouts. We walked out to the field together, warmed up and played pepper, bantering about our shortcomings the whole time. He owned a rifle of a natural throwing arm from the hole between third and short, and labeled me a rag arm. But I covered much more ground in a low crouch and called him "turtle." I was a line drive hitter, but he had more power, and called me a "punch" hitter. I called him Mr. Whiff. Two Mexican kids, a senior and junior who started the year before, also tried out for short, and they treated me with the scorn I had coming as the privileged son of an ex-big leaguer. My attitude was one of essential arrogance implying they didn't belong on the same field with me.

I realized I did not have a strong arm, especially from the overhand release. I threw three-quarter arm and at times side arm if I was moving toward my target, and I had perfected from hours of practice a quick release of the ground ball from the low fielding crouch that compensated for the lack of velocity in my peg. I seldom straightened to throw, but completed the entire process of catching and throwing out a baserunner in one single motion; an automation that enabled me to seldom think

Del Franklin
Short Stop

Posing for the high school team, with some "free advice"
from my teammate and pal, Walter Jones.

too much and commit an error. I didn't even have to look at my
target, knowing the ball would get there.

After a couple of days, coach Edgmon moved the two Mexican kids off shortstop and began a competition between Walter
and me. In a practice game, a big Mexican pitcher named Jorge
Rubio sized me up and planted a fastball in my back. I knew it
was retaliation for his two pals being demoted and I took it. I
refused to rub. As I trotted to first, he eyed me and I ignored
him. When I was on first, he still eyed me, and I took a good
lead. He turned to get the sign, got into his stretch, and I took a
huge lead. He threw over. I got back easily. I took another huge
lead. Richard Poplar, a senior, 200 plus pounds, slapped another tag on me as Rubio came over again. Poplar wouldn't talk to
me. He had marked his territory as a racist and had brawled

Walter Jones
Second Base

It could never be said that Walter lacked confidence.

with Blacks trying to put a foot in Senior Square on the main quad, a place no Black student had dared enter over the years. There had been near riots when a Black girl won out over four white girls for homecoming queen. Wayne Tatum, my Roosevelt teammate and a big league prospect as a pitcher, had followed Poplar's lead, drove around with him in Rich's car and had made varsity as a starting pitcher. If possible, he was more full of himself than I was.

I stole second easily, popped up, stared at Rubio, who stared back, and took another ridiculous lead. He threw over twice and then I stole third and popped up and smacked the dust off my pants and took another lead and yelled out at Rubio.

"You can't hurt me with your shit! Hit me again! It's an automatic triple!"

I sensed his hatred of me. I didn't give a shit. The game was mine. He was an interloper. Nothing could stop me. I was all about the game. Nothing else mattered or interfered. Nothing.

* * *

I made varsity shortstop. Even with his strong arm, coach moved Walter to second. There was no gloating. We still picked on each other, but also spent hours after practice working on the double play until we were slick. We talked baseball. Walter was calm and cool while I was fidgety and intense. When I made a suggestion on how he should hit, he just stared at me. I felt everybody should hit as I'd been taught by my Dad.

The early morning of our first varsity game, I walked down Alondra Boulevard with a few of my old neighborhood pals, cork-offs, clowns, card players, pussy talkers, virgins, all of us. We always passed Dad's store, which was between a liquor store and insurance office and across the street from the Richfield gas station on the corner of Santa Fe and Alondra, a busy hive.

Beyond the wide front window, behind a long waist-high counter, Dad conducted business with a crowd of shoemakers eating his donuts, drinking his coffee, buying his merchandise while he held court. Summers I'd worked for him as a stock boy and knew most of these customers, and no matter how busy he was he always noticed us kids lollygagging by, and if he didn't I'd pound on the window and double up my fist and shake a menacing fist and challenge the old man to a mock-fight. Right off he'd get the killer look and rush to the doorway and start taunting me.

"Hey bird-boy, who've you whipped lately? You can't whip nobody."

My friends, all of whom were terrified of Dad, the most notorious bad ass in town, watched me shadow box. "You're old and slow, Dad. I'm Sugar Ray."

"Look here, bird-boy, when you're twenty, and I'm fifty, I'll still whip you, and when you're thirty, and I'm sixty, I'll still whip your ass. And when I'm seventy, God willing, and you're forty, I'll STILL whip your ass!"

But this morning it was different. He came to the door with a big smile on his face and said, "Relax and rack that pea, Dell, and have a good game. I'll try and get there if I can."

* * *

A contingent of neighborhood pals, most of whom I'd known since grammar school, were in the stands of the windswept pasture of our Compton High ball field for my debut.

I got up four times and banged out three singles, walked, stole a base, and played errorless in the field, and we won. Coach Edgmon flashed me a fatherly smile afterwards and patted my butt. My friends stood after my last hit, gave me an ovation, and left. Walking home by myself, I was literally floating along the sidewalk about half a mile from home, on Alondra, when Dad pulled alongside me in his Nash Rambler station wagon. He stopped and I got in and instead of driving off he just stared at me with an expression indicating he was severely disappointed.

"I went three for three, Dad," I exclaimed proudly, hoping to wipe the look off his face. "I stole a base, walked, no errors, and we won."

"I know," he said, still not smiling.

"I didn't see you there," I said.

"I was there. I saw everything. Saw you looking all over the place when you're supposed to be paying attention to the game. I saw you visit Tatum on the mound twice and tell him how to pitch. An infielder NEVER goes to the mound unless he's called in to discuss strategy by the manager. Who the hell are YOU telling Tatum how to pitch! You want your teammates telling YOU how to play? Bush! A disgrace. Just because you got a couple hits you're telling everybody how to play the goddam game...since when does a 15-year-old hot dog tell everybody where to play?" I started to answer but he cut me off. "That's Edgmon's job. Next thing you'll be telling HIM how to run his goddam team."

My stomach churned with instant hot nausea. "Guess nothing I do satisfies you..."

"It's not just about playing the goddam game, it's about conducting yourself like a ballplayer, not strutting around like some rooster who acts like he invented the game, craning his head all over, looking at the girls, looking at your friends, looking at the scouts...I've never in my life seen such horseshit behavior on a ball field."

He started the car and headed home in silence. I went straight to my room and slammed the door shut, lay on my bed staring at the ceiling, wanting to punch savagely the face of the man that told me it didn't like me, nor what I'd become, or was becoming. Oh, maybe like most fathers he loved me, but that didn't prevent him one iota from finding me disgusting and even revolting.

When I finally got to the dinner table, mother looked agitated and unhappy. I'd heard them arguing from my room. Mother had made pork chops and mashed potatoes and peas and I speared three pork chops off the platter and slapped them onto my plate. Dad flashed me the evil eye.

"What have I told you before?" he growled. "Take one. You eat one, then take another. You don't take three. Those chops aren't going anywhere."

"I always end up eating three," I protested.

He speared two off my plate and dropped them on the platter. "You always take the three biggest chops. A pig. It's time you learned some goddam table manners."

"Murray," Mom protested. "Do you have to notice everything he does? Let the boy eat!"

He pounded the table, rattling dishes, causing sister Susie to wince and come close to tears. "You stay out of this!" he snarled viciously at Mom. "I'm in charge here! Stop protecting him! His manners are a disgrace and if it's the last thing I do, if I have to starve the wise-ass, I'm gonna teach him some goddam table manners!"

As I poised my fork to spear my chops back, he tightened his most murderous look.

"Don't do it, I'm warning you..."

My fork was barely in the chop when the lights went out. Next thing I was all the way into the living room, on my back, shaking out the cobwebs, feeling at my jaw. Mother hovered over me, and Susie was crying and had out her baton, ready to do battle in defending me from Dad, who sat in his dinner chair, a gloating grin on his face.

"That was just my Betsy Ann shot," he called. "A love-tap, bird-boy, not my Susie Q." He doubled up his left-hook fist.

I stood and began screaming at him. He rose and came toward me and I picked up his windbreaker as he came over and whipped it across his face and ripped a small chunk out of his bald head. He grabbed his head and his eyes flashed with murder and I took off out the front door with the old man on my ass. Of course, he couldn't catch me. I stood out on the sidewalk while he threatened to "break me into a thousand pieces" when he caught up with me. I gave him the finger while he reached up to halt the flow of blood from his head. Evidently I'd gotten him with the zipper-end.

I turned and began trotting. I wandered over in the darkness to Roosevelt Junior High and ended up walking down Long

Beach Boulevard and then Atlantic, just walking, boiling, thinking about taking out my savings and hitch-hiking off into the sunset, and the only reason I wouldn't was because of baseball. I was exhausted and starving and thought of visiting my grandparents on my mother's side a block from us, but knew my dad would be looking for me there. I knew also that after he cooled off he'd calm down, though this was the first time I'd ever struck back at him. He'd had me on the ground a couple times over the years and Susie always clobbered him with the baton while mother screamed and beat on him. I'd deserved it then, but not now.

Later, much later, on the verge of collapse, I reasoned Dad was in bed because he had to mind the store early, and knocked on the back door of my grandparent's house. Grampa was up—a night owl who went to sleep in the wee hours, slept late, ate eggs and only eggs; then, in his white short-sleeve shirt, black baggy pants, Dobbs Fifth Avenue hat and black shoes, walked all over Compton and clear into Long Beach and sometimes into South Central LA where he was known as "the walking man." He smoked a pipe and cigars. He studied religion and hated them all and cornered door-to-door preachers and corrected them on their spiels. He read the Russian authors, the German philosophers, listened to classical music, had played the oboe and flute in small town bands back in Wisconsin and was a tailor all his life who had no patience with customers and terrified all my cousins in his house and wouldn't let them make any noise or touch anything but favored and spoiled me because he'd been my surrogate father for two years while Dad was away in the war.

Mother always said, "Grampa knows you better than anybody."

He was the only non-Russian Jew in the family, a French-Belgian born outside if Liege, who came to America as a child and had no accent.

He let me in, smelling of pipe smoke. He was completely bald and because he seldom wore his false teeth, his chin nearly touched his nose. Dad claimed he looked like the cartoon character, Snuffy Smith. He knew why I was there. Gramma got up and made me bacon and eggs and poured as much milk as I could drink. Dad had come looking for me earlier. He was angry but they calmed him down. Grampa put me up on a couch in the den, which had a piano. He liked to sit in his den alone and read and listen to Rachmaninoff or Beethoven or DeBussy or Amos and Andy on the radio and smoke his pipe. Tonight we sat and talked.

"Your father, he's a good man," he explained, "but this baseball stuff, it's not you. It's just a game, Dell. You don't know it now, but you're a scholar, and an artist." He grinned at me, false teeth out, puffing his pipe. "Like your mother."

The Feud Rages On

Dad and I were not talking, nor offering apologies. Our feud seethed with such acrid resentment we refused to look at each other. When passing his store mornings with my crew I skittered on. Tension was taut at the dinner table. A welt from my flogging him with his jacket was scabbed over on Dad's pate, and occasionally he glanced up at the ceiling, where a smudge of grease was left from the pork chop that flew from my grip after I was punched out, reminding me. Mother tried to break the ice by asking me how I was doing in baseball, but these overtures received only stony silence or grunts.

In league play I was holding my own at the plate as lead-off hitter, but my fielding had begun to fall apart—specifically the accuracy of my arm, never a problem before. Coach Edgmon was easy and fatherly on his players, and especially me, clapping his hands and urging me to shake it off when I booted one in the field or ground my teeth, barely holding my temper when I made out.

"You can't get a hit every time," he told me. "Relax. Get 'em next time. You're hittin' over three hundred." But I wanted to hit .400.

At shortstop, I was trying to compensate for my average arm by hurrying or loading up my throws instead of going with my natural rhythm, and tossing balls in the dirt. I was "thinking" too much. I knew I should talk with Dad, who always solved my problems instantly with small, subtle tips that were often just as psychological as mechanical. Several times I could not control my temper, throwing bats, kicking dirt, and Poplar and Tatum were grumbling about my performance and alluding to Edgmon "coddling me." Worst of all, I grew tight, tentative. Overnight I'd gone from cocky and confidant to fearful of muffing one.

Edgmon finally took me off shortstop, switching me to second, replacing me with Walter.

"You're a little nervous out there at short," he told me in his trophy-laden office, where I pleaded with him to let me stay at short and work things out. He shook his head. "I figure the shorter throw'll take the pressure off you, son. Walter, he doesn't have your range, but he's got that strong, steady arm. I think you're gonna be the best damned second baseman in the league. I'm doing this for the good of the team, and your good, too. It's the right move."

Walter did not gloat, but instead encouraged me.

When I got home, I didn't tell mother about Edgmon's decision. She was studying down in the den, about to get her teaching degree from Long Beach State to go along with her nursing degree so she could be a high school nurse. She made straight A's. One minute Dad called her an "intellectual egghead with no common sense or understanding of the business world," and the next he bragged to his shoemakers that she had an IQ of over 150, which she did.

She saw I was down in the dumps and gazed at me, full of adoration, understanding and compassion, "the motha look," as Dad described it, so sappy, and I began squirming, though Mother was my true confidante, which Dad interpreted as her protecting me.

She sat me down. "Dell," she said firmly, looking me straight in the eye, like she did everybody, unnerving many. "It's up to you to be the mature one in your relationship with your father. You must make an effort to understand him and be a bigger, more tolerant person than he is. He can't change, but you can. We both know your father is domineering, and controlling. He thinks he has to be. He can be a bully. He's very jealous and petty, and he's vengeful. You have no idea how he tried to dominate me early in our marriage. This was such a shock, because during our three years of engagement he was a perfect angel. Then I learned this whole other side of him. He forced me to quit the air lines as a stewardess because he didn't want other men looking at me. He cheated me in cards for twenty years before I caught him. He tried to teach me to drive and humiliated me so I almost left him. The same with golf. You must understand that NOTHING you do in life will satisfy him. Your father, bless his heart, is insecure, he is, well, a belittler, and the reason he is this way, believe it or not, is because he is frustrated and disappointed he never got as far as he should have in baseball, and if you let him drive you crazy, honey, you will be unhappy, and I can't bear to see you this way, so miserable, hating your father who loves you more than you can imagine. Dell, listen to me—if you take your father, and baseball too seriously, I fear it could have a very, very dangerous influence on your life."

She sighed, still gazing at me. "You are NOT just your father, you are also of me, and you should not be ashamed of that. You are much, much more sensitive than your father. You see and feel things he doesn't, and you see gray, where he only sees black and white." Still gazing at me with the 'motha look,' she leaned forward and kissed my forehead, an act I'd been discouraging since becoming a teenager, and I squirmed, but she smiled, understanding my squeamishness at all things emotional. "Please start talking to your father again. He's always sorry when he knows he's wrong, but he's not going to admit it, and honey, his heart is breaking. Since the day you were born he has loved you like no other. You are his pride and joy, and you must put yourself in HIS shoes. That is the secret to living—putting yourself in everybody's shoes. Be big. Remember, Dell, as my mother says—'nobody is that wonderful, and nobody is that terrible.' The only way I have been able to survive your father is to understand him, and forgive him. There's no harder man to live with, but I could spend a lifetime trying to find a better man, a more decent man, a man as unique and interesting as your father, a man with his kind of character. You must be the adult in the relationship."

I knew she was absolutely right. I nodded. "I'll talk to him, if he wants to talk to me, but you've got to tell him I don't want him at my games, because Mom, he makes me too nervous, and I feel so much pressure that sometimes I can hardly think or breathe out there."

She looked deep into me, and nodded. "Okay. It'll hurt him, but it might be the best thing to do right now—for both of you."

BIG MOE

Gehringer

Charlie Gehringer of the Detroit Tigers was considered the greatest second baseman of all time. He was a home-grown Michigan native who'd been holding down second base since 1926 and was going to the Hall of Fame. There was no more popular player in the history of the franchise, and that included Cobb and Greenberg. He was a darling of the front office and the fans and press. He was probably the most fundamentally sound player in the game, a guy who went about his business as a total professional, and a master of every phase of the game—running bases, sliding, bunting, hitting behind the runner, going out on pop flies, making the double play, going to either hole, stealing a base, getting you a scoring sacrifice fly, anything you needed to win a game.

He was a quiet, reliable guy who, like DiMaggio, never made a mental error and could freeze you with a look if YOU made one, because you were hurting the club and taking food out of his mouth. He was the kind of leader you didn't want to disappoint, all business, respecting the game like a religion, and if you didn't respect it the same way, and disappointed him, you were gone.

He hardly said boo to me when I came up, never went out of his way to help me or give me advice, and he knew who I was, knew I'd been a top infield prospect in the organization and being groomed to take over his position even if I was a shortstop, and he knew he was just about finished as a ballplayer, but he wasn't about to give up his position to some interloper written about in the local paper as his replacement.

Gehringer knew that helping me meant helping the ball club, and the ball club for years had been his life's blood, and it was obvious he was hurting the ball club, because he could no longer hit or cover any ground. The team knew it, he knew it, everybody in the league knew it, and finally, in '42, they kept him on the roster mostly as a pinch hitter, for the fans; and then one of the writers who got a thrill out of making somebody miserable wrote a column with headlines in the Detroit paper saying I, Murray Franklin, was taking over his position.

He never said a word to me that day in the clubhouse. And when the game started and I was announced as the second baseman, the entire packed house booed me, and they kept right on booing me when I ran on the field. And when I ran off the field at the end of the first inning, a bunch of wolves near our dugout dumped garbage on me, coat hangers, corn cobs, filthy rancid stuff, and they cussed me and insulted me like I'd murdered Gehringer, telling me I'd never hold his jockstrap, and Gehringer sat in the dugout and never said a word or looked at me, and the booing and insults didn't stop until I pulled a single into left field.

I was relieved to go on the road and away from those Detroit fans. As for Gehringer, he never warmed up to me, never offered any advice or encouragement, and I never held it against him, because that was the nature of the times—you didn't want anybody taking your place and you never felt secure. He was a proud man, a legend. He'd been so great, and it couldn't have been easy to see somebody else playing a position he'd held down for 20 years.

Cowardice at Second Base

We had a big game with all-Black Centennial High, our cross-town rival. We played them at Cressey Park, a fine municipal stadium with symmetrical fences and stands wrapping around from third to first base and lights and a press box, where Howard Handy, sports editor of the Compton Herald American newspaper, sat and reported on games. The ballpark was located in the Black part of town, off Central and Rosecrans Boulevards. Like us, Centennial had some good prospects, including smooth switch-hitting sophomore shortstop Roy White, who would go on to have a big career with the NY Yankees, and several formidable player—strapping, mercury-quick kids with fierce us-against-them attitudes. The stands were filled with mostly Black folks.

Tatum, already drawing scouts with his live fastball and excellent control and poise and confidence, pitched, and it was close, a tense game. A very powerful senior outfielder who played linebacker on the football team, was on first base, and he began talking to me at second base. "Comin' down, skinny white boy, gonna cut your balls off, gonna take your skinny ass out!"

Walter cupped his hand to his mouth. "Don't pay him no mind, Rag Man. He's all jive, just bluffin.'"

"I been sharpenin' my spikes, boy, gonna cut you up good."

Sure enough, the hitter slapped a ball in the hole between short and third. Walter backhanded it and in one motion snapped me a perfect waist-high peg. I heard the baserunner thundering down the line screaming that he was "coming for me" and for the first time ever I hopped like a frightened hare across the bag too quickly to avoid his spikes-high slide. The ump called him safe in a voice that seemed to boom and echo in my ears for unendurable minutes. I never completed the throw to first, gripped the ball tightly, head down, unable to look at my team-mates or anybody as the baserunner stood, staring at me with utter disdain as he brushed himself off.

I heard the Centennial dugout's chorus: "Cluck cluck cluck! Chicken boy! Cluck cluck cluck!" I heard the baserunner whis-per, "Footsteps." Finally, I faced Tatum, who'd stepped off the mound to deliver me a look of pure loathing and disgust. "Gut-less motherfucker," he fumed.

"Gutless yourself," I growled back, finding my strangled voice. I gunned the ball at him so hard he staggered to catch it. Then I heard Poplar at first: "Guess you didn't inherit your old man's CAJONES, huh?"

I couldn't look at him. Centennial broke the game open, and when the inning ended I went to the far end of the dugout and sat. Even Edgmon left me alone. Walter finally sat beside me, stared straight ahead, patted my knee. He never said a word, and on the bus ride back to campus, after we lost, he sat beside me in the back.

"Everybody has a day like you did," he said softly. "Next time, you'll get 'em back. I know you will. That's how you learn."

"Walter, sometimes I wish I was you," I found myself telling him. "Black, with no Dad as an ex-big leaguer, and folks expec-tin' me to be like him."

He gazed at me. "If you feel that way, like you wanna be me, well, my friend, you are in powerful big trouble."

When I got off the bus last, Edgmon waited for me, put his arm around my shoulder and walked me toward the locker room. "Son," he said. "I'm stickin' with you no matter what. I'm in your corner. What happened today, it'll never happen to you again. I guarantee it. You got spooked. I been spooked. You got too much heart and character. I know you, and you got the right stuff."

At the dinner table that night, I felt like it was extra quiet. Dad acted as if nothing in particular had happened, and though I didn't see him at the stadium, I'm sure he'd heard about it. When you prove yourself a coward, you're sure the whole world knows about it.

Transfusion

Dad and Mom got into a savage argument that erupted at the dinner table a day after my act of cowardice. Every point Dad made was shoved down his throat with barbed venom. Finally he grew so exasperated and enraged that he fired a fork at her, and it made a direct hit, sticking in her tender bicep. Mother stared at him coldly and pulled it out, calmly walked out of the dining room, but not before telling him in an arctic tone of voice to "pack his bags and get out of the house." Susie ran from the table, shrieking.

This was a first; he'd never touched her, and she'd never booted his ass out. He packed a bag and moved into a shabby motel in Compton. The relief of tension in the house was instant. We were at last calm. Mom made a show of being happy, but I knew things couldn't go on like this, especially when cousin Bob, Dad's right hand man at the store, came by to inform us Dad was a mess and would probably get in a fight over a traffic altercation and end up in jail if Mom didn't take him back. He was so irritable in the store he was driving everybody crazy, working 70 hours a week.

A week into his absence I was sitting on the porch still moping over my craven display when Dad drove up in his Rambler wagon, bounced over a curb and back down into the gutter, coming to a crooked stop. Mother was instantly on the porch, hands on hips, looking cross. The shot-gun door opened and Dad fell out onto the strip of grass separating the sidewalk and curb and, on his hands and knees, vomited profusely into the gutter. I walked over to stand near him as neighbors piled out of their homes to observe the toughest, most famous guy in town resemble a skid row drunk. It was a Saturday afternoon. I'd never seen Dad this drunk before. I'd seen him happily lit with his baseball pals, but never like this—never.

While I stood over him, he peered up, and muttered. "Yer motha, she knows everything! Never wrong. Shit." He spewed out bits of vomit, hiccuped several times. "Go tell yer motha I'm comin' home. That's my house, too. I goddam worked for it. I paid for it. I won't be a goddam mouse in my own house!"

He sat up, holding his head. He tried to rise but teetered and I held him up. He smelled foul. I hoisted him by the armpits and dragged him like a 6 foot heavy bag toward the front door of our house. Mother and Susie stood on the porch looking like executioners. They turned away abruptly and made sour faces as I grunted and pushed past them, hauling Dad. I got him into the house and led him to the bathroom where he sat on the side of the tub.

"All I do is work!" He shouted. "And I'M the goddam villain. I'm no wifebeater. I'm not Black Bart!"

Doors slammed. I peeled off his sweat-drenched, vomit-sprayed shirt, pulled off his shoes, then his pants. He stood, wavering, and I caught him as he slipped out of his boxer shorts and led him to the shower. I got him in the shower. I turned on the cold spray full blast and savored his shuddering cries. I handed him a tooth brush with paste.

"In case she ever kisses you again, Dad."

"Very funny."

I kept an eye on him so he didn't collapse in the shower and cut himself to ribbons on the glass door. After more of his howling and growling, I got him out, tossed him a towel. He wrapped it around his waist and headed toward the bedroom where he collapsed face first on the bed and was immediately snoring loudly through a thrice broken nose. Mom and Susie were gone. I was stuck with Black Bart.

* * *

Next morning, late, Dad stood in the kitchen drinking coffee, his face doughy and stubbly, eyes bloodshot.

"You know your father's no drunk," he told me. "Your mother knows it, too. She knows she's gotta go pretty far to me to throw a goddam fork at her." He belched. "Anyway, thanks for taking care of your old man." He stared at me for a long time, appraising me with those bleary eyes. "Now," he said. "Go get the bag of balls. We're gonna hit."

We hauled the gear to the Roosevelt rock pile as churchgoers returned for yard work and stood with garden tools observing us. As we warmed up, Dad wore his grim game face. Then he grabbed a bat and said he was going to hit, because he was to play in an Old Timer's game at Dodger Stadium. Last year, down in San Diego, he hit a 385-foot homer at Westgate Park in an Old Timer's game and his arm was still pretty strong.

I tossed some normal BP and he pulled half a dozen ropes into left field. He waved the bat at me and implored me to throw harder. I did. He laced two balls that nearly took my head off. "Harder!" he shouted, a superior smirk on his mug, digging in. I wound up and fired one up and in and he tomahawked it, the ball soaring and curving over the heads of some young neighborhood kids who began shagging in the outfield. God, could he hit!

"KNOCK ME DOWN!" he bellowed, waving his hand at himself, taunting. "Come on, bird-boy!"

I fired a medium fastball and instead of ducking he took it on the shoulder and snarled at me. "That all you got? My my, the mosquitoes are biting early this year, aren't they, bird-boy... Goddam mommy's boy!"

I fired a ball as hard as I could before he could get set and he took it on the backside; then tossed the bat at me like a spinning propeller and I jumped over it. Then he was striding toward me. "Now you hit." He said, eyeing me like somebody he'd like to punch.

I took my stance, preparing for a duster. He made me wait; then lobbed a big slow curve down the middle for a strike, and when I froze and took it he jeered and then before I could get set he quick-pitched me a fastball inside which I fouled off. He loaded up and I rifled the next pitch into left field. Then he planted one in my backside, a hummer. I refused to acknowledge the bruising sting. Then he side-armed one at my ankles and I jumped over it and went down on my ass while he horse-laughed, holding another ball, flipping and catching it, in his glory.

"Ready to hit, birdie?"

"Fuck you! Bring it on!" I jumped up, dug in.

He was so happy, happier than I'd seen him in some time, needling, competing, confronting, like he was playing again, and not working his ass off in his shithouse and driving all over hell and back, even if he was his own boss and making way more money than he'd ever made in baseball.

I rifled three of his fastballs into left field before he dusted me. I made sure to hug the plate and took a low outside curveball and ripped it up the middle and nailed him on the foot and he went down in a heap and sat on the mound cursing and grimacing in pain. I waved my bat at him, "Get up old man, knock me down with your weak shit. I OWN you!"

He stood and grabbed balls from the bag and began feeding me fastballs, one after another, and his tricky off-speed curving drop, and I hammered everything. Something had busted loose in me. I wanted him to hit me. I wanted the pain. I was so relaxed, felt outside my skin looking in instead of inside looking out; an exhilaration and sureness coursed through my blood. My stroke was simple, level, compact, quick, a perfect extension of my father's swing, the swing I'd learned and copied from him, even adopting his mannerisms of touching the plate and digging in and pumping the bat twice before laying it on my shoulder while I eye-balled the pitcher, and I realized, as I hammered out line drive after line drive with violent precision, that the demented man on the mound was part of me and I was part of him, that indeed we looked the same, smelled the same, and the same wild Russian blood ran through our veins, and that no matter what happened from here on out we were one and the same and I could not escape him, whether I liked it or not. I must deal with it.

Finally, panting for breath, bent over at the knees, he looked up and grinned at me as balls came rolling in from the kids shagging in left field. He walked toward me, flipped me his glove. "Look, you know making the pivot at second you never let the baserunner intimidate you, I don't give a fuck who he is, you hit the sonofabitch between the eyes with the ball when he comes in high, and I guarantee he'll never come in high again, unless he wants a hair-lip or a new nose."

Dad grimaced as he talked, no doubt because of his toe. "You let these kids hit now. Pitch to 'em." He smacked me hard on the shoulder and set off toward the house, limping badly, neighbors, out in force, looking on. When I got home an hour later, mother was back. They were in the bedroom, Dad was face down on the bed, icepacks under his toe and on his back, mother massaging his neck. An ugly purple welt was on his backside. Mother looked up at me as I stood in the doorway. She shook her head, but there was a glimmer of accepting good humor in her eyes. "You two," was all she said.

Racial Rumblings

My parents were discussing moving out of Compton to a safe all-white suburb 18 miles away. They fretted over our house going down in value due to the influx of Blacks in town, and they feared for Susie going to Compton High, where Black girls beat up nice white girls. When they asked me about moving I went into a rage. We had a nucleus of players at Compton High that could win everything. Moving was unimaginable.

Meanwhile, the Compton American Legion post refused to sponsor our team, which infuriated Dad, who called members "pompous cheapskates and phony patriots." Some of the Compton and Dominguez high players signed on with Legion teams in LA and Long Beach, while my teammate Paul Schaal (who would play a decade in the big leagues) and I signed on to play third base and shortstop for the Bellflower team, 10 miles away.

Bellflower was all clean-cut white kids, a former farm community. Paul owned a black '51 Ford coupe and drove us to games all over San Gabriel Valley. Right off we produced. Our coach, the father of a senior pitcher, was overjoyed to have us, left us alone. Except for a powerful but slow-moving left-handed hitting catcher named Milt Swift, who was a prospect, Paul and I were their best players. We were free agents having nothing on our agendas but baseball, talking baseball, so dedicated that the Compton Connie Mack League team picked us up to play our positions among kids up to 19 years old. Now Paul and I played weeknight games and weekend day games, including Sunday doubleheaders.

Dad wanted me to get a driver's license and an old jalopy like Paul's so I could help him out with deliveries at his store, where I was working part time stocking, writing out orders, waiting on trade, and trying not to fight with him when he warned me to not "go so goddam fast!" I agreed to get a license. When Dad tried to teach me to drive with the Rambler, he made me so nervous I almost crashed. So mother taught me on her automatic transmission Pontiac, and much to Dad's sourness, I passed the driving test, and with my savings I paid for a 1952 Chevy coupe, a real pig, according to my cousin Bob.

So now I was making deliveries and alternating with Paul on our baseball excursions. We played our games, stopped for burgers afterwards and discussed our dreams. Paul had a rifle arm at third and a quick release, great wrists, and, like me, was an instinctive player though his swing was loopier than mine and thus more powerful when he connected.

Our Connie Mack team was superb and stocked with some tough kids, including the toughest fighter I knew, Jim Rooker, our pitcher/first baseman/outfielder/leader. We shared Cressey as home park with an all-Black team in the same league from South Central LA and Watts, and, since most of the guys on our team were racists, the rivalry was especially vicious. Many of the players on the Black team were from Centennial High, including the bruiser who intimidated me at second base. We beat them our first game, and in the rematch a couple weeks later, Dad coached because our regular coach went on vacation.

The all-Black team's desire to beat us that summer turned into a rabid and savage crusade, similar to the old Hollywood Stars/ LA Angels rivalry at its most heated, and on this night we had trouble keeping our poise. From their dugout they blistered us with personal abuse. Dad instructed us to ignore them, but it seemed these guys, without supervision from their coach, were obsessed with repaying centuries of white man's abuse of their race on our cocky white asses. Poplar was ready to do battle, whatever the odds, with the crowd ten-to-one Black over White—on their turf.

I came to bat in the bottom of the 9th with the score 3-2 in their favor with runners on first and second and two out. Dad was coaching third and hollering down to me to "get a good pitch!" I stared at the lanky Black pitcher and fouled off a pitch that was eye-high. I was a notorious "bad-ball hitter," and Dad hurried down the line to meet me at the plate.

"Relax. Be patient. Slow down," he advised, white spittle caking the corners of his lips. "Don't get behind and hit HIS pitch!"

"I hit best with two strikes, Dad. Leave me alone. I know what I'm doing."

He grimaced, jogged back to his coaching box. The next pitch was a snake of a hissing fastball at my knees, on the inside corner, an area that generally gave me trouble, but this time I lashed it on a rising line between the left and center fielders. I tore down the line and rounded first as the center fielder gave chase and Dad waved our runners around the bases, the ball rolling toward the fence on the dew-chilled grass. I was churning hard around second base when the left fielder blindsided me with a vicious football block at my knees, sending me airborne, head-over-heels to land face-first on the dirt infield.

When I looked up, Dad had the kid by the throat with his left hand and was smacking him hard in the face with his right hand as the kid back-pedaled into center field, his head bobbing back and forth like a speed bag in a boxing gym. Finally Dad dropped him in short center field, where he lay like a broken doll, and turned to hurry back into the infield, where our entire team had gathered, some wielding bats as Jim Rooker pulled me to my feet, a wild, gleeful look in his eye. My legs were fine. Jim's older brother Wayne was with us, bat on shoulder as the Black team and their fans trickled onto the field, outnumbering us by a huge margin. They milled ominously, many in trench coats. Then Dad was among us, gesturing to close ranks, like a western movie where cowboys were surrounded by a whole tribe of Indians. He instructed us to drop our bats and form a circle. The massing crowd, closing in on us, was cut off by their powerfully built catcher, George Hill, an all-league lineman on the Centennial football team. I'd played against him in junior high. He grabbed me by the elbow, faced my father. "Mr. Franklin," he said. "You folks line up behind George, and he'll get you out of here."

We quickly gathered our equipment at the first base dugout and in single file followed big George through and past the growling, baleful mob, out to the parking lot adjoining the spacious park. We jumped into our cars quickly, and in a caravan moved out onto Rosecrans Boulevard, with the mob stood looking on.

Driving slowly, Dad said, "He was just a kid, Dell, but I did what I did because nobody messes with anybody on our team, whether it's you or anybody else. There's no place in the game for what that kid did. He's lucky I didn't kill him."

A week later we were slated to begin the regional playoffs at Cressey, but only a few players showed up, including Rooker, Schaal, and Poplar, and Jim's brother and Paul's dad and brother as our only fans. There was a good crowd on the other side. Our cast of five sat in the dugout while the opposing team from the Valley warmed up. A bunch of kids from the Black team we'd beaten on my winning hit entered our dugout in humble posture, including the kid Dad had bopped around and nearly strangled. He walked directly to Dad, who stood.

"Sorry, sir, I lost my head." he apologized, his voice a faint rasp from Dad's strangling.

The Black kids, one-by-one, approached Dad and apologized, caps off. None of them glanced at me or my teammates, and the kid who'd cut my knees out from under did not apologize. One of the kids asked where the rest of our team was, and when Dad said he didn't expect them to show, he said, "We'll play for you, Mr. Franklin. We'll play for you anytime." His teammates nodded. Dad thanked them, wished them luck as ballplayers.

We forfeited the game.

BIG MOE

Beaned

In 1942 I got beaned by Phil Marchildon of the Philadelphia Athletics, one of the hardest, wildest throwers in the game. His fastball clipped me on the top back of my head as I ducked down and away and caromed to the screen, so I didn't get hit flush. But I was dazed and woozier than hell and they took me out of the game, sent me to the hospital, where the doctors cleaned the cut on my head and bandaged me up.

They wanted to keep me overnight for observation, said I had a concussion. I had a pretty good headache and Rose was very upset, didn't want me to play, but hell, I'd worked my way into some steady playing time after five years in the minors and waiting my turn behind a bunch of donkeys, I was going good, and you didn't want to get the reputation of a guy who couldn't play hurt or lost his courage after a beaning, because we had guys on Detroit that were waiting to take your job, you didn't want somebody coming in and getting hot and putting you on the bench. So I talked our manager, Del Baker, who wasn't my greatest supporter and who I didn't care for because he never went to bat for you, was strictly a front office stooge, into playing me the next day.

Well, in those days we didn't wear these protective helmets, you took your life in your hands when you hit, and as I stood at the plate I felt my ass turning to jelly and easing out—it was like I couldn't control my ass or my legs, they were pulling out. So I had to step out and gather myself, talk to myself, knowing everybody was watching and wondering, and force myself to keep my ass in. It was a real struggle. I took a pitch and got my bearings. Soon as you take that first pitch you're back to being familiar with things. I literally pushed my pelvis in and sucked in my ass and moved up on the plate, and settled my legs, and worked the count, and I knocked a single between third and short.

I was okay after that. I always knew how to get away from the ball, how to pivot on my back leg and duck, taking it on my hide. I had that confidence in my reflexes, and in all my years of playing ball that was the only time I got beaned, and I was dusted dozens of times, but I never got hit that much, even standing close to the plate.

The guy who got hit the most, the bravest hitter I ever saw, though, was Minnie Minoso, who I saw when I played in Cuba. One of the top pitchers in the league, a very hard throwing Cuban, beaned Minoso and he went down like a sack of potatoes, and he lay there motionless. We thought he was dead. The ballpark was quiet as a morgue. Minoso was a tremendous ballplayer and should've been in the big leagues years earlier. The doc gave him the smelling salts and suddenly he jumped up and ran down to first base. He stole second and third and next time up he stood on top of the plate, like he always did, leading the league in getting hit by pitches, and drilled a double off the wall.

Every time you start to think you're tough, you look at a guy like Minoso, and it humbles you.

Beaned

Our Bellflower American Legion team played a little better than .500 ball and finished in the middle of the pack in our league. Not much was expected of us in the 80-team prestigious Anaheim tournament at La Palma Park. We didn't have enough pitching, or a prospect at that position. Our prospects being scouted were Schaal, Milt Swift and me. At bat I had run into a brief slump and Dad told me I was too anxious, and although it was alright to be aggressive, with my quick wrists, I didn't need to be jumping at the ball; I could wait.

We won our first two night games and I hit several line drive singles and doubles and the scouts in the stands picked me as shortstop on the regional all star team. I stayed overnight at Jerry Stephenson's house the night before our next game. We spent the entire day working out. I had dinner with his huge family. Then we were up all night talking baseball, baseball, baseball. I got very little sleep. We kept going on and on about our dads, this player, that player, whether they were in high school, college, the minors, majors. Both of us wanted to sign baseball contracts out of high school. Jerry was an excellent student, I just got by making B's.

That night we played Torrance. They had a very tall right-handed pitcher who threw hard, but he couldn't get his curve over and my first two times up I whistled line drives past his ear into center, knocking in runs. He had a slow move to first and I stole bases on him. My third time up I didn't pick up a fastball up and in quick enough and the ball smashed into the bottom-back of my head and helmet and sounded like an explosion going off inside my skull. Next thing I remember was sitting in the dirt trying to get up, my dad and coach urging me to stay down, stay down...I refused and stood up when a doctor came down.

I was not wobbly. My helmet had ended up at the screen behind home plate and was partially shattered. Dad and coach wanted me out of the game. The doc wanted to look into my eyes. We were ahead in the game. I don't know why, but I started to go after the pitcher, who was apologetic and back-pedaled. Dad grabbed me.

"He wasn't throwing at you. You lost the ball in the lights. Leave that kid alone, he's as shook up as you are."

I shrugged Dad off and sprinted to first base. The ump came over to ask was I okay. I told him I was fine. My ears rang and my brain buzzed, like a faraway ocean. The pitcher, a prospect, was so shook up he walked three straight hitters, not coming close, always outside, and they took him out. When I came up next, I felt my ass oozing out of the box. I didn't step out. I swung at the first pitch and blooped the ball into right for a single. But I realized I was flailing to get the hell out of the box as the public address announcer boomed out I was the son of Murray Franklin and I got a huge ovation from a packed house as I stood on first.

After the game, Dad told me I should have taken the first pitch. Mother was irate at my staying in the game and wanted to take me to the hospital for x rays. I refused.

"You don't have to be like your Dad!" she scolded.

Dad said, "He's okay now. He knows what to do. This might never happen to him again."

My pals who didn't play baseball were often in awe of my style of hugging the plate and almost daring the pitcher to come in tight on me. I tried to explain to them that hitting and all that went with it, including getting away from balls at your head and body, were just part of it, and though a huge part of it, something I was used to, and that wearing a helmet added a whole new dimension to fighting the fear every hitter felt when he watched a hard thrower warm up or stood in against a wild flame-throwing prospect where the ball literally hissed as it jumped that last foot into the catchers mitt and made that resounding pop echoing throughout the stadium.

This was the ultimate challenge and why I played, why I could not wait to test my courage and dig in against these pricks with the "serious terrifying velocity and heat," and who reveled in intimidating you, like Jerry Stephenson, who told me more than once that he would "dust" me if he faced me because of my aggressive, arrogant crowding of the plate. Jerry, while warming up before high school and American Legion games, always fired a wild pitch over the catchers head from the mound as the first hitter stood by, to "plant a seed" in that hitter's and his teammates' minds.

Our next game I was fine. I took a pitch. I realized my initial response would be to jump at that first pitch to convince myself and whoever was watching that I was not frightened, but I was frightened, and fought it off. I pretended I was playing pepper, just tried to calm down, stay back and meet the ball, and stroked a single to left.

But we lost the game and were eliminated from the tournament, and so I did not make the all-tournament team as the only shortstop out of 80, and realized also that though I had more range and quickness than the other shortstops in contention, and had a quicker release of the ball, they all had stronger arms than me, powerful "major-league ready" arms, which I did not. I had big-time major league speed and range, something Dad said could not be taught or coached, but he also added you couldn't teach or coach a stronger arm either—you either had it or you didn't. I was determined to overcome this deficiency. At any cost.

Suburban Blues

There was sudden upheaval in my life as we moved into a 3-bedroom home in the planned suburb of Rossmoor, which was on the fringe of Orange County and had no downtown, no community center, no churches, schools, stores or gyms, no Blacks, Mexicans or hooligan white trash, no crazed dogs chasing you or your car down the street, only identical freshly minted homes in a perfectly symmetrical town-size grid—a sprawling mosaic walled in and isolated from the world. All the trees were new and small. The streets seemed deserted and devoid of the hum and babble of block life, where everybody knew everybody. There was no visible dissension among the white collar families slipping in and out of electrically opening and closing garage doors in their shiny sedans and station wagons. I was exiled from all I'd ever known and sentenced to this strange and utterly vapid sameness that had me unnerved and feeling like I'd lost all individuality and identity. Nobody waved to me, asked how I was doing in baseball, or how my parents were. I had no crew to run with.

Worst of all, I would not be playing at Compton High, beside my pals, Paul Schaal and Walter Jones, where I was established as an important entity.

I now attended Western High in Anaheim, a crosstown rival of Anaheim High, where Jerry Stephenson starred. I drove eight miles to school in my jalopy. The Orange County kids were cheerful, wholesome, directed, white, the schoolwork harder than at Compton, where many of the Black kids migrated from inferior Black schools in the south. The baseball coach, Roy Merk, a compact, bald man, rose quickly when I entered his trophy laden office and shook my hand, welcomed me to his program, informed me Coach Edgmon had called and given him a glowing report on my character and baseball skills.

"He didn't need to," Coach Merk said, smiling. "I saw you play in the Anaheim tournament. You're a helluva a ballplayer. We're more than pleased to have you aboard. I think you'll like our kids and we'll have a pretty good team." I was already aware that their team last year had been terrible.

While we talked, a stocky kid with coke-bottle glasses and a big friendly grin came into the office, and I was introduced to the football team starting guard and baseball catcher, Dave Sturrock, a senior. We shook hands.

"I saw you play at La Palma. You're a great player. I can't wait for baseball season to start. And hey, I grew up in LA and idolized your Dad when he played for the Stars. I'd be honored to meet him. I've still got his autograph from Gilmore Field."

It wasn't long before Sturrock was at the house meeting Dad, who now drove 18 miles to work. By the time baseball season arrived, I'd met all the varsity players through Dave, my immediate good friend, and more than a few of them made the pilgrimage to meet Dad, who regaled them with baseball stories while they admired his silver bat. Gone from our walls were the framed baseball pictures that filled our den in Compton. Our new modernistic furniture was uncomfortable. Mother was now school nurse at Bolsa Grande high school in nearby Garden Grove. Susie took a bus to school.

In Rossmoor, everybody seemed well dressed and well off, except me, as I still wore rags. Our neighbors prevailed in a sort of smugness, as if they had achieved a level in society higher than ordinary folks like those in Compton. I felt alienated. Something brewed inside me that I was struggling to comprehend—an attitude of denial I was part of this plasticized utopia, and a rancorous disdain for what so many had aspired to all their lives—the American Dream and all its luxurious trappings. I despised this place. I wanted no part of it. I itched to get away from it so I could breathe again. I refused to go into our pool, of which Dad, though no swimmer, was so proud.

When I tried to explain my new feelings to Mom, she said, "You'll adjust and make new friends and everything will work out. You'll discover that people are essentially the same everywhere and observing them and getting to know them will enlighten you. Change can be good."

When Dad sensed my discontent and asked what was eating me, I shrugged, and said I couldn't stand Rossmoor. He seemed confused. "All I ever wanted is to give you a better life, Dell, and better things than I had."

"I don't want any of it, Dad—it's bullshit."

He just stared at me, as if to say, "Is this my fucking kid?"

Feeling Low at Western High

The ball field at Western High was second rate and the school, without athletic legacy, had been converted from a junior high. Our first practice coach Merk put me at shortstop. I felt quicker, faster, stronger, and watched my batting practice grounders eat infielders up. We started out the pre-league schedule winning four straight, and because we had nowhere near the talent of Compton, I felt it was my responsibility to lead the team by example and production. I was an established prospect and played with swagger, knowing I made a difference. We were excited about being league contenders instead of perennial doormats. I was the "Big Dog," perhaps to my new teammates a savior, seasoned by continuous winter league play with the Red Sox, with other prospects like Andy Etchebarren. I was almost "there."

We continued winning in league play and were to play first place Anaheim at La Palma Park—their home field—in a game highly publicized in the *Orange County Register* AND *Anaheim Bulletin*. Anaheim was strong, with a great tradition, led by Stephenson and a gifted shortstop, big, raw-boned Frank Peters, a kid with enormous hands and a cerebral application to the game. Frank, a power hitter, also played winter ball for Boston and alternately exchanged banter with me as we vied for playing time. He told me: "Jerry says he owns you—he knows your weakness."

IN LA PALMA STADIUM

Western Hosts Newport In Sunset League Crucial

Junior Lary Lawson will trek to the mound tomorrow afternoon to defend Western's first place tie with Anaheim in the Sunset League standings as the Pioneers take on Newport Harbor.

Coach Roy Merk's Pioneers have a 7 - 2 mark and have won seven straight league encounters. The Tars have been a very hot club as of late and are in third place with a 6-3 record.

Western started its win skein with a 1-0 win over the Sailors as Dennis Yoken gave up two hits in the shutout.

Lawson, who came on in the fifth inning to quiet Anaheim while his teammates hung a defeat on the Colonists to tie the league lead, is a righthander. He will be opposed by Tars' Mike Murphy, who pitched a three-hitter while Yoken shutout Newport in the first round. Murphy too is a righthander.

Tough Game

Newport mentor Andy Smith stated that "Western will be in for a tough game with us" as he looked forward to the contest. He said that the Pioneers have been getting the hits with the men on bases to ring up their win skein.

The Pioneers have a .357 team average in second round action. They will face a stern test in Murphy, who has good control and throws at most speeds.

Third - sacker Russ Rapp has replaced Western's Fergie Olver as the league's leading hitter. Rapp has a .483 average compared to Fergie's .462. Olver has yet to collect his first hit in second round action. Sunset hurlers have been pitching the centerfielder more carefully causing Olver to "press" for hits too much.

Back Up Pitcher

Backing up Murphy in the pitching department are Tom Call, a righthander, and Dale Townsend, who will start in right field. Townsend came in to bail out Murphy, who ran into trouble with powerful Fullerton last Tuesday. Newport won though, 6-3.

SUNSET LEAGUE STANDINGS

TEAM	W	L	GBL
WESTERN	7	2	
ANAHEIM	7	2	
Newport Harbor	6	3	1
Fullerton	5	4	2
Santa Ana	4	5	3
Garden Grove	4	5	3
Huntington Beach	3	6	4
La Habra	2	7	6

/GAMES BEHIND LEADER

FRIDAY GAMES

NEWPORT HARBOR AT WESTERN; ANAHEIM AT SANTA ANA; Huntington Beach at La Habra; Garden Grove at Fullerton.

Olver continues to lead the Pioneers in hitting. Four batters own averages over the .300 mark. Tom Quick, who homered in his last game, has a .391 average. He is followed by Dennis Painter and Del Franklin with .333 and .323 averages, respectively.

Painter's .571 leads the second round averages for the Pioneers. Mike Mathias and Dan Cook are close behind with .556 and .500 marks, respectively.

The Pioneers, who have not lost a game on the road the entire season, travel to Garden Grove next Monday for an important contest with the Argonauts.

more

NEWPORT HARBOR (6-3)
Barry Wallace, ss
Bill Voss, lf
Russ Rapp, 3b
Rich Rizon, cf
Bob Liljeswall, 1b
Don Sherman, 2b
Dale Townsend, rf
Bob Thompson, c
Mike Murphy, p

WESTERN (7-2)
Nick Odowick, lf
Mike Mathias, 3b
Del Franklin, 2b
Fergie Olver, cf
Tom Quick, rf
Dennis Painter, 1b
Roy Nash, ss
Gary Martin, c
Lary Lawson, p

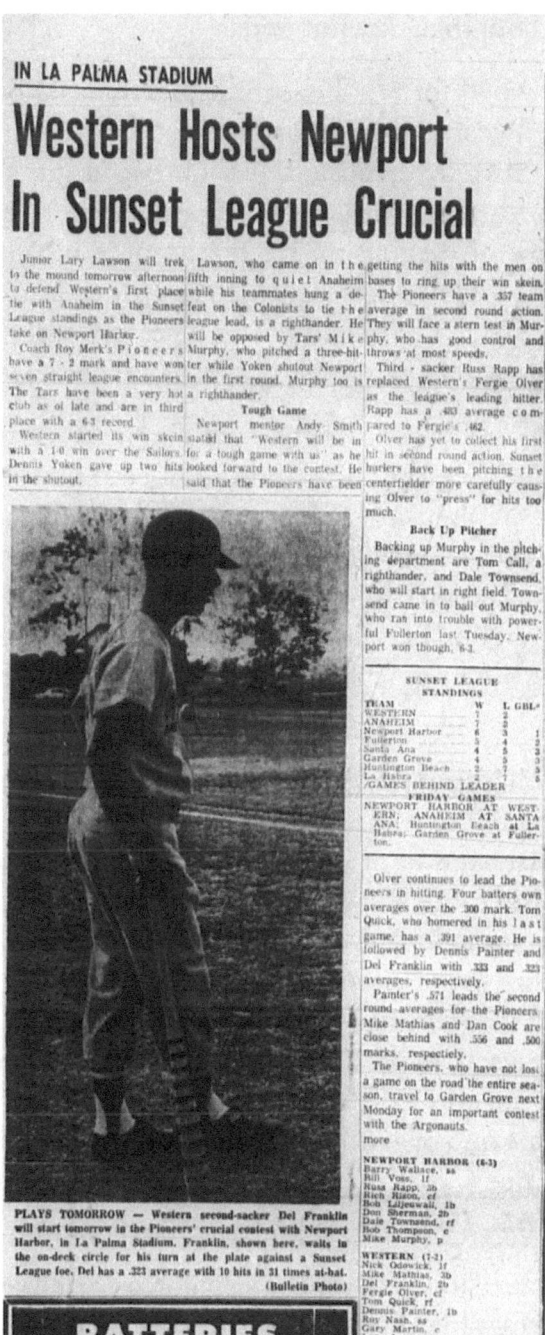

PLAYS TOMORROW — Western second-sacker Del Franklin will start tomorrow in the Pioneers' crucial contest with Newport Harbor, in La Palma Stadium. Franklin, shown here, waits in the on-deck circle for his turn at the plate against a Sunset League foe. Del has a .323 average with 10 hits in 31 times at-bat.
(Bulletin Photo)

BATTERIES

High school baseball in the area was highly competitive and got a lot of attention in the papers.

"We'll see about that," I countered.

I was so pumped for Stephenson, with whom I'd been talking trash for two years, I could hardly breathe when I came up to hit, batting third. As expected, Jerry brushed me back on the first pitch with a ball that hissed by me like a freight train. I made a show of digging in. He threw me a bunch of sliders away, which I fouled off. He jammed me with a fastball, which I fouled back. Then he froze me with a perfect slider on the low outside corner, the first pitcher to strike me out all year.

I was furious, my brain roaring. Anaheim bombed our pitcher. Frank hit a homer into the stands, lumbered past me at short, head down. Stephenson shut us out, got me to hit two ground outs. Afterward, Peters paused as he headed toward their team bus as we racked up our equipment. I was smoldering. "Don't feel bad, Franklin," he said. "Nobody's touched Stephenson all year, except me in practice games. Someday I might give you my secret."

The Anaheim loss burst our bubble. We went on a losing streak. Our pitching fell to ruins. I tried to do too much, began pressing at the plate and went into a tailspin, feeling responsible for each loss. The more I pressed and fought myself, the worse I played. The stunned and disbelieving looks on my teammates faces gave me pause as to my own sanity when they watched me kick and throw things, fulminating, cursing savagely, losing control of myself and entering a mindless derangement I felt consuming me and which I was helpless to combat or escape. Coach Merk came over and told me to calm down. He seemed concerned, peering at me as if I was some new person he did not recognize.

I needed Walter Jones to set me straight, as he always had, but now I was the "Man," a supposed leader, and only Sturrock, whose batting helmet we shared, was furious when I kicked it so hard the bill tore off and he had to face a pitcher with a helmet

Pioneers Beat Oilers; Sunset Decider Friday

Righthander Dennis Yoken came within one out of hurling his second Sunset League shutout yesterday but still humbled Huntington Beach 5-1. The win was Yoken's second over the Oilers this season and was Western's 11th Sunset victory.

The Pioneers are deadlocked with crosstown rival Anaheim with only the Friday afternoon contest between the two schools remaining in circuit action this year. Both have 11-2 records and both are expected to receive CIF playoff berths despite the outcome of Friday's decider.

Western wasted no time in getting on the scoreboard as they drove starting pitcher Dave Wilhelm from the mound with only two out in the first inning.

First Run

Wilhelm got Nick Odowick on a close play at first but surrendered a walk to Mike Mathias. Second baseman Del Franklin forced Mathias for the second out of the inning, the last out while Wilhelm was on the mound.

Franklin stole second and coasted home on Fergie Olver's single to left. Tom Quick rapped a double to score Olver with the second run.

The Pioneers scored single runs in the third, fourth and sixth frames.

Franklin opened the third with a double. After the Pioneers loaded the sacks Roy Nash tallied the

run with a sacrifice fly.

Odowick scored Western's fourth run on a wild pitch by reliefer Paul Sweigart. The small left fielder had opened the inning with a double and was advanced on a sacrifice by Mathias.

Quick drove in his second run of the day after successive singles by Mathias and Franklin combined with a free pass to Olver had loaded the bases.

Ed Sulka rapped his second double of the contest to score the Oilers only run. Pinch hitter B Haines was nicked by a pitch and stole second before Sulka doubled.

Hollypark Opens Racing Schedule

INGLEWOOD (UPI)— Colorful Hollywood Park, the track of lakes and flowers, opened its 22nd season of thoroughbred racing today with the running of the $20,000-added Hollywood Premiere Handicap.

The 6-furlong sprint, which traditionally gets the 55-day summer meeting under way, drew an unexpectedly large field of 14 when entries were taken Tuesday.

Probable favorite and topweighted at 126 pounds was Revel who last week at Golden Gate won the Sacramento Handicap in 1:08 3-5, fastest time in the nation this year.

The Premiere Handicap is the first of 33 stakes at the meeting which is featured this season for

the first time by the installation of "daily double" wagering on the first and second races.

Hollywood has offered the most prize money of any track in the world to horsemen and this year expected to distribute an estimated $3.6 million in stakes and purses. The stakes program is highlighted by four $100,000 added races with the guaranteed $162,10 Hollywood Gold Cup July 15 the top attraction of the meeting.

Duren Joins Angels Today

LOS ANGELES (UPI)— Ryne Duren, former New York Yankee star reliefer, was expected to arrive here momentarily to join the Los Angeles Angels.

Angel Manager Bill Rigney told newsmen Tuesday night that Duren informed him a mixup had occurred at Dallas, Tex., on his plane reservation and that he was planning to catch the first plane available.

Duren was one of four players traded by the Yankees to the Angels Monday for the outfielder Bob Cerv and reliefer Tex Clevenger.

HUNTINGTON	AB	R	H	RBI
Sukla, ss	4	0	2	1
Darrow, lf	3	0	0	0
Johnson, cf	4	0	0	0
Rapp, c	1	0	0	0
Strother, 2b	3	0	1	0
Parker, 3b	3	0	1	0
Bartholomew, 1b	2	0	0	0
Haines, X	0	1	0	0
Spillers, rf	1	0	0	0
Vela, rf	2	0	0	0
Wilhelm, p	3	0	0	0
Sweigart, p	3	0	1	0
TOTAL	34	1	5	1

WESTERN	AB	R	H	RBI
Odowick, lf	4	1	1	0
Mathias, 3b	2	1	1	0
Franklin, 2b	4	2	2	0
Olver, cf	3	1	1	1
Quick, rf	4	0	2	2
Painter, 1b	3	0	1	0
Nash, ss	3	0	1	1
Brouwski, c	3	0	1	0
Yoken, p	2	0	0	0
TOTAL	27	5	9	4

SCORE BY INNINGS

		R	H	E
Huntington	000 000 1—1	5	1
Western	201 101 x—5	9	2

SUMMARY

Runs Odowick, Mathias, Franklin (2), Olver; Sulka. Errors Johnson, Quick, Nash. Stolen Bases Haines, Franklin. Sacrifice Hits Mathias, Nash. Two Base Hits Odowick, Franklin, Sulka (2). Runs Batted in Quick (2), Olver, Nash, Sukla. Double Plays Franklin, Painter (2); Yoken, Franklin, Painter. Credit Victory to Yoken. Charge Defeat to Wilhelm. Left on Bases Western 11. Struck Out by Yoken 6, Wilhelm 10, Sweigart, 4. Bases on Balls Off Yoken 6, Wilhelm 1; Sweigart, 3. Hit with Pitched Balls Haines, Rapp. Wild Pitches Yoken, Sweigart.

Sunset League Standings

TEAM	W	L	GBL
WESTERN	11	2	
ANAHEIM	11	2	
Newport Harbor	8	5	3
Fullerton	8	5	3
Santa Ana	5	8	6
Garden Grove	5	8	6
Huntington Beach	3	10	8
La Habra	2	12	10

GAMES BEHIND LEADERS

FRIDAY'S GAMES

WESTERN AT ANAHEIM (LA PALMA STADIUM 3:15)

Fullerton at Santa Ana; Newport Harbor at Huntington Beach; La Habra at Garden Grove.

SAFE AT HOME — Anaheim's ... despite last second attempt by ... to make the tag. Action took ... yesterday's game, won by Colts ...

I was able to shine at Western High, but turmoil within me had begun.

looking like something a Nazi trooper wore. He let me have it, calling me a "goddam spoiled baby." This stopped me. He also came over later as I sat seething quietly in the corner of the dugout, put a hand on my shoulder, and said, "I know it means everything to you, but I'm worried you're going to seriously hurt yourself the way you're thrashing around."

Dad, not able to catch my games very often now that he was working so far away, finally sat me down one night. "You're so goddam herky-jerky and nervous, I've never seen anything like it. Since when do you start throwing things around like a half-cocked busher? You can't throw your goddam bat every time you make an out. You're gonna make out six or seven times every ten times at bat, even at this level, because that's just the way it is. You're up there fighting yourself after one pitch. You've got to stay on an even keel if you're gonna play this game, Dell. You can't go hangdog when you're stinking it up, and you can't think you invented the game when you're going good. And goddammit, the worst thing about you acting like a damn maniac is it's selfish, you're only thinking about yourself, and your teammates and your coach'll end up hating you." He put a hand on my shoulder. He was genuinely worried. "If the game's gonna drive you crazy, take a little rest. I mean it."

To counteract what was happening to me—feeling like a prisoner to my moods and emotions—I found myself clowning. In practice, I ran the bases backwards; I imitated a penguin and made crazed slides into bases and had my teammates laughing, though strangely. I realized I possessed a slapstick talent that had people rolling over, holding their bellies. This act seemed to relieve the pressure somewhat and turn my game around, even as my new teammates called me "Flake," "Clown," "Mad-Dog," and "Psycho."

When we played Anaheim the last game of the year, I no longer felt like "The Man." I had become some other person over the course of the season. Peters launched another homer and

Stephenson shut us down. I made three outs, none hit hard, but didn't strike out. Anaheim won the league, and it was announced by the public address system after the game that they would enter the state playoffs, representing our Sunset League, and that Peters and Jerry made first-team all league. They posed together for the photographer from the *Orange County Register*. I scooted quickly to the bus, avoiding them.

On the bus, my stomach roiled stabbing cramps. I felt like an utter failure, as if all I had aspired to was in shambles. I began to wonder, for the first time, if I was suited for the game, the life; then immediately expelled such an idea with a shudder. What the fuck was I thinking?

BIG MOE

The Bench Jockey

Birdie Tebbetts was a fine catcher and knew the game inside out, and especially pitchers. He knew just how much gas a guy had left in his tank, when he was losing his stuff and ready to get shelled, and he could get on guys pretty good, really get under your skin. He was smart and had a piercing, twangy voice, which was why they called him "Birdie," an obnoxious, irritating voice that carried all over the field and cut right through you, and he had a sarcastic way of saying things that always got your goat—he was a first rate needler, a sniper, an original, maybe the best in the game. He was what you call a bench jockey, a lost art these days, what with all these guys making so much money and swapping teams and having agents and fraternizing like bosom buddies.

One afternoon in St. Louis Tebbetts was on a pitcher with the Browns named Vern Kennedy, a guy he'd caught a few years earlier with Detroit, a strapping guy from Kansas, a former track star and football player. It was very hot, sweltering, and it doesn't get any hotter than it does in St. Louis in the summer. You can't breathe on a day like that, the outfield grass is baked brown and the field hard as concrete, almost like the field breathes fire. Birdie was riding Kennedy. At first it was playful, because they were old teammates and all, but then Kennedy started struggling, and Birdie's saying he ain't got this and he ain't got that, "you'll be gone by the fourth inning, Kennedy, your fastball's straight as a string, you're dead meat," just sniping away, and sure enough Kennedy doesn't have it that day, gets knocked around, and by the fourth inning he's gone, and Birdie's crowing and gloating, and Kennedy, he's sopping wet, got beat up for a bunch of runs suffering in that heat, watching line drives whistle past him and bounce off the fence and guys circling the bases, and he gets an unmerciful booing when he walks to the dugout.

Birdie's on the bench that day, not catching, and he keeps right on crowing and gloating when Kennedy walks to the dugout. But instead of leaving for the clubhouse and taking an early shower, like all pitchers do after they get their brains beat out, Kennedy sits down in that stifling hot dugout with a towel around his neck and takes his cap off, and he sits there like that for the rest of the game. Well, our ball club has to get to our clubhouse through their dugout, and when the game ends and we pass through their dugout, it's empty except for Kennedy, who's still sitting there, towel around his neck, a very quiet and polite gentleman who minds his own business and never has anything bad to say about anybody. He stands up and asks Birdie if he has anything more to say, and before Birdie can open his mouth Kennedy decks him with one punch, knocks him down and out, hits him so hard that for a minute or so we think he might be dead.

Kennedy picks up his glove and cap and walks out of the dugout, the towel still around his neck, and we carry Tebbetts into the clubhouse and lay him down on the training table where the doc tends to him. He's pretty groggy, and the next day he's real quiet, and misses the game, and everybody on the club's on his ass, calling him "One-Punch Tebbetts" and "Old Canvas Back." He took it pretty well in stride. Birdie knew the business and took it as well as he gave it out, and the next time we played the Browns and Kennedy pitched, Birdie got on him again, but he made sure to stay away from the personal stuff, and nothing came of it.

A Season of Troubling Failure

During the summer I worked for Dad and played American Legion ball for West Anaheim. Three mornings a week I followed Dad in my Chevy to arrive at the store at 7:30, where a dozen or so shoemakers awaited him in eager anticipation of donuts, coffee and kibitzing, Dad's mood was instant sunshine the second he arrived, no matter how worried or pissed off he was about other matters. These men were not only Dad's customers, but friends whose life breath was attuned to their morning visits, which were lively and full of laughter and gossip, led by Dad, who always had new stories, jokes and "hot poop." He made a fuss over each shoemaker as if they were special, and it occurred to me that they relied on him and the camaraderie happening in his business.

Though Dad and I clashed frequently when we were backed up and behind and I was "going too fast," when he asked what I wanted to be paid, I told him to give me what I deserved or the minimum wage. He insisted I was worth more than the minimum wage despite being a chronic pain in the ass, because I did work hard and besides needed a little extra money—for the girls. But I had no girlfriend. Most of the girls at Western High looked upon me as a clown-around baseball player or a morose idler in class, staring at breasts and asses and fantasizing. Whenever I worked up enough courage to talk to a girl in hope of perhaps making a date, I was gruff and blurted out questions or statements, and felt like I was regarded as a pestilence.

Nights when I wasn't playing ball, I drank beer and whiskey with Sturrock and a few teammates.

Our American Legion team was as big a mess as the high school crew, with a sprinkling of junior varsity players and John Huarte, a jut-jawed All American high school football quarterback from a nearby Catholic school. A pitcher with mediocre stuff, he was a phenomenal football player headed to Notre Dame and became our unquestioned leader who tried not to show his disgust when we flailed miserably and I continued kicking at things and flipping my bat and cursing savagely, feeling like a penitent little boy beside John, who was the epitome of excellence and character. But I couldn't help myself, was like a tortured dog biting himself up and down, gnawing at fleas.

Our coach, Frank Blunt, a tall, thick man who loved baseball but had never played much and knew less, was too intimidated by my being the son of Murray Franklin to offer me advice on how to play and conduct myself. He'd enlisted an assistant coach named Bill Lentini, a small, curly-haired man with intense brown eyes who owned a tire store in Stanton. Lentini was a street guy who knew little about baseball, had never played much, but, like Blunt, was so in love with the game he donated free balls and bats and helped run practices. He was excited about all aspects of baseball and indeed possessed a visceral instinct about the guts inside a player, and a person, and stroked me with flattery every time I screwed up, almost as if he was trying to single-handedly rebuild in me what had been reduced to ashes. Bill became friends with and worked as a bird-dog for Chicago White Sox head scout Doc Bennett and reiterated to me over and over that "you have everything there is to be a great big leaguer—those wrists, those wheels, your instinct..."

In my all-consuming negativity, I thought he was making this up to salvage me. I began to consider getting away from baseball for a while and started to seriously consider that perhaps I lacked some vital ingredient to succeed in this game, had a flaw in my mental make-up that held me back, that caused me to lose hope when things went bad, to get too down on myself and distrust the encouragement of a generous, compassionate man like Lentini.

But without baseball, what would I do, and what was my life, other than a passage not worth living? And how would Dad feel about his son being a quitter? So I played out the season, started hitting again, stopped throwing temper tantrums, but was disappointed when we lost our first game in the Anaheim tournament. No all star game this year.

The Write Stuff

Without consulting Dad or Joe Stephenson, I decided to take winter ball off, but Dad was more disgusted with my grades in school than my not playing baseball, wanting me to go to college like he did, preaching that I needed a college degree to succeed in this world.

My grades sunk to below C as I shirked my studies. I wanted no part of school. My only meager talent seemed to be in English, where my teacher, Mr. Robert Korfman, a square fuddy-duddy in vested suits and bow ties, exercised no-nonsense control over his class while verbalizing a passion for literature that was not to be compromised. He shocked me by reading one of my compositions of fans at a ball game to the class. Students roared with laughter and hung on every word, unlike with other readings, where they yawned and dawdled. Girls, and especially a popular beauty named Shari, who'd previously cringed at the sight of me as I slouched in the back, actually turned to smile at me, like I was an actual human instead of a deadly disease.

Mr. Korfman, a Kansan, had me stay after class and looked me in the eye as he asked me to sit down. I complied, clutching my ragged notebook. "You, Dell Franklin, are NOT just a jock. You're a writer, whether you like it or not. You possess all the sensibilities and instincts of a writer, even if you are so confined in your development you can only write about buffoons sitting in the bleachers at ball games. You have a rare gift. Don't waste it being a one-dimensional person. The fact that you're a terrible student should not matter if you pursue a passion for reading and writing. You might even surprise yourself some day. Sometimes the most errant kids, the worst students, go on to do great things in the arts."

Despite myself, I was flattered. "So what should I do, Mr. Korfman?"

"There's a creative writing class run by Mrs. Rogers. I can recommend you and you can pay her a visit. The class has been going on for a month, and some of the students are skilled and been writing seriously since they were young. But none of them have what you have..." He smacked his gut. "I see a seed growing there. Water it. And when you report to Mrs. Rogers, be sure to make an effort to be humble. Tell her you want to write. I'll put in a good word for you. I'm counting on you now."

I was inspired by Mr. Korfman. I did like writing. It went hand-in-hand with my propensity to entertain, embellish, relate stories from what I'd observed on a daily basis, like Dad, who was a riotous story teller at baseball Hot Stove meetings. Often I amused Sturrock and baseball pals with tales of the shoemakers at the store and off-beat characters I'd observed in Compton.

When I reported to Mrs. Rogers, a heavy woman who wore baggy dresses, she immediately informed me it was too late to enter her hand-picked class of budding prodigies who worked on the school paper, the yearbook, were members of the poetry club, and entered fiction contests.

"What have you written so far, Mr. Franklin?"

I explained my baseball piece written for Mr. Korfman. She sighed, rolled her eyes. "There's simply too much work to make up."

"Ma'am, how many assignments would I have to make up?"

"Several essays and two short stories."

"I'll do them all tonight. I'm a fast worker. I've got ideas."

"I'll have to talk to Mr. Korfman." She dismissed me.

Next day, Mr. Korfman informed me Mrs. Rogers wanted no part of me in her class. He was smiling at me. "She finds you exceedingly arrogant and feels you'll be disruptive. So you see, Dell, perhaps you will learn a lesson. You should have said you'd TRY and write the assignments you were behind on in a few days or a week, and you wished to write about subjects other than baseball, instead of bowling her over with your confidence."

"I was going to write about a bunch of shoemakers, sir. With all due respect for one of your fellow teachers, Mrs. Rogers is a pompous snob."

He erupted into laughter. "Well, whatever your views on that subject, it would have given you the opportunity to write." He placed the tip of his pencil against his chin, scrutinizing me severely, yet with a glint of humor in his eyes. "You could have LEARNED something. It would have been a good experience to get thrown into a different mix. Now I can only implore you to write on your own, and to read voraciously. Read the American masters first—Twain, Steinbeck, Hemingway. Read everything you can get your hands on. I can recommend other writers as you grow. Good literature will train you to think and force you to feel, and you will become more in touch with your emotions and intellect, and better able to cope with what life throws at you. I'm counting on you to read and write, young man."

"I promise I will, sir. And thank you."

Taken Under Fergie's Wing

I was eating lunch at a bench by myself at school when a kid who looked to be around 25 came up and introduced himself as Fergie Olver. He'd heard I was the star baseball player on campus and informed me he'd moved down here from Moose Jaw, Canada to pursue a professional baseball career as a center fielder. He was stocky with a husky voice, wavy black hair, heavily lidded eyes and a bold, direct manner. He told me he played junior hockey and had a chance to turn pro in that sport, but much as he loved hockey, he loved baseball more. His family had sold their home and moved everything they owned to this area because it was a baseball hotbed where he had a better chance to "sign." He said there were hardly any scouts in the vast regions of Calgary, so his family had taken a big gamble for him. His dad, a plumber, had managed to find a good job and his older brother, a roughneck, worked and lived at home.

We began hanging out and one afternoon pitched batting practice to each other. He was strong, fairly fleet and graceful, had a level pendulum swing, and did things right. He didn't have a strong arm. He poked me in the chest afterwards.

"I hear yer a bloody primadonna, throwin' temper tantrums like a little kid. Christ, I wish I had half yer talent. An idgit can see yer a fuckin' natural. But I ain't playin' with a bloody flake. This is our senior year, and I'm shapin' yer ass up, because this is OUR team, your team and MY team, and since yer gonna be my best friend, I'm gonna take yer sorry ass under my wing, and we're gonna win this league and we're both gonna sign and be playin' pro ball...okay?"

I became his personal project. Right off it was obvious he had a way with the girls, like it came second nature. "Listen, I've got more pussy than you might get in your whole life. I been at it since I was thirteen. I already got my eye on a couple hoo-ers. These babes down here are dynamite compared to the farm heifers back home." He poked my chest. "Yah just gotta know how to talk to 'em. You don't. Yah never look at 'em when yer talkin' to 'em, because a blind man can see yer afraid of girls."

"Bullshit."

"Oh yes yah are. First of all, yer a decent lookin' guy, but yah dress like a bum. First impressions mean a lot. And I seen the way yah gawk at that goody-goody Polly Puritan Shari Lackey. Stay away from that wench, and follow the Big O, and I'll set yah up with a bloody hoo-er, and once yah nail one of them, all of 'em'll be after yer scrawny ass if yah throw 'em a good fuck. All yah gotta do, Dell, is hang out with the Big O and let me do the talkin', and you'll get laid."

The Big O, like me, didn't give a hoot about school. We spent our time in pool halls in Orange County, where the big players shot for money. Fergie grew up above a tavern and was a crack shot able to run rack after rack in straight pool. He corrected my bridge and taught me how to hustle and soon we were gambling every weekend. Fergie befriended perfect strangers with his big innocent and disarming smile and instant charm. We began making money, the Big O always making the final kill against older, more experienced players. "Don't mess with the O," he whispered to me after each conquest, his eyes dancing with mischief and conquest.

When we hunted down girls—mostly gum-chewing twitchy-hipped sophomores in tight dresses who seemed drawn to Fergie as if he was Elvis—he watched me act interested in them and try to make friendly conversation, and chastised me afterwards. "Just feed 'em the Southern Comfort," he urged. "They don't give a flyin' fuck about what you got to say. What yah do is give 'em a buncha shit, keep 'em off balance, maybe make 'em cry, then make up, and then they're fulla passion, and yah nail 'em like yah love 'em, only yah never get stupid and TELL 'em yah love 'em, because then they either get bored and drop yah, or they try to trap yer ass in marriage."

I didn't dare admit to him I couldn't stop thinking about and keeping my eyes off Shari of the porcelain skin and perfect posture and prize-winning smile that oozed easy self-confidence and was pursued by the student-body president and those already headed for American Dream success. I hated being attracted to her, like I was a traitor to myself.

When Fergie came to our house in his brother's big smoke-spewing Packard, my parents looked him over pretty well and he talked baseball with Dad. Mother winked at me and said Fergie had "the devil in his baby blue eyes." Dad was thrilled I had a baseball buddy, mentioned that Fergie was much more mature than me, which was "good for me."

"Yer dad, he's something, he's a real presence, he is." Fergie said. "I can see how yah ended up such a great ballplayer with a dad like that, but Dell, if I were you I'd sign and get out from under his shadow and play ball a thousand miles away."

BIG MOE

Ted the Temperamental Genius

Nobody hated sports writers more than Ted Williams, and I don't blame him, because you couldn't trust most of them. Ted was fair game, and didn't play up to any of them. Some guys, like Boudreau, went out of their way to accommodate writers and never had anything bad to say about anybody, knew how to hold court and schmooze, and in the long run it helped him and his team, but Williams was the opposite, wouldn't bow down to anybody and let his hitting do his talking. He didn't care about getting along with people. He was his own man, and refused to wear a tie and nobody could get him to wear one, not even the President, who he didn't like anyway, being a dumb-ass republican like Feller.

As players, we mostly liked him. He was a stand-up guy. You couldn't help but like him. He was like a big kid that wouldn't grow up, looked like a big gangly kid. He was always gung-ho about the things he liked, like hunting and fishing, and pooh-poohed what he didn't like, and that was the way it was with him—obstinate, opinionated as hell. If he was going to do something for somebody, he didn't want anybody, and especially the press, knowing about it. He got enough glory being the greatest hitter in the game. He liked to hobnob with the trainer, the clubhouse boy, the groundskeeping crew at Fenway. He could be himself around those guys, and he made sure to help them out when they had family or financial problems. On the other hand, if you were a big general in the Marines, or a politician, and wanted your picture taken with him, well, he didn't come to you, you came to HIM, because he kissed nobody's ass.

When I played short against him I positioned myself behind second base, because as a left-handed pull hitter he refused to hit to left field, disdaining the "Williams Shift" that was originated by Boudreau, who knew Ted was too stubborn to do anything but blast the ball right by you or through you. When I played second I was always in short right field, while York played deep behind first base along the line, and he still ripped rockets by you. He hit the ball harder than anybody, and hit it with a topspin that caused the ball to explode off the ground and eat you up, and you'd better by God wear your cup when Ted was hitting! I've seen him hit line drives at Briggs Stadium that never got over 12 feet high, caromed off the right field wall and bounced back into the infield for a stand-up single! I remember Ted hitting balls that ricocheted off infielders' chests and knees, and afterwards he'd stand on first looking up at the scoreboard, knowing the official scorer was a sportswriter, and sure enough the scoreboard would put up an E-3, or E-4, or E-6, and the crowd booed, and he'd glare up at those guys in the press box—"Knights of the Keyboard" he called them—and he'd spit in their direction, because he not only hated them, but also blamed them for not voting him Most Valuable Player in the American league when he hit for the triple crown and every ball-player in the game knew he deserved it.

When the scribes came around the clubhouse fishing for stories, if he wasn't in the trainer's room, he insulted them with profanity, called them gutless, stupid, you name it. He always did things the hard way, his way, probably lost several points off his lifetime batting average. Ted was as difficult as he was brilliant, and who knows, maybe all geniuses are temperamental pains in the ass.

Redemption

Coach Merk pulled Fergie and me into his office before our first practice, and sitting at his desk, said, "I know you two don't give a hoot and hell about school and I know you're running amok. Well, here's my advice: If you're going to skip class, don't get caught, and make sure you do enough to stay eligible. We're going to have a great team this year if we get any kind of pitching and you two stay out of trouble." We promised in unison to stay out of trouble. Then coach looked me in the eye. "I'm moving you to second base, so you'll be more relaxed. At second, you can become the best ballplayer in the league, in any league anywhere. Dell, you have unique insights into the game, a second sense, so I'm giving you the green light at the plate and on the bases. I'm also making you, along with our catcher, Gary Martin, co-captain. I expect you to lead this team and set an example. You know what to do. I believe in you."

All business, I began running practices for coach. No more clowning. Fergie, Martin and I were the first ones on the field, hauling out the equipment, playing pepper while the rest of the team straggled out. I pitched batting practice until coach had his pitchers prepared. Some of the JV's who played Legion ball were improved, and we had some decent arms on the mound, though nobody special. When the pre-league schedule began, we pounded good teams from large schools. I hit third and

Fergie clean-up. I held my temper at all costs but still cussed and drew complaints from a couple religious members who recoiled with distaste when I wrathfully informed them cussing and and insulting teammates was a vital part of the game.

Coach remained mum when I blistered teammates for dogging it or playing stupid. I began to execute with discipline and key into every situation, every hitter. I crowded the plate with belligerence. Our flashy new shortstop, Roy Nash, who had good hands and a cannon for an arm, grudgingly accepted my harsh goading as we worked for hours on the double play. I encouraged and chastised him. A finicky switch-hitter with a picture-book swing but a hole in it inside, he took too many good pitches, and I knocked him down in BP when he took a strike and nagged him constantly to be a "fucking hitter and swing the bat, stop being a goddam beggar!"

In games, I took gigantic leads and either bluffed a steal or stole. My speed had improved, allowing me to challenge and outrun all the top sprinters on the track team in spikes. The game was mine again. I was on a mission, riding the crest, capable of doing magical things. I was a frothing animal on the field, wishing to cut the guts out of my opponents, bonding with my teammates like a fanatical marine. Coach nodded at me, winking. He knew me inside out, knew the best way to handle me was to leave me alone.

Dad said, "Looks like you're finally arriving."

Our league was one of the strongest in Southern California. Every team had prospects drawing scouts—Stephenson, Peters and a pitcher named Ron Yett at Anaheim; pitcher/shortstop Ed Sukla at Huntington Beach; Rich Rison at Newport Beach; Jim Campanis and a catcher named McCauly at Fullerton; hulking pitcher/outfielder Roy Gleason at Garden Grove; Fergie, Nash, myself and a tall, goose-necked outfielder named Tom Quick, who had blossomed at Western.

We started out winning in league and ran neck-and-neck with Anaheim, a team on a crusade as Stephenson dominated like a colossus. Before our first game against them at La Palma, Peters sidled up to me, unaware I'd made it my personal agenda to hate all opponents, and said, "Guess you're doing it all this year. Must be less pressure at second, huh? Maybe short was too much responsibility."

I walked away. We battled Stephenson and beat him in a tight game. I walked and reached first on an error and unnerved him on the bases, causing a wild pick-off throw, though I still hadn't got a solid hit off him. After the game, I went out of my way to avoid Jerry and Peters. I was one hard-bitten motherfucker.

I was choking up on one of six of my dad's model bats from Hillrich & Bradsby in Louisville that he'd ordered straight from the manufacturing plant and pounding out a plus .400 average, balls exploding off the major league grain and finding gaps in the outfield, my level top-hand swing creating topspin on hard grounders that ate up infielders. I was on a tear. Guys pitched around me, and the Big O feasted—a one-two punch.

I had not forgotten the day I lost my guts on the double play against Centennial as a sophomore at Compton, a bad dream that still haunted me. In the game against Huntington Beach at La Palma Park in which I'd already pivoted on two double plays, a burly football player named Tom Parker—a notorious hard slider—was on first base. Sure enough, our crack third baseman, Mike Mathias, fielded a bouncer and flipped me a strike at second. Parker was on top of me with a big jump, yelling like a Kamikaze and neglecting to slide in an attempt to run me over. I straddled the bag and in one motion turned and released the ball at his face, causing him to dive just short of the bag as the ball carried to first to complete the DP. Parker lay on his side. I stepped over him and jogged off the field as Fergie, on the run, slapped me hard on the ass.

EFFORT IN VAIN — Huntington Beach's Tom Parker (17) flies through the air at Western second baseman Del Franklin (partly hidden by Parker) in the second inning of yesterday's Sunset League contest. Parker's rough tactics went for naught as Franklin got the throw off to complete the double play. Franklin participated in three twin-killings during the contest. He has been the key man in nine double plays during 13 loop games played by the Pioneers.
(Bulletin Photo by Mike Robinson)

Pioneers Beat Oilers; Sunset Decider Friday

Turning the double play was always a priority for me.

The following day the *Orange County Register* had a front page photo in the sports section of Parker hurling his body at me while ducking at the last minute as the ball flew an inch from his ear. Under the photo was the caption: "Tom Parker's rough tactics go for naught as Dell Franklin completes his third double play of the game." An accompanying article went on to report I led the league in DP's, doubles, stolen bases, had made only one error, and struck out once this season. The same game of the three DP's I roped two doubles. Dad was at the game, sitting with Baltimore and Milwaukee scouts. When I got home that night, he said, "You're really racking that pea, but you're not getting enough steam on your double play relay. You can nail these high school kids, but in the big leagues you need more carry on your peg."

"I thought I hung in there pretty good."

"You're supposed to."

A Pox on the Prom

"Yah know, Dell," Ferg told me, the wild glint in his eye. "If rogues like us make it to the big leagues we'll be fightin' off the pussy, and they'll be cream of the crop. Any guy ever wore the big league uniform's had more women than he can count."

And he twisted my ear.

On the ball field, we continued to win. The *Orange County Register* and *Anaheim Bulletin* wrote up our team, and the student body, always obsessed with football and sometimes basketball, filled La Palma Park for the first time ever. Walking down the corridors with Fergie, fellow students—even girls!—smiled and waved at us like we were celebrities. The most popular pretty girls began to show up at our games with members of the political class of striving achievers, stomping during rallies and cheering our successes.

One afternoon, sitting directly behind my dad and a cluster of scouts, was Shari. As always, she was clad in billowy ankle-length skirt revealing nothing, high-necked sweater, hair perfect, posture prim and self-assured, occasionally clapping, a smiling queen paying homage to her minions. We won the game, and I hit some rockets and ran the bases like a wild man, dirtying my uniform.

Next day in English class I slouched in back studying her white neck in the front row. She had the clearest, pearliest skin, the bluest eyes, wore no make-up. When she talked she looked right at you. She listened intently and liked to smile. When class ended, she stopped me outside the door.

"Dell, I just wanted to tell you what a good game you played yesterday. You are such a good baseball player."

I shuffled and grunted as she held her books against her ample chest. "I also think you're a very good writer, and should be in Mrs. Rogers creative writing class."

"Yeh well." I shrugged. Fergie lurked down the hallway, holding hands with Tammy, who he was fucking on a regular basis in his brother's car at the drive-in movie, and his eyes twinkled with lascivious mischief.

Shari stepped closer. "Dell, I don't think you're anything like you act. You put on this tough-guy act, so gruff, but inside I think you're soft as a marshmallow. The act is just a cover-up, because you're afraid of being sensitive. I think deep down inside you're really a nice guy."

"I ain't so nice."

"Why must you talk like a...street thug? You're not fooling me one minute, Dell Franklin." She smiled at me in a very wise and knowing yet fond manner. "I think you're an interesting person."

I blushed. "Yeh? Well, yah wanna go out some time then?"

"Well, right now I'd just like us to be friends."

I turned abruptly and walked off. Fergie winked as I caught up with him. Peering back, Shari looked stunned and hurt.

"Yer bloody sweet on her," Fergie said after she stalked off. "Look, she's a really high-quality girl, the kind that'll get under yer skin and fuck with yer baseball. She's a bloody virgin, I'd bet, the kind yah take home and marry." He leered at me. "She's comin' to all yer games, eh? Settin' yah up for the bloody kill. All you want right now, mate, is a bloody piece of arse."

* * *

We continued winning, and I continued ignoring Shari. One of her poetry class friends stopped me in the hall and asked who I was taking to the prom. I informed her I didn't go to proms. She said a bunch of guys, including one of the brainy social climbers, who was going to Brown, had asked Shari, but she hadn't yet made a decision. At dinner, Dad asked, "Who's the girl with the flawless skin and pretty blue eyes?"

I shrugged. "Just another devoted fan."

He winked at mother. "Nice girl, Rose. He's like his old man—good taste in women." He glanced back at me. "You still a fighter, or you a lover?"

Shari again pigeon-holed me outside English class. "Who are you taking to the prom—Fergie?"

"I hate proms. I ain't wearin' a damn monkey suit for nobody. I hate dancing. I hate everything about the whole stupid tradition. I'll go to the all-night party and get drunk."

She rolled her eyes. "You takin' Fergie to the all-night party, too?"

"He's taking Tammy. Maybe you can give him a big graduation kiss, eh?"

She issued me a look that said I still was not fooling her one iota and walked off, but came to my game the next afternoon, sitting directly behind my dad and the scouts, and when I happened to glance over at her she looked right at me, and smiled.

Taking Infield With "Big Klu"

A scout from the newest expansion team in the big leagues, the LA Angels, asked me to work out with them at Wrigley Field during their first series with the fabled New York Yankees. I arrived early, and dressed beside Ted Kluszewski and Steve Bilko, two immense first basemen, possibly the strongest in all of baseball, who platooned against right- and left-handed pitching. Both men were late in their careers and weighed around 250 pounds of solid muscle and nodded at me in a kindly manner as I slipped my 160 pounds into an Angels uniform. As a child, I had baseball cards of both behemoths. Kluszewski was one of the great power/high average hitters of his generation, a borderline Hall of Famer with a perfectly level pendulum swing, while Bilko languished, though still popping prodigious tape-measure home runs.

I hit early batting practice against their pitching coach, Marv Grissom. I was overanxious, trying to hit balls out, kept pulling low line drives foul, hitting the fence twice. Grissom gestured for me to calm down. I hit the fence twice more at 340 feet and then went out to shortstop as the Angels hit BP and began flagging down their wicked shots, wanting to impress whoever might be watching me.

Kluszewski, wrapped in an olive-green nylon sweat jacket, glove in his back pocket, walked out and stood by me as I pretended I was in a big league game. Somebody hit a hard ground ball his way and he skipped out of the way.

"Pretty dangerous out here, kid—a guy could get hurt."

I found my voice. "I figure I got to stop the hard ones if I'm gonna be any good, Mr. Kluszewski."

"Klu," he said. "Call me Klu." He watched me. "You got a good pair of hands, kid, and you swing level. But stay back." Then: "I got a helluva a knuckleball. Maybe some day they'll let me pitch." Then he wandered out into left field, where a cluster of pitchers kibitzed with outfielders, sneaked up on pitcher Art Fowler, enfolded him in a headlock, talked casually to the group, then dragged Fowler by his neck into center field to discuss something with outfielders Albie Pierson and Lee Thomas, and then continued into right field, where he released Fowler and resumed conversations with other Angels.

When starting shortstop Joe Koppe joined me at short, I moved over, and the first ball hit to him took a crazy hop and broke his nose. Blood spurted and he hustled into the training room. When we finished BP and I ran to the dugout, Angels manager Bill Rigney asked me if I wanted to take infield at 7:45 while they set Koppe's nose. Of course I did! The Angels retired to the clubhouse while the Yankees took the field and I remained in the dugout to watch them hit BP, their power hitters—Skowron, Maris, Berra, Howard and John Blanchard—popping home run after home run into the stands in right field or over the left field fence.

When Mickey Mantle came up, there was an electric buzz around the cage as sportswriters closed in and Yankees joked with Mantle after he missed the first pitch. He grinned and then, left-handed, launched a ball that left his bat with a different sound than the others and cleared the right field scoreboard like a golf tee shot. Nobody else had even reached the towering scoreboard wall; his blast had gone a hundred feet farther than the rest. His show of power was otherworldly.

When we took infield in front of a full house, Kluszewski was at first. I fired the first ball hit to me over his head and nearly hit somebody in a box seat and he told me to calm down. From then on I was snappy and accurate, except on the 3-6-3 double play, when Klu had me lurching awkwardly trying to corral his knuckleball and remain slick on the return throw. He gave me the knuckler on every throw and kept a straight face, and when we ran off the field he slapped me on the ass with his glove. Rigney nodded at me, very affirmative.

I showered and sat with Fergie and a couple teammates and their parents high up in the stands, including Fergie's mom and Dad. I asked Fergie if he'd watched the Angels take infield.

"Of course I did. Watched everything. Some arms out there, ey?"

"That was me at short—all alone."

"Yer bloody full of it."

"Joe Koppe broke his nose during BP. That was me, Big O, throwin' to Big Klu, my buddy. How'd I look?"

"Tell yah the truth, I couldn't tell the difference."

Fergie's mom chimed in, "He looked slick as the pros."

Meeting "The Kid"

Dad had no interest in going to ball games, did not follow the big leagues, but consented to take me to a Red Sox/Angels game at Wrigley Field when Joe Stephenson left us box seats. The game was unexciting, and Boston, with Ted Williams recently retired, was an uninspiring team. We left in the 7th inning to avoid traffic so Dad could get home early and sleep before going to work in the morning. The bowels of the dank old stadium were nearly deserted, concession stands closing as we hurried toward a ramp that would take us to the parking lot. Near a concession stand I recognized a tall, familiar figure talking on a pay phone attached to a post. I grabbed Dad and pointed.

"Dad, that's Ted Williams over there."

He halted, peered. "I think so. I think that's Ted."

"You know him, right?"

"Well, we said hello a couple times twenty years ago. He's a loner, Dell, doesn't like to be bothered. He can be a real pain in the ass."

"I thought you said he was a good guy."

"He is…"

"I gotta meet him! He's the greatest hitter of all time. You said it!"

189

We walked up to him as he talked on the phone. Williams wore a loose fitting sport coat over a plain white shirt open at the throat. He alertly eyed us, looking trapped and edgy, like a cornered animal. He finished his conversation and stared at us in a confrontational manner. Dad quickly told him he'd played against him before the war, with Detroit, and introduced himself. Ted's face softened and he smiled, shaking hands with Dad.

"I remember you, Franklin—line drive pull hitter, good anchor, level swing. I always played you near the line." He relaxed, asked Dad what he was doing these days, and when Dad told him about his business, Williams said he was glad to see a fellow ballplayer doing well, and then he glanced at me, as if he'd just noticed my presence, winked at Dad, and nodded toward me. "Who's the kid, Franklin?"

"That's my son Dell, Ted."

"Ballplayer?"

"Helluva ballplayer. Good prospect. Infielder. Got the good hands."

Williams appeared insulted. "Hands? Hell with the hands. Can the kid hit?"

"Got a double, triple, home run today, drove in six runs. Hitting over .400. Great pair of wrists."

Ted's face lit up and he offered me his paw, which shook mine lightly while I squeezed hard. "Thattaway, kid. Keep swingin' that bat." He shook Dad's hand again. "Good to see yah, Franklin."

Then he was gone, like a phantom. Dad placed an arm around my shoulders as we walked out of the stadium. "Quite a day, huh? Worked out with Klu, went three for five, and met the greatest hitter of all time."

"He played you on the line. He knows your game."

"He knows everybody's game. He probably remembers every goddam pitch he ever hit or didn't hit. He's a mad scientist. That's why he's great."

"They Don't Like Individualists"

The showdown with Anaheim for the league championship at La Palma Park was a huge Orange County event. The *O.C. Register* sports page ran a feature story on both teams with pictures up front. The stadium was packed with parents, boosters, students and scouts and fans interested in both teams. There was a special feeling of excitement in the air of a big game, where your ass was on the line and you were tested before a sold-out crowd.

As Stephenson warmed up, I considered dragging a bunt on him, especially since their third baseman played me deep. Whenever I got on base it unnerved him, because I knew his move to first and took liberties on the base paths that might embarrass him. I felt baserunning, more than any aspect of the game, defined a ballplayer, and that scouts often missed out in judging a player only by size, power, arm, and straightway speed instead of instinct and instant acceleration—my fortes. I felt my instincts were a weapon that enabled me to single-handedly intimidate and disrupt a team, especially in a close game, where my daring baserunning and taunting inspired my teammates and excited the fans, and that every eye was on me when I got on base.

But bunting Stephenson implied I couldn't HIT him. Anaheim scored 3 runs on us in the first inning. When I came up to the plate there was nobody on and two outs. I took a fastball on the outside corner and lashed it into right field for a single and rounded first hard, skidded to a stop, staring at Jerry, who stared back. I took a ridiculous lead, bluffed a steal, drew several pick off throws; then stole second easily. But he struck out Fergie.

That afternoon I got two hits off Stephenson and ripped two other pitches right at somebody. We came back to go ahead 4-3, but ended up losing 5-4. Stephenson went all the way and beat us—the best-hitting team in the league. After the game Jerry and I visited. Both our teams finished with brilliant records of over 20 wins and were going to the playoffs as favorites. Our dads stood nearby conversing as folks filed out. Several young kids sought and got our autographs. Jerry was contemplating signing a big bonus with the Red Sox back in Boston. He suggested I play Legion and Connie Mack this summer and build up more of a reputation and sign the following year.

Bill Lentini, my puppy-dog friendly and excitable American Legion coach approached me, grinning like a child, shaking my hand with genuine enthusiasm.

"I know you lost the game, tiger, but you were magnificent today and you've been magnificent all year. Nobody attacks the game like you do. You play with a vengeance. The game is yours. You're exciting. Nothing can stop you now. I can't wait till Legion season. You got it all, kid. You're the best damn ballplayer in the whole damn area, trust me, and I've seen em all."

I knew Bill believed everything he said. Still, I couldn't quite believe him.

As I walked off, Shari found me. "I'm so sorry you lost, Dell," she said. "I know how much it means to you." A couple of her girlfriends were standing back. "I hope to see you soon."

When I ate dinner that night, Dad said, "You need a haircut. Your hair sticks out of your cap. And you wear your cap too low.

And your uniform always looks sloppy. It doesn't look good. All that stuff matters to college coaches and big league scouts." He issued me a long appraising look. "They don't like individualists."

Well, truth was, since I was in grammar school, the last thing I wanted to do was look like everybody else, much less wear a uniform. They could take me as I was or shove it!

BIG MOE

A Nod From the Yankee Clipper

Scuttlebutt passed around by players was that DiMaggio was so quiet when he first came up to the big leagues that he'd go days without speaking to anybody and it wasn't because he was unfriendly, or a snob, but that he was shy and awkward around people. He'd been very poor as a kid, like most ballplayers, and uneducated. His first few years as a Yankee he had such a problem speaking he went to diction lessons with a private tutor so he wouldn't embarrass himself around the press, because hell, he was the biggest celebrity in New York, and probably in the country, outside of heavyweight boxing champ Joe Lewis and President Roosevelt, and here the guy could hardly express himself.

I've never seen a ballplayer make the game look so easy. He was never a guess hitter, because a guess hitter can't be consistent (except for Rudy York), but Joe just seemed to know what was coming, had an instinct or knack for knowing a pitcher's patterns, and it was almost scary the way he couldn't be fooled at the plate, all spread out in his stance with a short step into the ball. Same thing on the base paths. He always knew when to go from first to third and never got thrown out, and he always knew when he could score from second on a single. Even when he booted one, he never looked bad, had a way of gliding effortlessly in the outfield. The year he hit in 56 straight games he only struck out 13 times as a power hitter! I don't care much about statistics, because statistics do not always make a ballplayer, but that statistic was the most amazing.

Joe didn't trust many people, just a few teammates. He was well liked by ballplayers, though there was a certain amount of jealousy and carping among guys who played against him, guys who liked to poke fun at him and say he was dumb and stupid and arrogant and of course he was a Yankee, and nobody liked the Yankees, they held themselves aloof from the rest of us, like they were royalty, which is probably something I hate to have to admit is true. They had a great farm system, players who came up out of the same mold, so to speak, and the moment they put on those pinstripes and walked on the field, especially Yankee Stadium, they smacked of an arrogance that galled you. You hated them. They were intimidating. They were just men like the rest of us, but they seemed special, and Joe, he was a king even among that bunch, though he never showed off and quietly went about the business of beating your brains out.

I saw him in the hotel lobby where our ball club stayed whenever we came to play the Yankees. He had a room there. In those days, there were strict unwritten taboos about fraternizing with players on other teams. You didn't say boo; they were the enemy. But hell, I was a rookie, and like everybody else I was in awe of DiMaggio, or the Big Dago, as he was known among ballplayers. He was having an incredible year, doing it all, in his prime, on top of the world. There he was, by himself in the lobby, standing browsing a newspaper, perfectly dressed and groomed, a polished man by this time.

I went up to him and offered my hand and introduced myself, told him how much I admired the way he played ball and respected the game. He put down his paper and shook my hand. He wasn't the kind of guy to stare at you, being so shy, and stand-offish, almost like he was embarrassed by being who he was.

But he kept his eyes on me. "Franklin," he said. "I know about you. You're hitting the ball pretty good yourself." He kept staring at me. "Is it true you're a college man—that you got a college diploma?"

"Why yes, Joe," I said. "The University of Illinois."

Those dark eyes dropped, looked inward, then back at me, and I thought I saw real sadness. "I envy you," he whispered.

"You're an Outcast, Franklin, an Outlaw"

We reached the quarterfinals before El Segundo slaughtered our pitching staff with booming home runs, one by future big leaguer Bobby Floyd, and our high school careers were finished.

School now consisted of Fergie and me playing pool and barely graduating, so that a couple major colleges wrote me off as a student/athlete because of my terrible grades. I had no desire to pursue college. I wanted to play ball. I wanted to play every day or night, out from under Dad's shadow. In Connie Mack and Legion I played shortstop and began tearing up both leagues in the summer, hitting over .400 and driving in more runs than anybody in the line-up, stealing bases and tearing around the bases like a precision madman. Bill Lentini wanted me to sign and felt I could steal 50 bases in the minors. He told me it was a natural course that I, like any other kid my age, sign a contract, get away from home, and spread my wings playing ball somewhere a thousand miles away.

He told me Doc Bennett, his White Sox boss, who was sold on Fergie, would sign me at his behest. I asked did he LIKE me?

"He's scared of your temper, and he's not sure about your arm, but he'll sign you if I ask him to. He trusts my judgment."

When Dad and I discussed the possibility of signing, he said, "Listen, a guy like Lentini, he's never played ball, he doesn't have the sense to realize you're not ready for pro ball. When the time comes that you are, well, you're a late bloomer like me, and you're going to be better than any of these 18-year-old kids like Fergie. None of these kids'll last a season in the minors, trust me. I'll know when you're ready."

Sometimes Dad sat with scouts at my games. I had no idea what they talked about, but realized no scout could bullshit my Dad about baseball. One of them signed Bob Bailey for over $100,000. Stephenson got around $60,000 and through a loophole was able to pitch for our Connie Mack team, a literal Orange County all star team. Jerry was spectacular, mowing down hitter after hitter with an overpowering fastball and tight slider, throwing shutouts. Fergie signed with the White Sox. Tom Quick and Nash signed. Our Legion team won a few games in the Anaheim tournament and this year, though I played shortstop, I was picked as the starting second baseman out of 80 teams to play the Dodgers rookies team. Every player on our team was scheduled to sign, except Keith Erickson, a shortstop who went on to play pro basketball in the NBA. Several of the all stars made the big leagues.

"Just be patient," Dad urged. "You're blossoming, getting stronger and faster. It's a big advantage if you start as a man, not a kid."

"You waited until you were 23," I countered. "By the time you got to the big leagues you were 28 and the war started. I'm playing better than any of these guys who've signed."

"Look, you're not gonna get a big bonus because you're not strong enough yet. In a couple years you'll have more power, you'll be mentally more mature to deal with the ups and downs, you'll be strong enough to hold up to the grind of a long season, and you'll get more money, believe me. Right now you'll just be another expendable kid with a small bonus, playing for $400 a month, Fergie, Nash, Quick, none of 'em'll last a year, trust me."

If I didn't sign, I'd have to play in junior college. Already Mike Sgobba, coach at Fullerton High and due to be the coach at Fullerton JC, promised I'd be their starting shortstop. "You demolished our pitching staff," he told me. "I think you're the best ballplayer in Orange County. Come play for me. I can't promise you much at the JC level, but I'll get you a job."

Lentini told me to go play for Sgobba, a fair man who knew baseball, if I didn't sign. But the school was over 20 miles away. I began to consider nearby Cerritos JC, a baseball power dominating its level of ball and felt to be on a tier with most major colleges, and with a great coach, Wally Kincaid. I made up my mind to visit him, with no idea what I was getting into, feeling I was good enough to play anywhere and relishing going against the grain with a big chip on my shoulder.

In Wally Kincaid's office, which was ensconced in a first-class athletic complex, I announced that I wanted to play baseball there. Kincaid leaned back in his chair at his desk, not quite prepared for me, then sat forward and shook my hand without a lot of conviction and removed a toothpick from the corner of his mouth. He was around 37, about 6 feet tall, with small features, short hair.

"I watched you in a high school playoff game," he said. "You threw your bat after hitting a ground ball and argued with the umpire after you got thrown out and I thought it was pretty bush. Frankly, Dell, this is not personal, because I think you're probably a good kid, but you strike me as a hothead and a bit of a hot dog. I don't need that in my program."

I watched him replace the toothpick back and told him I realized I was all of what he described me, but that I was working hard to mature and was embarrassed at being a damn busher and that beneath it all I was a team guy who pulled for my teammates and "went to bat for them."

Kincaid was inscrutable as he moved that toothpick around, not really looking at me. He took the toothpick out. "There's no doubt you can play. There's a lot of kids in this area who can play, and I don't recruit them all, because some of them don't fit. Can you understand that?"

"I sure can, coach."

He leaned back, sized me up. "I usually trust my first impressions." He sighed. "I'm going to tell you right off there are no promises. But I'll give you as good a chance to play as any of the kids I've recruited to play for me, because I do think you can produce. I like the way you run the bases. And you can steal. And you can hit. We can use that."

Coach Kincaid stood and we shook hands and he welcomed me aboard. Kincaid had already won several championships and, like an assembly line, fed players to major colleges and the professional ranks and also bird-dogged for the St. Louis Cardinals. Crew-cut, he wore sunglasses and positioned his cap just right. I felt his persona was one of darkly-shaded windows into which one couldn't see, though he could see out. He talked slowly with no regional accent. He seemed methodical and meditative. He had not only established this baseball program, but pretty much designed their state-of-the-art ballpark and clubhouse.

Kincaid sent me to my class counselor, basketball coach Caine, who sat behind his desk studying my high school transcripts, then paged through my entrance exams, raising his eyes to survey me with some concern.

"You scored in the 90 percentile in math and English." He told me. "Those tests indicate you're an extremely bright underachiever as a student. You won't have to take bonehead English or remedial math, like a lot of these jocks. What happened with your grades? You kept going downhill from your sophomore year on and barely graduated."

"I didn't study. Just read stuff I liked."

"Well, you don't study here and maintain a C average, you won't play ball." After he got me my classes, he told me I should get a haircut the minute I left his office and then he led me through a tour of the athletic complex. While doing this, two scary-looking marine-like football coaches snapped at me to "get a goddam haircut!"

When school started, I made sure to attend all classes and found studies more stimulating and the environment less restrictive. Certain classes were conducted in cavernous lecture halls, and when the professors paused in a meaningful manner, students scribbled feverishly in notebooks before looking back up. I characterized these fellow students as on missions to earn diplomas that would enable them to find good jobs and become vital cogs in the machinery of American commerce. But I scoffed at them condescendingly because I was going to be a professional baseball player and avoid this predictable path set down before me by my parents and the parents of all my friends and just about everybody else who preached education, career, family, suburbs, etc.

My new teammates to a man were well groomed, preppily dressed, hair cut close at the neck and around the ears; polite, quiet, serious students. The only one who seemed to relate to me in even the most minute way was a third baseman named Fred Dyer, who I remembered as a fellow Anaheim tournament all star. Tall, rangy, muscular, with a blond bowl cut hairdo over a suspicious, worried face, Fred was from Whittier, where he'd been all league in baseball and basketball, a good prospect with a power bat. We shared two classes and struck up an interest in literature that led to exchanging books, as Fred was a rare intellect among jocks. Early on we both agreed we were wary of Kincaid. I asked him why he chose to play for Kincaid, who'd nicknamed him "Grumpy."

"He wanted me here. I was going to go to UCLA, and I could've signed, but I'm not ready to leave home. I want to graduate college. I think Kincaid's the best coach around, and I can learn a lot from him. What I'm trying to figure out is what YOU'RE doing here. If anybody isn't Kincaid's type, you're it. You're an outcast, Franklin, an outlaw."

"I like going against the grain, Fred—doing it the hard way."

"Why? We're talking about your baseball career, your future, your life. We're talking about going where you're wanted. Look at Mike Sgobba at Fullerton. He doesn't care if you grow a beard as long as you can play. He's a good guy. I almost went there. Why didn't you when he wanted you?"

The Misfit

When I showed up at our first practice, Kincaid checked out my John F. Kennedy haircut, wriggled the toothpick around in his mouth, and mentioned I might be showing off for the girl he saw me with in the student union, Shari, who'd somehow become my girlfriend and fellow student at Cerritos. She'd broken me down into a helpless victim of a young girl's beauty and acumen. I was love-struck and fully engulfed. She was planning our future and believed in my greatness as a ballplayer and as a potential serious and successful grown-up family man and provider.

During batting practice, Kincaid tinkered with my method of bunting, which I learned from Gene Handley, a master of bunting. No coach had ever tried to teach me anything, and didn't dare tinker with what Dad had taught me. Kincaid wanted me to keep my right foot back in the hitting stance and twist my hips forward to bunt in the usual crouch. I told him I was used to bringing my back foot up even with my front, which gave me a better look. Only time I kept my back foot in place was when I dragged a bunt for a hit.

Kincaid sighed. "Let's try it my way and see how it goes. The game is constantly evolving, and sometimes a new, innovative way to do things improves your game and helps the team. I understand you have sound fundamentals. I know who your father is. I'm not trying to undo what he's taught you. But I want everybody on this ball club doing it my way. So far we've been pretty successful."

I tried it his way, laying down several bunts. Kincaid nodded his approval. He was right. While hitting, he observed my propensity to pull every pitch. He asked me to go to right, and when I did, he nodded his approval. Then he suggested I didn't need to choke up the bat too much with my kind of strength and felt I should cock it a little lower on my shoulder. He felt what I was doing was too exaggerated. I told him I'd hit this way all my life and had good success.

"Try it my way, just to see what happens. You've got a good level swing. I'm not messing with your swing. I'm trying to make you better."

I stubbornly conceded, realizing I'd considered doing exactly what he suggested in the past. Kincaid was a sound, studious baseball man who'd dedicated his life to the game, his players, the program. But he seemed strictly by the book. He was a general, holding himself aloof from his players, occasionally showing his personal side by initiating traditional baseball pranks, like having one of his veterans put itching powder in my jock. It was Kincaid who did the kidding, orchestrating everything that took place on the field and in the clubhouse, and it was Kincaid who nicknamed us, referring to me as "Peanuts" after the comic strip character. Dyer felt Peanuts was all wrong.

"Kincaid knows you, Franklin," Dyer said. "But in some ways he doesn't."

Kincaid had played semi-pro/barnstorming ball, but not pro ball. He was a bright man. He worked with his players, getting out on the field, going over technical points, but he never, like my dad, fielded or stood at the plate. He was never excited. He was low-key, seldom smiling or raising his voice. There was an imperious aura about him that I felt served him well. I actually liked him.

"What's this guy like?" Dad asked.

"He knows his baseball."

"I asked you what he's like. What's his make-up? What kind of man is he?"

"I'm not sure yet, but I think he's a pretty solid guy."

"Well, you don't seem too crazy about him. You should've found out something about him before you went and played for him. That fella from Fullerton, Sgobba, he's a helluva good guy and a pretty fair baseball man, and he raves about you, thinks you're a great kid. He believes in you. He's the kind'll go to bat for you, Dell, and you don't find many of those in this business, trust me." His eyes penetrated me, the hard eyes that flared with disappointment in his son. "Where did Kincaid ever play? My guess is nowhere. Well, what can I say? You made your bed, so you sleep in it, make the best of it. Keep your mouth shut and go along with him and play ball. What bothers me is I know a lot of good college coaches who like your game, like Dedeaux at USC and Winkles at Arizona State, and I could've gotten you in there despite your rotten grades and horseshit attitude toward school. But you never consulted me, your father, who if anything has your best interests at heart more than anybody else."

"I realize that, Dad. I wanna do things on my own, my way."

He was baffled. "Okay, let me ask you this: how do you stack up against the kids Kincaid recruited?"

Most of Kincaid's kids had been all league at local area high schools. I'd played against most of them and felt I was better because I was faster and I could hit with anyone and play anywhere. But Kincaid wanted a certain kind of player and person and had a plan, a mission, something he'd spent his life researching and working at. And this mission was not to be fucked with.

"None of Kincaid's players are better than me, Dad, but they're different than me."

"Different? How?"

"They're like a fraternity of squeaky clean boy scouts who feel it's an honor to play for Kincaid. They are the model of the image Kincaid wants his team to project. They are a bunch of really good kids who study hard, and they're smart, but they're quiet, too quiet for me, and they ain't Fergie and they ain't me." I gave my dad a look he didn't like. "Maybe I should've signed, huh? I could have, you know, Baltimore and Chicago."

"Jesus Fucking Christ," he fumed, flailing his hand at me in disgust and walking off.

BIG MOE

Greenberg

Hank Greenberg and I got along well right off because we were fellow Jews in a game where there was hardly a handful of us in all of organized ball, much less the big leagues. Hank was a sophisticated man and had good taste in everything—books, clothes, restaurants, women. At that time he was a bachelor, a tall, handsome man, cultured, reserved, far more polished than most of the guys who played in that era, what you call a classy person. He dated Ziegfeld Follies girls. He always had a book to read. His philosophy on hitting was unique and on the money for a power hitter.

What I remember about him most was how hard he worked to make himself a better defensive player. Although he was one of the best average and power hitters in the game, he was like Gehrig in that fielding did not come naturally to him, and he worked as hard on his fielding as he did his hitting. He'd get the clubhouse boy, a coach, or anybody he could find connected to the club to hit him grounders after a game. He'd take ground ball after ground ball and throws in the dirt, sweating for hours long after everybody else went home. He made himself a good fielder because he wouldn't settle for mediocrity at any part of his game.

When it came to the Jew baiting, Hank, unlike me, didn't have the reputation of nailing a guy in a heartbeat if he heard somebody make a dirty comment about Jews, but at the same time he drew the line when it came to putting up with that kind of bullshit. He was not the trained boxer and fighter I was, but people knew better than to mess with him. He was a proud, serious Jew, and he didn't like it any better than I did when the front office brought down the rosary beads to the clubhouse. Hank was too successful a player, too big a name, to screw with once he established himself as a Hall of Fame caliber player.

He was the first ballplayer to join up when the war started.

Back in 1955 he wrote me when he was General Manager of the Cleveland Indians. He wanted me to manage a bunch of kids they'd signed for the California League up in Visalia, wanted me to teach and groom these kids for the big leagues, and at the same time he wanted to groom me for the manager's job at Cleveland in a year or two, no more. He promised me that job. He trusted me, knew I understood the game and had the respect of the players and was a good teacher.

But I had to turn him down. I was doing too well in business. I was stable and in one place and didn't want to leave home and beat the bushes and drive around in buses, and even if I got the Cleveland job there was no telling what would happen if I had a bad year because players weren't ready. Hank could get the ax himself or quit out of frustration from putting up with the idiots in the front office, and then I'd be left high and dry, out of work, at the mercy of the baseball fraternity, the organizations. You have to try and hook on with somebody else as a base coach, or as a scout or minor league manager or a front office toady, and that's the last thing I needed in my life, so I had to turn my old friend down, and he understood.

As it turned out, Kirby Farrell, a pretty sound baseball man, got the Visalia job and managed the big club in '57 and lasted one year and of all people was replaced by the biggest front office ass-kisser of all, Bobby Bragan. Hank didn't hang around long either. He was too smart to. We weren't great friends. We never hung out together, because he was gone in 1942. What we had in common was that we were ballplayers, and big-city kids, and Jews, and there would always be that trust, that bond, landsmen, and that was enough.

Warming the Bench

In early spring Kincaid gave me the second base position and in preseason games I hammered the ball and played airtight defense. I felt I was set. Kincaid seemed to have accepted me despite his initial misgivings. Then he brought in a highly regarded second baseman named Jerry Harmon, who'd gone to the University of Arizona and been disenchanted with the program and transferred to Cerritos. Harmon was a speedster, built like a whippet, appearing streamlined when he ran, but he was nowhere as explosive at the start or as fast around the bases as I was. He was a good ballplayer with an average arm and an awkward-looking slinging sidearm motion. Quietly intense, serious, private, Kincaid immediately gave him second base and moved me to the outfield as a platoon player. He liked me in center but said he had a kid coming out from the football team who had played that position.

I felt he had to play me somewhere to get my bat in the line-up, but he had his outfield set and sat me down when we played Fullerton. I watched some of my ex-teammates and kids from Fullerton and La Habra who'd witnessed me tearing up the Sunset league and Legion and Connie Mack ball. I felt ashamed and could not look at Sgobba or any of them. They played us tight, and in the bottom of the ninth, down a run, men on base, Kincaid pinch hit me. My teammate and friend at Western,

Gary Martin, was catching. "What the fuck are you doing pinch hitting?" he asked from his squat. "Sgobba can't believe you're on the bench. I haven't seen one guy in their lineup who can hit or play like you."

"Gary, I don't know what the fuck's going on. Christ, I'm hitting around .400."

"Why are you playing for a guy like Kincaid? You should be with us. You know all our guys, and they know how crazy you are. You'd be our best player. You're getting the royal shaft, man. This makes me sick, Dell. I ran into Fergie and he says you've lost your fucking mind."

I ended up anxiously hacking away at every pitch and then took a half-assed curve on the outside corner from a pitcher I hit .700 against in high school. As I walked off the field, Sgobba stood staring at me, shaking his head slowly. Kincaid was silently furious, as if we'd lost the final game of the college world series, which detracted from our reputation of invincibility, like the Yankees. He would not look at me or say a word, and I felt a cold draft from his coaches and second-year players. I'd let everybody down.

From this point on I was relegated to pinch runner. No matter how hard or well I played in practice games, I didn't play in games. I was ignored, a scrub, and began to feel estranged from my teammates, except for Dyer, who had injured his elbow and expressed a desire to leave Cerritos, which he felt was a bit of a "meat factory."

"Franklin," he said. "I hate to say it, but Kincaid's not gonna play you."

Dad wanted to know "what I'd done to get benched." He wanted to confront Kincaid. I told him to stay out of my business and let me handle it, not wanting a scene. On a Saturday afternoon I pinch ran and Kincaid gave me the steal sign in a tight game and I stole second and scored a big run on a single to left, thundering across the plate. Kincaid clapped his hands and smacked my ass and exclaimed "thataway, Peanuts" as his coaches got in on the adulation.

I hated the nickname, and it became more and more evident I didn't fit in with his chosen recruits. I was an oddball, a contrary kid incapable of conforming to a certain brand of college uniformity and rah rah bullshit. I didn't hang out with any of my teammates except Dyer. We began haunting a pool hall between classes. I warmed the bench for several games, watching Cerritos roll over mediocre teams and licking my lips at mediocre JC pitchers. Everybody was happy but me. I was slowly becoming unhinged on the bench, could not sit still, having never warmed a bench, in the past having found it intolerable coming out for one inning! I began secretly rooting against teammates, hoping they'd fuck up so I could get into the line-up and impress Kincaid, but it was beginning to dawn on me that he was not going to play me, and I wondered was he trying to deliver me a message he felt I needed as a person and a ballplayer.

When I peered up in the stands to spot some of the same scouts I'd seen over the years, one of whom offered me a contract, I felt like crawling into a hole and dying.

Dyer felt I should be playing. One of our tall, right-handed pitchers, Steve Wright, who had already been offered contracts, whispered to me before a practice game that he was going to "pipe" me every pitch. He did and I whistled two ropes for singles into left field. It did no good. Dyer was right—he was not going to play me. Fergie, Sgobba, my dad, they were all right.

I said nothing to Kincaid, who treated me like there was no problem between us. Dad and Mom sensed my despondent mood and tried to talk to me, but I locked myself into my room. I had no idea what to do. I didn't want to talk to anybody, and especially Fergie, who was headed to Spring Training with the

White Sox and scheduled to play in Harlan, Kentucky. I could have been with him if I'd stuck with Bill Lentini, whom I could not bear to face.

And Shari was beginning to sour on my moods and drawing away. We went to movies and afterwards necked and panted in my stinky, cluttered car as I tried to pry my way through her panty girdle, a literal fortress. I was no Fergie.

Introduction to the Real World

I was hanging out in no-man's land in the outfield during BP when I noticed my dad confronting Kincaid near the first base dugout. All activity on the diamond ceased. My heart thumped deeply in my chest as Kincaid lowered his head and looked to the side as Dad, arms-folded, gave him the "look" as he talked to him. When Kincaid finally spoke, he lifted his head slightly, at one point spreading his arms in a gesture of futility. Then Dad strode off in an angry gait and I steered clear of Kincaid, showered and quickly and drove home, where Dad fixed me with his hard, angry eyes.

"I can't stand a man who wears sunglasses when you talk to him. I can't stand a man who chews a goddam toothpick and mumbles and won't look at you. That man doesn't have a hair on his ass."

"I told you to stay out of my business, Dad!"

"I watched his team. I'm not saying this because you're my son, but nobody out there is any better than you and none of them can carry your bat. I don't know what you did to piss this guy off, but he's not the kind of guy you should be playing for." He sighed. "You really screwed yourself." He shook his head slowly. "I know how you're feeling, Dell, believe me. There's nothing tougher than sitting on the bench and watching somebody who can't carry your jockstrap. I watched guys like Bloodsworth and Hitchcock and Mayo and Webb, guys who were downright horseshit, playing my position, and it's an organizational thing, and it drives you crazy, you feel like you're losing time, it beats you down, but you can't let it, you've got to keep your daubers up, and we'll see if we can get you signed."

But the looked we exchanged said something different.

* * *

On a road trip to Visalia for a JC tournament, we took a caravan of mini-buses. Team managers and Kincaid's assistant coach, Howie, did the driving. Howie, a muscular, burr-headed ex-marine and former Kincaid catcher at Cerritos, drove our van, Kincaid sitting shotgun. I sat in back. Harmon and a few infielders sat in seats up front. Unlike the riotous banter and non-stop chatter of my high school team, these guys were cautious clams, treating conversation as a disease and clubhouse cut-ups and kidders like myself as heathens.

At one point Kincaid nudged Howie, and cracked, "Franklin's pretty quiet. Must be going crazy back there with nobody to talk to."

Visalia had a cozy minor league park. We stayed four to a room in an old hotel with fire escapes on the main drag. That evening Howie assembled us in his room and told funny stories of past Cerritos teams and his days in the marines, which "shaped him up when he was a cocky lost soul with no direction." Rock solid and brutally honest, he kept his eyes glued on me when mentioning a certain person on the team who would "benefit by going into the military, where they'd force him to grow up." There were lots of glances and nods.

After he excused us, I managed to corral Dyer and a big, amiable second-year outfielder named Charlie Neal, who I recognized immediately as minimally corruptible and not quite a Kincaid clone, down to the Dairy Queen on the main drag where we tried to pick up girls but ended up paying a wino to get us a bottle and a six pack. We watched the locals drive up and down the boulevard and struck out with the girls and eventually showed up slightly tipsy in the lobby an hour after curfew to discover Kincaid sitting in a chair and peering up at us from a magazine as we tiptoed sheepishly past him to our rooms.

Kincaid never said a word. The tournament was rained out and on the bus ride home he never said a word, the entire trip grim and silent. The next couple games I did not pinch hit or pinch run, not even when the situation glaringly called for it. In a rout, Kincaid used everybody on the roster but me. We were all anticipating a prestigious JC tourney in Fresno, another road trip as defending champions. When I walked into the clubhouse to read the traveling roster, my name was missing. Everybody else was on it. I gazed at Dyer and he shook his head and then his eyes widened with extreme alarm at the sight of me as I made a beeline across the clubhouse toward Kincaid's office. Two pitchers, Bailes and Raines, tried to waylay me but I shrugged them off, pounded on Kincaid's door, ripped it open and burst inside to find myself facing Kincaid as he sat in his swivel chair behind his desk, toothpick drooping in his mouth.

I felt myself the maniacal version of Murray Franklin as I started toward his desk. He stood facing me, no longer the phlegmatic stoic. Howie was behind me. I was breathing too hard to talk. Kincaid glanced at Howie and nodded toward the door, and he left, closing the door while I stood snorting fire at Kincaid.

I said something like, "What the fuck are you trying to DO to me? Why the fuck am I not on your goddam chickenshit traveling roster?"

Very evenly, toothpick out, he said, "You fell asleep on the bench. That's inexcusable."

"What?" I was aghast. "Bullshit. You can't be serious."

"I asked you twice to grab a bat, and you ignored me. Your cap was pulled low over your eyes. I figured you were sleeping, or else your mind was on anything but baseball."

"That's bullshit, too, and you know it. Goddam lying bullshit."

"And you're off the team. Get out of here. I've had enough of you. I never asked you to come play for me. You're a disruption. I've got 25 kids here. I'm running a program. You don't have the first clue how to be a teammate."

I began trembling. Maybe thirty seconds passed. Kincaid stood leaning forward in his sweat jersey, hands balanced on his desk. He shook his slowly, wearily, revealing deep creases in his face. "Look, I don't dislike you, Dell. I think you're a good ballplayer, but you'll be better off playing on another team, for another coach, but not here, not for me."

I was utterly depleted. Speechless. Kincaid sat on the corner of his desk. He seemed to be studying me, his first display of some shred of personal interest. "Have you ever considered doing something else, besides playing baseball?" Suddenly he seemed sympathetic.

"No."

"Look, baseball isn't everything in life, especially if it drives you crazy. Be a painter, a lawyer, a doctor, a carpenter, a teacher, try something else. Maybe you're really good at something you don't even know about."

I couldn't look at him. "I was out of line busting in here. I know better. I'm sorry."

He looked troubled, but at the same time I realized he was relieved to have me out of his hair. "You know, I had battles as a kid," he said. "So I joined the military. It gave me direction and purpose. I saw how the other half lived, got a bigger picture of the world, and where I might belong. I thought about what I wanted." He looked straight at me, sans shades. "I'm not telling you to do the same, but it's an idea."

By this time my legs were noodles. I was about to collapse.

"Listen," Kincaid said. "I'm truly sorry the way things turned out. If you intend to play somewhere else, I'll try and help you. I would never do anything to hurt the career of you or any kid."

I walked out of his office realizing I didn't give one iota about his team, or any team. It was dog-eat-dog and we were all obsessed with getting ahead in our own baseball careers, using every level as a stepping stone—Little League, high school, Legion, college. Team spirit? Bullshit. I hated the whole concept. In the stock still clubhouse, none of my former teammates said a word as I cleaned out my locker. Steve Wright flashed me a look of commiseration. Only Dyer came over to say tough luck and we'd hook up soon.

BIG MOE

War Time

Almost everybody in baseball who was young enough and able-bodied (hell, we were professional athletes, in our prime, cream of the crop of American manhood) went off to war, or at least joined some branch of the military. It wasn't a time to think about yourself, or your career. Joining up was the decent and honorable thing to do. You didn't want anybody patting you on the back for it, even though you were giving up everything you'd worked for all your life. A pro ballplayer only has so many years, and here I was, 28, just finding my niche, in my prime, and I had to go, knowing I was going to lose my best years, years I could finally make some decent money and establish myself, knowing the guys taking my place were either too old to go, or young guys who found a way to get out of it for their own good.

We had this young kid, about 21, 22, Hal Newhouser, a big left-handed pitcher, a real horse, had just about the best stuff in the league next to Feller, and he said he wasn't going, and his mother supported him. He was a Momma's boy, spoiled, arrogant, a bratty kid, couldn't stand to lose or not get his way...and then the big dummy went on radio in Detroit and popped off about why he wasn't going, something about fighting his own people, and ended up getting some kind of medical deferment.

A couple of our players were cleaning out their lockers and getting ready to check out and go into the service, and they bounced him around pretty good. Tebbetts really went after him, boxed him around, called him yellow, and believe me, there were a bunch of us who wanted a piece of him.

I thought about guys like him when I was overseas in the South Pacific, living the dog's life, the heat so bad the ground cracked and you went a little crazy, and the malaria, the crotch-rot, and wondering if you were ever going to get out of this hell hole alive or in one piece; and you wondered about some of those poor kids storming those beach heads, little guys from the end of the line, taking it on the nose for the rest of us, doing the right thing, and you think about this big strapping kid back in the states, having his biggest, best years, winning over 20 games, throwing more innings than anybody in the big leagues, making a reputation for himself, getting famous, a hero to kids, an all star, making good money, and you wanted to puke.

The fans, they forget, because they're fickle, and later on all you hear about is a guy's great years and great records, and he WAS a hell of a pitcher, I admit, but as a man everybody on Detroit knew he was a horse's ass, selfish, no guts, put himself before his country while the rest of us did the dirty work while he took the easy way out.

Sometimes in life it's the things you don't do that haunt you, but then sometimes you have guys who don't know any better, or do know better but don't give a damn, and guys like that, well, you wouldn't change places with them for anything in the world, because at least you wake get up in the morning and look at yourself in the mirror and know your team-mates see the same guy you do.

A Mother's Soothing Balm

Driving the few miles home from the Cerritos athletic complex through the flat, featureless boulevards wedged in between housing tracts and strip malls and the dwindling dairy farms, everything looked different and seemed suffused in a gray pall. Slowly infiltrating me like a clammy fever was the bludgeoning reality that not only for the first time in my life was I officially extricated from the love of my life, baseball, but that there was a change going on in me that was not good; I did not understand it but it was verified by the looks of my ex-teammates as I left the clubhouse—this kid is a fuck-up and there is something very, very wrong with him. I was isolated and exposed as a psycho, trapped in the shell-shocked ruins of my surroundings like the last man on earth.

When I got home, mother had just returned from her job as school nurse at Bolsa Grande high school in Garden Grove and was in the kitchen preparing dinner. I didn't want to face her in this state, but she took one quick look at me and dropped everything to ask what was wrong, and when I explained what had transpired her eyes filled with far less sympathy than I expected.

She calmly told me to sit down. I sat down. She sat down. "Sometimes," said my mother. "certain things are meant to be.

Nature must take its natural course, and for whatever reason it ultimately works out for the best. Sometimes an experience you feel is terrible turns out to be a blessing in disguise, despite the pain I know you're feeling right this minute and will feel for a while."

"I don't see any blessing in disguise, mother. I should've signed. I could be off with Fergie, beating the bushes, instead of wallowing in this...goddam suburb. I hate it."

She looked me directly in the eye. "Dell, I know it seems hopeless right now, but whether you come to realize it or not, you are the kind of person who is going to have to bear up to some very tough periods in your life, a lot of pain and disappointment, because you are not like other people. You don't accept things as they are. You have always been independent, and rebellious, and people who are like that pay, always. In the end, this will make you a stronger person who sees more, and feels more." She actually smiled at me. There had never been a time when she didn't make things feel better for me at my lowest moments.

"How lucky you are, believe it or not, to be more perceptive and sensitive, to suffer more, because there will be that much more to experience, so many more horizons to cross! You're never going to be dull, and the world is full of dull people. Who you are and what you're going to be are as opposite from the limited world of baseball as you could possibly imagine, and believe me, I was in baseball with your father for a good many years, and I know what you'd be up against. Your father, in case you didn't know, knocked heads with coaches and managers and the front offices all his career, and he paid for it, and I'm not sure HE was cut out for that life, but he was such a brilliant athlete, and loved baseball so much, he didn't seem to have any choice. In an era when men ended up doing what their parents wanted them to do, or took what was available, your father did what HE wanted to do, and so will you."

Later, at the dinner table, Dad said, "Well, a blind man could see the writing on the wall." He gazed at me, not happy. "What about school? You staying in school?"

I was thinking, it was shameful to be eating my Dad's food under his roof like a freeloader while my friends were either away at college or playing pro ball or working. "I don't know what I'm gonna do, Dad."

"Well, if you're not going to school, you can work for me."

"Maybe I'll join the marines."

"Don't go off half-cocked for Chrissake! You've already screwed up one part of your life—don't ruin everything."

"He is NOT going in the marines," stated mother. "Not over my dead body."

Later, mother came into my room, where I lay on my back staring at the ceiling. She sat on the side of my bed. "I think you should seriously consider writing. That English teacher at Western thought highly of your talent and felt there was something inside you that was a writer. And I think as long as you're living here you should find a job other than working for your father. I think you need a change. You need to think about things. It's been baseball baseball baseball since you were a little boy. Maybe down the line you can play again, honey, but right now you need a break from it."

She kissed me on the forehead, smiled at me in a way that said things would be okay, and left the room.

Disneyland

I quit school and applied for a job at Disneyland, presenting myself to the interviewer as a clean-cut college student, and was hired as a sweeper at the "Happiest Place on Earth." I was issued a white uniform and clip-on black bow tie and handed a broom and dustpan and sent to scoop up butts and all small debris in Fantasyland, my territory, as one of the employees keeping Disneyland spotless and wholesome for swooning, camera-toting tourists. My supervisor, Roy, was a clean-cut guy around 30 in dark slacks, dark string tie, black shoes, white short-sleeve shirt, with a chain of keys dangling from his belt and a row of pens in his breast pocket. He was an intense team player who immediately set forth to motivate me: "If you work out, Dell, there's no telling how far you can go. This is the greatest place to work in America. You could end up a ride operator, or a supervisor, like me. Sky's the limit!"

Since Disneyland was non-union, everybody was underpaid but supposedly ecstatic because it was a privilege and honor and a status symbol to work at Disneyland. I was paid $1.67 an hour to sweep. Right off I found myself gravitating to implement my new trade at an area close to the Fantasyland snack bar, which was operated by a crew of pretty college girls with chirpy, upbeat attitudes, like Shari, who accused me of being a quitter and an immature child, gave me the boot, further broke my heart, and was engaged to a fraternity boy.

To keep my mind off the demise of my baseball career I volunteered to work six 10-hour shifts a week and Roy was very pleased, though he warned me to cease hovering around the snack bar and distracting the girls who were there for customers only! The deadening, mindless job was transforming me into a detached, robotic dullard. I began to despise Disneyland and its contrived, aggressive PR campaign of wholesomeness. I made no real friends and sought none. I worked, went home, ate, read in my room, avoided my parents; spent my day off body surfing in Huntington Beach.

Meanwhile, at the lunch benches during breaks, I tried to make time with the plethora of good-looking girls (the only kind Disneyland employed) and, on my own, sans Fergie, struck out over and over and began to see myself overall as a loser.

Fergie Tries to Rescue Me

Fergie was back in town after a summer of playing ball in Harlan, Kentucky, where he had a respectable year considering he was hobbled by a bad knee. The swollen, ugly knee needed surgery, which would be paid for by the White Sox, who had released him (as Dad had predicted) and the organization was peeved because they felt Fergie's knee was damaged (in hockey) before they signed him, a secret he kept from Bill Lentini and Doc Bennett.

Always confident and optimistic, he was a little subdued but not disillusioned or demoralized. He conceded there was very little glamour in the bushes, only hardship. In Harlan he could be playing a day or night game and hear gunshots from some of the Hatfield/McCoy-like mountain people downtown shooting at each other over century-old feuds in front of innocent bystanders who took it all in stride as a way of life in that blighted region of America. Fergie described Harlan as poverty-stricken, poorest of the poor, meanest of the mean, kindest of the kind, all in all good folks.

"What about the girls, Big O?"

"Awh, Jesus, Dell, you could spend a lifetime there and never find a girl half as good lookin' as the average ones back here. Yah gotta feel sorry for 'em, havin' to hook up with the uncouth bastards gonna end up treatin' 'em like shit. The half decent ones'll do anything to get knocked up by a ballplayer and get out-a that poor coal mining region.

Yah gotta feel for those folks, but I'm glad I'm out-a there and back home."

He'd lived in a boarding house with several other players who were either hicks or city kids and they had little in common but their individual ambitions to make the big leagues. The bus rides were miserable, the food terrible, the caliber of ball probably no better than college, the life draining, sleep-deprived, no privacy, lonely. He was almost glad it was over.

"I only saw one player on our team with a real chance of makin' the White Sox, a guy named Ken Berry, the best outfielder you'll ever see. He could play center in the big leagues right now, he's that good, but he doesn't have much of a stick. You're a much better hitter. I didn't see a guy in the league any better than you. I can't believe how yah fucked up, and went and played for that poop at Cerritos when yah could-a signed or played for Mike Sgobba. I never seen a guy fuck up his career worse than you. It just makes me sick. I talked to Bill Lentini and he just shakes his head. I thought you had some brains. I mean, you're twice as smart as me, cuz I'm just a bloody hard-headed hockey player from Moose Jaw, but you don't have a lick of sense, Dell. Jesus fucking Christ!"

When I got off work, we shot pool. I told him about Shari giving me the boot and he issued me the usual razzing over my stupidity and ineptitude around girls. He had made up his mind to use his experience as a pro ballplayer to try and get into radio and TV broadcasting. He could do hockey and baseball. What about an education? Fergie flashed his winning smile, pointed to his noggin, winked.

"Don't worry about ole Ferg. He's got an education all his own upstairs, and he'll come out smellin' like a rose. It's you we gotta worry about. I gotta get yah playin' ball again. It took me about a month to see I'd never make the big leagues, not with my abilities. If I hung on as a player I could maybe reach double A ball and later be a coach. But I don't want that low-payin' dog's life. But you? Except for yer arm, you can go all the way, and there's ways to cover up the arm if you can catch up with the high heat and run the bases and play like you do. I'm gonna talk to Lentini. Yer a sorry-ass excuse for what yah used to be right now, but Ferg's gonna take care of his buddy. If I gotta get yer ass signed, I bloody well will. Yah fuckin' weasel, yah don''t deserve as good a friend as me." He grinned and slapped my chest like a big brother. "Fuckin' Disneyland. What the hell yah doin' out there—imitatin' Mickey Mouse?"

I shrugged. "It's the cleanest, most wholesome place on earth, Ferg. Totally synthetic."

"Synthetic?"

"Artificial. Phony."

"Yeh, well, now yer talkin' about the world we live in, Dell, in case yah haven't noticed. Better get used to it or find a way to play the game, or yer in deep shit. Between that and the bloody crooked politicians, that's life."

"Well, I don't seem to fit in anywhere."

He placed a reassuring hand on my shoulder and looked me straight in the eye. "We gotta get you signed to play ball. If yah don't play ball, or at least give it a try, yah'll regret it the rest of yer life and wonder if you were good enough to make it." He squeezed my shoulder for emphasis. "We gotta get yah signed, if it's the last thing either of us do. You not playin' ball, lovin' it like yah do, and workin' at Disneyland, that's bloody criminal. It makes old Ferg sick in the gut."

I had not picked up a ball, bat or glove in months. Nights after work, and mornings when I awoke, were spent reading excessively, with a new-found hunger for literature. Steinbeck, Hemingway, John Dos Passos, Herman Wouk, Thomas Wolfe, Theodore Dreiser, Sinclair Lewis, Faulkner (with great difficulty), Upton Sinclair, Jack London, Bertrand Russell, Somerset Maugham, D.H. Lawrence, Mark Twain. My grampa Charley donated old, dusty paperbacks by the Russian masters. I was not ready for "Crime and Punishment." Dad was stumped by my hermetic reading transformation. It took him three minutes to fall asleep reading Harold Robbins blockbusters he kept at his bedside table.

"So what are you going to do with yourself, Dell? Work at Disneyland until you get drafted? Go back to school? What about baseball?"

"I need some time off from it, Dad. I'm waiting for the old itch to grab hold of me."

"You let me know when that itch starts. I know some people. All you've got to do is get on the field and show 'em what you can do." He smacked my knee in a fond manner. "And look, if you don't want to play ball, well, far as I'm concerned, it's all right with me."

"Mother's been talking to you, huh?"

"No, I've been thinking. I know it hasn't been easy for you, being a ballplayer's son, and especially a ballplayer like your old man. I've been hard on you, but it was always because I expected so much from you. What I didn't mean to do was make you so damn hard on yourself. I was always hard on myself, but in a different way, I guess. My dad was no athlete, so there was no pressure. Maybe things were less complicated for me. I could just go out and play, with nothing to lose, nothing expected of me. I was always loose in my approach to the game. I know baseball is a simple game, Dell, and it's not for a complicated person, who can't shut things out and thinks too much and lets the game drive him crazy. I could always concentrate on the game, and nothing else interfered or mattered. Then I became a professional when I'd never really considered it as a kid, because I loved it more than anything in the world. If it's no longer that way with you, well, like I say, that's okay with me, but if you still got that fire in your belly, I'll find a way to get you back in the game—if you miss it? Do you?"

I shrugged. Then: "Don't try and do anything for me, Dad. I wish it was like Little League, when nobody knew who I was and I made it. I feel like driving to Florida when Spring Training starts and just show up to see what I can do and what they think of me. Just some walk on. I'd even consider switch-hitting at this point. I don't know why. It's just a thought."

He was staring at me. "Damn boy, you're making a habit of doing things the hard way. You're working against near impossible odds."

I thought to myself, "If I don't play ball, it's the waste of a lot of talent for a game I love and know how to play, and of all the years I dedicated to it."

"We'll see how it goes, Dad." As I watched him walk away, not happy because his kid was not happy and on an unsure path. I felt bad for him, felt like asking him to play a little catch and pepper in the front yard, but it was far too late for that now.

BIG MOE

Facing Feller

When Bob Feller warmed up on the sidelines near the dugout before a game you actually saw his fastball rise about a foot, and the sound it made when it popped into the catcher's mitt was a sound unlike you heard from any other pitcher, even the hardest throwers in the league, guys like Virgil Trucks, who I played with, and Newhouser and Marchildon. It was like the difference between getting hit by Joe Lewis and some light heavyweight.

Certain guys got that "green-around-the-gills" look—like they were going into combat the first time—and came up with mysterious ailments on days Feller was scheduled to pitch, and certain guys up at the plate, you saw their knees shaking from the dugout. They were paralyzed with fear, couldn't get their bats off their shoulders. Other guys went up there and swung like they were going through the motions and in a hurry to get the hell out of there, because Feller was wild as hell and put the fear of God in you. He had a high leg kick that hid the ball until the last possible second, and his curve ball broke about nine inches to a foot very sharply when it was right on top of you at

Big Moe knocked down by Bob Feller during a Navy game.

nearly the same speed as his fastball, making it hard to distinguish what was coming at you, so a lot of guys were bailing out.

I always felt batting helmets ended the separation between the men and the boys. Without batting helmets you took your life in your hands when you faced Feller, and Feller knew that, fed off it, fed off the fear. He was cocky and ornery on the mound, had a big mouth, which he constantly shot off, even in the Navy, where it was common knowledge nobody popped off unless you wanted the brass to give you the shaft.

I faced him in service games on the East Coast before we all shipped out. We had great players on our Navy team—Hugh Casey, Peewee Reese, Phil Rizzuto. One game we turned six double plays. The best ball in the country was probably being played along the East Coast among service teams. Once, late in the game, I was up, Feller was pitching, with men on base, and an admiral, who pretty much put his team together and liked to have his say, like they all did, and bet on the games with all the other brass from all branches of the service like they all did, came out to the mound. This admiral tried to get Feller to walk me and load the bases, so he could face a weaker hitter he owned, a guy who couldn't touch Feller with a paddle.

I'd had fair success against Feller. I was a dead pull hitter and liked the challenge of hitting off him and you had to be that way or there was no use playing the game. But Feller was as stubborn a sonofabitch as there was in the game, and no goddam officer was going to tell him what to do on a ball field. He chased the guy back to the dugout and was so distracted he piped me a fastball down the middle on the first pitch and I sent it on a line right past his ear and drove in the winning run. This felt good, because he'd dusted me a week earlier.

He stormed off the mound, and that night on Armed Forces Radio he popped off about how no Navy big shot was going to tell him how to pitch and who to pitch to and so on and so forth, and a few days later they shipped him out, headed for the South

Pacific like the rest of us, and I hear he gave a pretty good account of himself out there, which doesn't surprise me. He was never short on guts or heart and he always stuck up for the Black players during barnstorming days when other guys wouldn't. He's what you call a good American, a patriot, and you have to say overall he's a good man, despite being a goddam mule-headed Republican and as tough to take off the field as he was on it. He was self-righteous as they come, and he could never keep his foot out of his mouth.

"You'll Never Be a Ballplayer"

Bill Lentini, who had been talking to Fergie, contacted me. He said he'd sign me right now if he could, and mentioned a few teams that were still interested in me, though nobody was going to give me any real money after getting kicked off a college baseball team—unless I was King Kong. He felt I made a mistake not signing out of high school while I had a chance to, but what was "done was done" and now it was time for me to "get back on track."

I visited him at his tire store and the diminutive Lentini put me in a bear hug. His big brown eyes were soft and melting. "How's my guy? Why haven't you called or come see me? I miss watching you play. You know I'm your biggest fan, Dell. You're like my own kid."

"Awh, Bill, cut it out. You're killing me." But it was good to see him and receive his always sunny support.

He poked me in the chest, kept his finger there firmly. "I know what's inside you, Dell. Going to play for that cold fish at Cerritos, you broke Bill Lentini's heart." He withdrew his finger. "I talked to Doc Bennett. I'm his right-hand man, his bird-dog. I told him I wanted you to come out and play for the White Sox winter league team. They play next Saturday."

Bill was the most relentless salesman and schmoozer this side of my dad. He convinced me to get myself in some sort of shape while Fergie went under the knife. I quit Disneyland and decided to re-enter Cerritos and change my major from physical education to English Literature. When I informed Dad that Lentini had gotten me a tryout, he grumbled, "I don't trust that guy. I've seen a thousand like him. They never played ball but they want to hang on and butter up the front office stooges."

"He's a good guy, Dad. He's intimidated by you. Everybody is."

My first game was to be played almost 40 miles away, out in the San Fernando Valley. When I got to the ballpark in my new heap, a dented VW, the White Sox were playing a team similar to those I'd played against with the Red Sox, who no longer had any interest in me, though I wore the same uniform Marco had given me. My hair stuck out from under the back of my cap. I saw a lot of decent prospects playing catch and partaking in exuberant chatter. I had not worked out or picked up a ball. Doc Bennett spotted me and barely nodded, a small, blunt-faced man with a fringe of white hair under a brimmed, light-weight hat of the like scouts wore. I felt he was not originally impressed with me and had been coerced by Lentini to give me a shot. When I reported to him he dismissively told me to report to Don Buford, who was running the team and riding herd on the players in a no-nonsense authoritative manner. I felt Bennett's attitude was a calculated tactic that old timers employed with new prospects.

Buford was a small, muscular Black man with the legs of a whippet. His uniform fit him perfectly, as if tailored. I remembered him as a terrific gutsy football player at USC, and as a baseball player he was an overachiever, a Nellie Fox-like self-made holler guy. Currently he was a highly regarded AAA player soon to be a big leaguer who'd paid his dues. Upon observing him this first time, his persona seemed fearsome, the kind of guy who had scrapped for everything and demanded nothing less from the kids now playing for him.

When I reported to him he sized me up from top to bottom. "Who the hell sent you?"

"Doc Bennett."

"He never said anything to me. Go warm up."

I got loose and fielded some grounders at second. I was rusty but strong. In the cage I dropped two perfect bunts down each line, and after fouling off a couple pitches I began rifling line drives to left, wanting to put on a show, for this was my showcase. Buford did not look at or talk to me or start me and I sat on the bench at the far end of the dugout, bored, not knowing anybody or wanting anything to do with anybody, listening to the little rooster talk baseball and display his keen knowledge of the game, which was exactly like mine. He was all business, treating this meaningless game as if it was the final of a World Series. In the eighth inning he told me to grab a bat, pulled me aside at the bat rack. "I want you to lay down a bunt."

"I didn't drive forty miles to lay down a goddam bunt."

"Either you bunt or sit down. We're trying to win a ball game."

I thought of flubbing two bunts so I could hit away, but a guy like Buford would see right through that ploy. Up at the plate, the first pitch was in my wheelhouse and I drilled it on a line into left field for a single. I hadn't returned from rounding first hard when Buford sent down a pinch runner. I hustled off the field into the dugout, found my bat and glove.

"You'll never be a ballplayer," Buford barked at me. "Get the hell out of here."

I was happy to leave on these terms and didn't bother to check out Doc Bennett in the stands. When Dad asked how it went,

and I told him, he grimaced, told me he didn't care how goddam far I drove, I should have bunted. Dad once said, "The
game I love is not run by people I like, but if you want to play,
you have to deal with it."

Creative Writing

At Cerritos, I decided to take only classes I liked—creative writing, English Literature, and a liberal arts agenda. I was now strictly a student. I associated with no one. My writing class, which was comprised of students who had been writing fiction, poetry and journalism in the past, and a few older people wishing to learn to write, was taught by a mop-haired, youthful man around 30 named David Edwards. He was rather shapeless, with a sensitive face. He wore baggy slacks and short-sleeve shirts. On our first day of class he delivered a detailed account of who he was and what he was about. He grew up in Hollywood. Went to Hollywood High with his dear friend Richard Chamberlain, star of the TV series, Dr. Kildare.

Edwards was proud of his Welsh ancestry and spent a summer at an estate in Wales partying and studying for his sabbatical with Richard Burton and Liz Taylor, whom "one could listen to for hours" as they recited Shakespeare or carried on between themselves while downing prodigious amounts of booze. Edwards' writing mentors were F. Scott Fitzgerald, "who wrote the truest sentences," Lawrence Durrell and Henry Miller. He shambled about clumsily and used his hands when he talked, seldom raised his voice, did not lecture, wished to be called Dave, NOT, God forbid, Mr. Edwards!

Our first assignments were to write about anything that came to our minds, so I dashed out a ridiculous vignette of a southerner named Virgil Pilch who was so lazy he "did less than nothing if humanly possible," and spent most of his time vegetating on the front porch with his dog, who was lazier than Pilch and rose up one evening to bite him on the ass after he expelled a ceaseless barrage of foul flatus.

I had no idea where such drivel originated, but I was nevertheless proud of my piece and read it over and over with increasing approval and self-congratulation. Mr. Edwards spent each class discussing writers and writing but taught no structure or plot, suggested no self-help books, renounced formulas, and instead urged us to read the great writers and the underground writers and learn from them, and, after we grew weary of imitating them, continue writing until we "found our own voice and style."

To my shock and mortification, after Edwards eloquently read a few clever short stories by students who I suspected sat up front and appeared *avant garde* and dressed in garish if utilitarian apparel, and whose pieces were accepted with relative civility, lukewarm praise and guarded criticism, he picked up a sheaf of papers and began reading my Virgil Pilch nonsense.

I instantly felt exposed, my stomach burbling battery acid. My face grew red-hot. I broke into a cold sweat. And although Edwards did not announce my name before reading my piece, heads began to swivel around to peer at the ex baseball player scrunched down in his chair in the back of the room. By the third sentence I was ready to sprint out the door and never return. People frowned at each other with quizzical expressions, as if to ask "who the hell could write this retarded bullshit?" Gruesome stuff. No story. No plot. No theme. Some coherency, yes, but no beginning, middle or end. A southern accent hokey and stolen from Thomas

Wolfe. Mr. Edwards finished, smiled, placed my assignment on his desk, then sat on the corner of his desk, and asked the class for commentary.

I was unprepared for the humiliation and excoriation that was about to come, and that was well deserved.

BIG MOE

Tuna Fish

Fred Hutchinson and I came up together in the Detroit organization and before shipping out to the South Pacific during the war we played ball on the East coast together and were in the Gene Tunney program, and since we were big league ballplayers the Navy made us chiefs. Fred was a ground-ball pitcher with good stuff. There was a lot of resentment on the Norfolk base toward us Tunney program chiefs among the old chiefs who'd spent their entire careers getting a chief's ranking. They were bitter, a tough, nasty bunch, and when Hutch and I—good friends—drank together in the club, well, these chiefs ganged up and gave us a pretty rough time, rode us hard, called us Tuna Fish, which is about as low an insult you can call a Navy man.

This went on month after month, and we understood it, took it in pretty well, but I guess these chiefs took this as weakness, and it got worse and worse, real personal and vicious, until these goddam chiefs were practically foaming at the mouth, embarrassing us in front of everybody, really enjoying themselves. They hated us, and I could see why: we had pretty young wives, we were ballplayers, the brass loved us

Murray Franklin posing with the Navy team in his usual spot, second row, second from the right.

and bet like crazy on our games, and if we won we got perks and so on, which were far and few between in those days, so that you almost felt guilty taking them.

Hutch was a big red-faced guy, some Irish or Scot in him, a serious man, but sweet-natured, a gentleman. But he had a long fuse and a temper that could blow quick, and he could fight. One evening we were at the bar having a few, and these chiefs were all around us and all over us, and it really got nasty and ugly as they tried to out-do each other. I finally looked at Hutch, and his face was redder than usual, and his mouth was tight, like one straight line, and his eyes went coal black, and his cheek was twitching. He said to me, very softly, Murray, let's take those goddam old salts outside and teach 'em a lesson.

We were in our pretty ice cream uniforms, all white and starched. I finished off my beer and so did Fred, and then he stood and pointed toward the door that led to the big lawn outside in front, and bellowed loud enough to be heard all over the base: OUTSIDE! The whole goddam bunch of you! We'll find out who's Tuna Fish, and who's Barracuda!

We went outside. Earlier in the year I'd put on boxing exhibitions for the troops with the world light-heavyweight champion, and Fred, he was like an angry ox, and we beat up six or seven of these chiefs, one at a time. A pretty good crowd formed, and it got bigger and bigger. We were hitting these chiefs so hard they were groaning and screaming. Chiefs were laying all over the lawn, moaning, crawling around on all fours, bleeding like stuck pigs, their uniforms full of blood.

Finally an older chief, one with all the chevrons who must have been in a few campaigns, with the big red boozer's nose, a guy with a real pus gut, he taps me on the shoulder and asks us to stop before the two of us kill all the chiefs in the goddam Navy. After all, he says, we got a war to fight with the goddam Japs over seas, and we're all in this together, and so we helped up the beat-up chiefs and got their caps for them and put their caps on their heads and led the poor bastards back into the club, and the chiefs bought all our beer and got us good and drunk, and pretty soon we were singing together, leading Navy cheers, and they toasted us, because we weren't Tuna Fish no more, we were Barracuda, and after that we could do no wrong with those chiefs.

Humiliation, Then Hope

"Well?" Mr. Edwards said, as he scanned the faces of those fellow students who were obviously embarrassed at the idiocy of my next story—which was about Clem Jark and a hillbilly woman—and hesitant to even lower themselves and comment on its debasement of the writing society. "Let's hear your comments."

A man around 50 with the old military buzz-cut, not far from me, stood. "This story...it did have some humor." There was consternation on his face. "But it went nowhere. It was just description. It was a...hodge-podge. I have no idea what he was trying to get across."

He sat down and a big, barrel-chested, bushy-bearded guy called J. Hampton Mills, who sat in the front row, stood. He published, edited, and was chief writer of a revolutionary weekly of about 4 pages that attacked the status quo with salacious and outrageous articles hoping to upset or arouse dull, impervious Cerritos commuter students who didn't give a crap about anything except a diploma that would lead them to middle class comfort, something J. Hampton Mills in his class tirades despised venally. He was ferocious, mid-twenties, and his voice boomed with authority; an imposing leader of the meager enclave of malcontents against the bomb, war, the gas chamber, America's inherent racism, and everything else that was wrong with the country.

"If this piece was a drawing it would be a cartoon for kinder-gartners…uh, excuse me, preschool kiddies just out of diapers. The scope was microscopic."

I tried to block out what came at me next like a barrage of suck-er punches to my very existence. Nobody defended me. It was decided that the writer of my supposedly anonymous piece did not possess the depth of a tapeworm, nor the knowledge and experience of an adolescent. But Mr. Edwards held up his hand like a stop sign.

"Humor," he said. "This is the only piece by this class with hu-mor, that actually caused a ripple. So I see promise."

Groans. Snickers. I was devastated. What the fuck was I DO-ING here? I should go back and kiss Don Buford's ass and Doc Bennett's ass, and Wally Kincaid's ass! I was a baseball player, an athlete, not a dork! When the class mercifully ended, I waited until everybody was gone so I didn't have to face any of them in the hallway. I was dropping the class! Shuffling out the door, head down, Edwards called to me. He sat behind his desk, grin-ning at me. He asked me to sit down, and in a trance I complied, in the front row.

"Don't get discouraged," he said. "I liked your story."

"Bullshit. It wasn't a story. It was garbage. I had no idea how bad I was, how stupid I was, what a disillusioned idiot I was until I heard that asinine gibberish. My crucifixion was justified."

He laughed; then sat forward. "Look, the purpose of this class is to expose the truth. You can't really write until you know your-self, and the best way to know yourself is to listen to your own words and see how they are accepted. It's painful, but writing is a painful business that calls for deep introspection. Life is pain-ful. Some people never consider writing until the pain in their life becomes unbearable and they have no alternative left but to write." He smiled at me, a big kid smile; eyes full of humor. "Let me tell you this, Dell: YOU are a writer. Most of the people in this class are aspiring writers who have been at it since they were young and they're pretty good at a certain level, but you are the only writer with an original voice. The first sentence I read, I KNEW you were a writer. Your words bounce off the page. Now don't make that sour face. Don't be so damn hard on yourself! Listen, I would never, ever misguide a student of mine. Dell, I don't know your background, don't know why you've chosen to write, or what made you want to write, but it seems to me this is your first effort, and there's a reason for that, and I'm here to make sure you pursue and develop this gift, because if you don't I would consider that a great waste."

I was dumbstruck. "What makes you think I can actually be a writer, Mr. Edwards—uh, David?"

"Dave...Dave."

"Arrogance. I don't know where it came from, but my God, you possess splendid arrogance. I'd pay to have it. You've got a fresh approach and a fearless verbal masculinity. It's inspiring for me as a teacher of writing to have a student like you in my class. Now you go home and get started on your next assignment, and think about the criticisms, and don't let them discourage you. I look forward to your next piece."

I was speechless. I found myself thanking him. He handed me a paperback copy of "Catch-22," by Joseph Heller. He informed me my first big steps should be to start my own library of classics, European and Russian masters and obscure underground books by modern writers. From them I would gain inspiration, joy, education, philosophy, understanding of the world and humanity, and the study of style. He said it was necessary I read "the bad stuff as well as the good stuff" so I knew what to do and what not to do. He didn't want any thanks. His gratification was from teaching and inspiring. Mr. Edwards.

Out in the hallway, striding past fellow students, I went from hating myself to considering I was special in some way, that I had a leg up on these pedestrian plodders with their narrow and limited ambitions. I was no longer a baseball player, I was a fucking goddam writer!

Transformation

Mother, upon coming home from her school nurse job, was careful not to disturb the budding genius clacking away on a $10 Smith-Corona typewriter in his bedroom. When she asked if she could read my pieces, my retort was, "Maybe someday."

Professor Edwards advised me to write about "anything that comes into my mind." Like pals, we sometimes met in the student union to drink coffee and discuss literature, writers and writing. I told him about my experience with coach Kincaid. He seemed amused, felt Kincaid a reasonable man considering he was a coach. When I pointed out Shari, sitting across the room with the handsome preppy she was engaged to, the two involved in intimate whispers broken up by sudden laughs, longing gazes, and tender touches indicating they were on fucking terms, I disclosed to Edwards she'd been my flame and dumped me because I was "defeatist and negative and without direction, and I didn't clean my car windows when we went to the drive-in movies."

Edwards burst out laughing. "Oh, heartbreak and rejection are great fuel for writers, Dell. I've found you can fall for many different types of women over the years, and the last thing you want at this point in your life is a steady who's planning out your future together. I've been in and out of relationships, and as a writer myself, it can be difficult. I'm still searching at 34. There are times I don't mind being alone. It was Somerset Maugham who wrote, 'No object is more deserving of pity than the married bachelor.' Seeing that young girl with that fellow, well, that's a sure sign she was never for you, but somebody else might be."

Edwards suggested I pursue sports writing. I could make a living and on the side write serious fiction. I'd ALWAYS be writing, and therefore improving. I informed Edwards I had a foul taste in my mouth from baseball and dreaded hanging out in clubhouses or locker rooms. Instead, I wanted to travel the world, then go in the military, and gather experience. Edwards said I already had plenty of experience and to write about my dad and our relationship, but right now I couldn't and instead found myself writing about people and subjects and situations I'd never experienced and knew nothing about. He did not discourage this, as long as I wrote.

Observing fellow writing students, I realized they had nothing in common with me or anybody I'd ever known. With the exception of a handful of 40ish adults, they were skeptical of established conventions and at times belligerently rebellious, often bickering with these older students who accused them of being naively idealistic. Edwards slyly orchestrated literary, social, political and even cinematic disputes and smiled as he observed them flower into snarling and vituperative shouting matches. Several of the more shabbily dressed girls, who seemed to purposely make themselves look the opposite of Shari, sided with J. Hampton Mills and hung out with him in a small clique in the student union. They read poetry and idolized the Beat Generation writers, especially Burroughs and Ginsburg. They were in love with Fellini movies, abstract art, and hybrid folk/protest music. Half the time I did not know what the hell they were talking about, but I could not wait to get to Edward's class and join the rousing debates, even if I was regarded as class stooge.

These days, walking around campus, I observed a vast sea of students with little inclination to question or rebel against the powers that be or test the authority of the system. They were sheep, searching for mates, pursuing a diploma and the gateway to soulless suburban anonymity, contentment, security, the procreation of more indistinguishable lives and the never-ending acquisition of material possessions and a tiny plot of turf on which to build shelter to justify their existences. My new classmates vilified such ambitions and in the process established themselves as eloquent haters.

This anger and hatred caught fire in my gut, providing me with a new, surging passion to express it. I hissed at the prissy and immaculate and well-endowed coeds I had previously drooled over and thought of as potential life mates. As for the girls in my creative writing class, whose attire approached mine in slovenliness, I viewed them with fascination, wondering what really lurked beneath the costumes and facades. They ignored me, except to roll their eyes and sigh when I expounded sententiously.

I began to take stock of myself. What was baseball, a simple game, in the great realm of discovery on this planet? How futile was it, poring over major league box scores with hunger every morning as I followed my idols? Christ, I actually had a brain! When Dad looked at me, the worry and confusion on his face was palpable and we had little to say to each other, though Mom and I seemed to be talking about subjects she'd always wanted to talk about with me, while Dad was suddenly odd man out.

* * *

Instead of hitting a ball around or playing basketball or hanging out with Ferg, which was what I usually did on weekends, I was invited to Professor Edwards's home for a writing seminar that was to be totally ad lib and spontaneous. I was to bring nothing but my typewriter. Dave lived in a slightly ramshackle turn-of-the-century Victorian home in a leafy part of old Whittier. Couches, chairs, sofas, futons, all blanketed, were scattered about in a spacious sunlit main room with wooden floors. Nearby was a kitchen, its countertop piled with dishes. A huge pot of stew simmered on the stove. Beer cans and wine bottles and glasses sat on ledges and tables. A stereo piped turned-down folk music. Everybody smoked and a few puffed marijuana. Did I want any? Uh-uh. I didn't even smoke—another reason to scoff at the stiffs. I did happily swig from a bottle of cheap wine and later grabbed beers from a fridge—all supplied by Dave.

The group consisted of about a dozen of the most venal anarchists—a few from our class—led by J. Hampton Mills, and various writers who'd studied under Edwards and gone on to four-year colleges or jobs or no jobs in the real world. Edwards told us to write about whatever entered our minds. I dashed out a slipshod account of an affluent girl from a prime suburban home (modeled after Shari) who falls to personal ruin and degradation and becomes a toothless, drug-bedeviled homeless harridan/prostitute. I titled it "Gidget Goes to Hell." Edwards, while reading this babble, had to halt a few times to laugh, though my cohorts refrained from such levity and exchanged glances indicating that they thought I was hopeless.

I remained aloof, observing from afar, a dog lost and wandering in the wrong backyard. These folks were self-righteous, intolerant, judgmental, sneaky, jealous of each other, cloaking their true feelings in lies lavishing praise on their precious, sometimes flowery, sometimes minimalist, didactic, acidic, amateurish, plagiary-ridden, bogus-experimental works. Dave occasionally winked at me, which helped soften my sense of estrangement and lameness, which I actually relished.

Mills actually lodged at the house. He found little salvageable in anybody's work. He now wrote a weekly column in the Cerritos school paper, for whatever that was worth in this institution of apathetic zombies. His main axes to grind were with our government and Americans, whom he felt were ignorant, intolerant, racist, greedy, cosmetically indulged, imperialistic, materialistic, complacent, spoiled, and, most irredeemable, indifferent to the misery of the under classes here and throughout the world. We were the most hated, hateful and monstrously despicable race on earth. Once, when I questioned his bombast, he called me a misinformed simpleton, and I called him a calculated eccentric and a pretentious fraud, to which he scoffed jeeringly and informed Mr. Edwards he must be "losing his marbles to allow a stunted suburban fool like ME in his seminar."

When the subject of Steinbeck, my new idol, came up, Mills said the great man was "written out, contrived, embarrassing..."

I countered, "You should worship Steinbeck, Mills. He fought for social justice and the underdog. They even called him a Communist, like they do you."

"Steinbeck's lost his way. You're a living, breathing cliché."

They had to separate us, Edwards in the middle. Mills retired to his room adjoining the front parlor. Edwards immediately warned me to watch what I said, because Mills liked to eavesdrop and collect material to use in his columns against his myriad enemies. I purposely lingered near his room and spouted my own particular brew of blasphemy, hoping to draw him out of the room for more confrontation, but of course he was non-violent and in contempt of all forms of competition (which was for children), his scholarly rejoinder being to lose himself in the clattering of his typewriter.

I drove home wondering what I was becoming and if it was any damn good.

BIG MOE

Front Office Whores

Bucky Harris and Gabby Hartnett were fine players in their days and a pair of true gentlemen. Hartnett was a Hall of Fame catcher, a guy I watched growing up in Chicago, and Harris played and managed half a century. They were almost too nice to be in baseball.

In 1946, when I returned from the service, they were at Spring Training with the Tigers down in Florida and were going to manage and coach our farm team in Buffalo. I'd had a great spring, hitting over .400, got myself into great shape after a three-year layoff. The general manager, Jack Zeller, called me into his office and told me they wanted to send me to Buffalo and start the season with Eddie Lake, Eddie Mayo, Bloodsworth, and Skeeter Webb, four guys who couldn't carry my jockstrap. Well, I refused to go down. I was half crazy with anger, and I wanted to kill Steve O'Neill, the manager, and the rest of the stooges in the front office running the team. I asked Zeller what was going on, because he wasn't a bad guy, and he knew I could play rings around those guys, but he said his "hands were tied." That's what they all tell you.

I asked to be traded. Zeller said he'd work on it, which was more bullshit. Hartnett and Harris told me to cool down and come up to Buffalo and play for them. Rumor was very strong they were both going to the Yankees the next season, with Harris as manager, and he promised he wouldn't go to New York without taking me along. He'd always liked me, believed in me, and he told Rose that, and tried to get her to persuade me to go with them, and SHE wanted me to go, too, but, like I said, I was too angry and fed up with the Detroit organization by that time to keep playing for a prick like Spike Briggs.

Harris and Hartnett understood and told me not to give up hope, because the Yankees wanted a Jewish ballplayer with some hitting punch to play third and utility. There was a huge following of Jewish fans in the Bronx. A perfect situation. When you're in a line-up with guys like DiMaggio and Henrich and Rizzuto, your batting average automatically goes up thirty points.

But hell, time was running out on me. I was 32 years old and felt Detroit would never trade me to New York, because they knew damn well I'd come back to hurt them and make them look stupid. So I was stuck between a rock and a hard place, really getting the shaft. Going to Buffalo at this point was humiliating, and so I got an offer to jump the big leagues and go down to Mexico for a lot more money than I'd make in the big leagues, and I took it, and told Briggs to stick it up his ass. A local sportswriter interviewed me and I told him, "I've always been good to baseball, but baseball has never been good to me, and I had to do financially what was best for my wife and son." I'd had enough of getting handed rosary beads before games and watching donkeys play my position.

In professional baseball, sometimes it's not just about playing the game, although it should be that way. I'm no Alibi Ike and I don't believe in sour grapes and I always look forward to the next step and never let the bad breaks keep me down and made the best of a situation, but sometimes you're in the wrong place at the wrong time and have no control over things and have to sit and watch the prime years of your career go down the drain, wasted.

And sure enough, in '47, Harris goes to the Yankees as manager and they win a World Series! If I'd listened to Rose, things would be different now. We'd probably be New Yorkers. But that's all water under the bridge, and you should never forget there's a lot of heartbreak in baseball, especially if you love the game and will go anywhere, under any conditions, to play.

And especially if the money's better.

Big Words

In the quiet of my room, mother made sure nobody disturbed the genius as I continued to churn out pages on my typewriter, having no idea where the words, ideas and scenes came from. I was influenced by anybody I read, and especially the last author I read. At class I was still going at it with Mills and his coterie and enjoying myself, even when one of his female followers told me snidely to "Get over yourself!"

Where was my best pal, the plain-speaking, plain thinking Fergie when I needed him? How I missed The Big O's uncomplicated views on everything. My father, like Mills, was equally repulsed by the "suburban hot dog" and mystified by his seemingly overnight transformation. There was no discussing anything with me now, especially since we'd never really talked about anything except baseball; though he often went to great lengths to impress upon me the benefits and joys of running his own business, watching it bloom, being his own boss answering to no one, a sly Jew outwitting his fellow Jews in competition and stealing their customers with better deals and cunning tactics, proudly screwing the government with ingenious and borderline illegal write-offs, putting people to work and providing them a living, possessing the freedom and new affluence to vacation in Hawaii with mother and buy an El Dorado Cadillac and eat in swank restaurants and fit mother in diamond jewelry and designer attire and put my sister and me, if I wanted, through college!

I would have none of it. I'd make my own way, my own money, thank you. The business to me was a waste of time compared to aspiring to be a writer. I mocked all the appliances, gadgets and gizmos he brought home on special deals with a sense of excitement. His sporting of success, his starting a business from rock bottom, "making gelt from dreck," was, to me, no big deal. To my mind his journey emanated not out of choice, but necessity, so that he was just another number punching a clock—be it his own—and controlled by a system drowning in material excess while wallowing in the American propaganda machine brainwashing us all into thinking having all this shit made us the greatest and happiest country in the world, when in truth, our blatant consumerism made us obscene and spiritually bankrupt in the eyes of great philosophical writers like Henry Miller and Jack Kerouac and most of Europe.

"Jesus Christ, where did all those big words come from, bird-boy?" Dad demanded to know as we sat at the dinner table. "You talk like a kid with a paper asshole. You don't know from nothin'. Go out in the world. And since when does a son of mine become so goddam uppity?"

Like mother and grandpa, now that I took a music appreciation class, I darkened the front room and listened to Beethoven, Tchaikovsky and Rachmaninoff, and even my sister gazed at me like I was off the reservation.

Dad turned to mother. "The kid's living under MY roof, eating MY food, he's making fun of his old man, and blowing so much smoke up everybody's ass we're all choking on it."

Mother retorted, "Oh, for God's sake, get a sense of humor, Murray."

One Last Gasp

A figure out of the past showed up at our house, somebody I hadn't seen since I was a small boy in Compton: Little Jules, Dad's old friend from the Mountain State League. He was bald as a marble, nattily clad, the same old lefty with hooked beak and the grotesquely bent arm from throwing decades of breaking stuff in the low minors. Exuding irrepressible effervescence, he was lavish in praise of our digs and Dad's success. He was now scouting for the Houston expansion team and working under head scout Fido Murphy, who was out in southern California trying to sign players to stock the rosters of their minor league system. Jules nearly crushed my hand when Dad re-introduced us, and regarded me with admiration.

"Look at the forearms on the kid, Murray, just like you, chip off the old block, spitting image, grown into a man." He grinned at Dad. "He's you with a good head of hair." I was sure Jules knew I'd been booted off the Cerritos team and run off the field by Buford and consequently tabbed a flake, malcontent, psycho. But Jules told us he'd heard I had "big league tools." He believed that if I had anywhere near the ability of Dad, which Dad quickly confirmed, there was no reason I could not sign and begin my climb to the big leagues, especially since I'd made the Anaheim tournament all stars. "Almost all those kids are playing pro ball somewhere, and those who aren't are in college and will sign someday. You're the only one who hasn't, and look, with ex-pansion, you got a great chance with the dilution of talent." He smacked my arm playfully. "It's the perfect opportunity."

Tryouts and exhibition games among prospects were being con-ducted on the UCLA home field at Sawtelle off Wilshire Bou-levard. I'd played there numerous times with Boston in winter league. I drove out with my old pal, Dave Sturrock, who was go-ing to Long Beach State to become a coach and wanted to bring me moral support. He kept reminding me I was the best ball-player he'd ever seen, better than all the guys we'd played against and that were now playing in the minor leagues. But when I ar-rived at UCLA I felt sluggish, like my body was in quicksand. For the first time ever, the sights, sounds and smells of a baseball diamond felt alien as I was surrounded by the smack of ball into glove and the knock of ball off bat melding with anxious chatter and a couple coaches yelling. The diamond was crawling with players warming up and taking infield. I'd never seen so many players on one field.

Jules spotted me and called me over and I was introduced to Fido Murphy, a very short block of a man at least 60 whose face resembled that of a rumpled bulldog with underbite. He stood along the first base line, his X-ray eyes quickly appraising my entire presence. "Jules here," he said in a gruff voice. "He tells me you're a good ballplayer, a chip off the old block. I remember your dad, and he was a helluva ballplayer. Good to have you aboard. Go warm up and we'll see if you're the player Jules says you are."

Among the excited, high-energy, chattering mob, anxious to display their wares, I found an older guy, perhaps 25, a first baseman, to warm up with. Most everybody out here was a free agent, and we were all looking each other over, and I realized I was the only one out here with a mop of hair protruding from under my cap like straw and a stubble of beard. I didn't FEEL like a ballplayer. Dad had urged me to get a haircut.

Fido had me at shortstop, where a few players awaited their turns to pounce on grounders and throw to first, reminding me of my Little League tryouts at age nine, a lifetime ago. I recognized a few players I'd once competed against. Some sleek Black kids were being timed running down the first base line after their last hit in BP. Fido's assistant coach rapped grounders to the infielders between pitches. Houston, like the Dodgers, was scouting Black track stars and trying to convert them into baseball players to intimidate teams on the base paths, like Maury Wills. I wondered did they possess the stealing and base-running instincts I did. Did they understand the fanatical, nuanced, neurotic blood feud of facing a hateful and hating pitcher? Did they have it in them to so infuriate an opponent with every tactic imaginable that it rallied your own team to go to war against them?

From shortstop, the field seemed slanted uphill and first base a hundred yards away. I felt a sudden urge to tell Fido I was a centerfielder, where, for a very short time, before I went into the doghouse at Cerritos, I felt a natural freedom and ease. Flat-footed, the first few ground balls handcuffed me, one bouncing off my chest. I didn't feel coordinated.

"Yer rusty, kid, hang tough," Fido hollered, and his coach lashed me another, which I trapped awkwardly on one knee (a no-no) to keep it from going through my legs. Then, not planting my right foot, I bounced a throw to first. The heavyset guy I'd warmed up with scooped it up, then pointed a glove at me and shouted, "Relax, kid! Take your time! You're okay, babe!"

Then Fido roared, "Where's the arm, Franklin? I thought you was supposed to have an arm. I thought you was a stud!"

I had no rhythm or feel for the game, continued to scuffle. I blocked balls, aimed throws that lacked zip—goosing the ball. "Jesus Christ," I heard Fido grumble to Jules, loud enough for me to hear, no doubt trying to motivate me, but clearly losing patience as I lost heart. "He looks like he's afraid of the goddam ball! He ain't half the player as his old man!"

Jules clapped his hands. "Shake off the cobwebs, Dell baby. We know it's been a while. Give the kid a chance, Fido."

Later, in BP, Fido and Jules stood by the batting cage while I hacked away. I hit one ground ball after another, but no rising ropes. Where was my pop and snap? The bat felt like 40 pounds of cement. The harder I tried to quicken my swing, the more I flailed away. I felt like slamming the bat over my own head.

"His timing's off, he's got a good level swing, like his old man," Fido conceded, "Okay, that's enough, Franklin. You got a game tomorrow night at eight. Yer startin' at short. Then we'll see what you're made of. Now hit one more and run down the line!"

I pulled one in the hole and took off for first and felt like I'd never get there. My uniform felt like a strait-jacket soaked in ocean water. Driving home, Dave said, "God, that Fido's an ass-hole, the prick couldn't stop bringing up your Dad. It's bullshit." At home, Dad asked how it went. I told him my timing was off at the plate and in the field. He asked had I practiced. I told him I had, but I hadn't.

One Dream Ends and Another Begins

I drove out to the ball field at Sawtelle for a night game in my old VW bug. Jules met me, clapping his hands; excited, telling me this was "my big chance, go get 'em, tiger!"

I sought out the burly first baseman who'd played pro ball and been released and was trying to hook on again, and we warmed up. He'd been friendly in a big brother way, encouraging me, but this evening I didn't say a word, and before we took infield he observed me closely and remarked that I didn't "look right." I shrugged.

Taking infield, the inertia began to infiltrate me. My arm, from trying to put too much on my throws the day before, felt like a rag dangling from my shoulder by a single tendon. It throbbed. I didn't care. I didn't care.

"Come on, fer Chrissake, let's see that arm!" Fido barked, scowling. "Let's see some hustle. LOOK like a ballplayer!"

My first time up, I faced a pitcher with average stuff. With men on first and second, I fouled off a couple pitches I should have nailed and finally bounced a ball to short. My journey to first base—where scouts had once timed me below 4 seconds—was one of those dreams where somebody is chasing you but you're in quicksand, and you wake up in a cold sweat just as you're about to be chased down by a monster. I hit into a double play, which I never did, unless I drilled a rope at somebody. And I didn't care.

Fido, pacing the dugout, was incensed. "Speed? Where's yer fuckin' speed? Yah LOAFED down the line. Yer a dog."

I booted one in the field. I came up again with men on base and hit into another double play, found myself slowing down as I approached first. Fido wouldn't look at me. I didn't care. My last time up I took a quick weak swing and dribbled one back to the pitcher and jogged down the line, holding onto the bat, wanting to smash something with it, anything, but mostly myself.

Returning to the bench, head down, Fido met me, bottom teeth bared over his upper lip in a vicious cast, as if I had personally insulted him and his way of life of some 60 years in the baseball business—surely sacrilege, akin to burning the American flag. I sneaked a pitiful glance at him, and his look said it all—"Get off the field you fucking disgrace!"

What he said was, "I seen enough of you, boy. Go sit on the bench. They sold me a bill of goods. You ain't got it. Yer no ball-player. Yer wastin' my time. I got kids here wanna play ball, not stink up the field. I can't believe yer Franklin's kid."

Jules would not look at me as I sat at the far end of the dugout. I didn't care; something was very wrong. I observed my tempo-rary teammates and felt a strange contempt for the game I had aspired to and been obsessed with since I was a tyke slapping a ball into my glove in the Hollywood Stars clubhouse as a 7-year-old. My head was spinning. I gritted my teeth. I hyperventilat-ed. Players along the bench stared at me. A cold black cloud engulfed me as I relived my lifeless slogs down the first base line, making me wince and cringe. Hitting into two double plays? Something was terribly, terribly wrong.

I rose and walked out of the dugout and without meeting the eyes of anybody, headed straight to the restroom, where I took off my uniform as quickly as possible and along with my cap tossed them in the trash can and walked out in my sliding pads and undershirt toward my car, hurling my spikes and glove into a thicket of bushes. I opened the trunk and found my shorts, put them on, closed the trunk, then swung my bat against a tree, my entire body vibrating with the impact, and then hurled the bat with my dad's autograph on the barrel like a javelin into infinity. Inside the car, I pounded the steering wheel and dashboard, then clenched my fists and punched myself in the head and face, bashing at my cheekbones and jaw, the hard clouts dazing me. I tasted blood. Slumped over the wheel, I unleashed a prolonged wail, a yowl, a scream, until my throat burned raw. Then I settled into quiet sobbing that would not stop.

BIG MOE

Mexico and Cuba

A bunch of us jumped to play ball in Mexico, including Mickey Owen, and a close friend of mine, Sal Maglie, who looked mean as a mafia killer but was as sweet and gentle a guy you'd ever want to meet. You were usually the only American player on your team, and winters, when I played in Cuba, you were usually the only white player.

In both countries, the fans were wild and packed the stadiums, and no matter where you played, that city pretty much closed down for the ball games. Those who didn't go to the games listened on the radio. Nobody loved baseball like these people, and the fans bet on every game, every inning, every player; they were madhouse crazies, but great fans, and if you played well they treated you better than you'd ever been treated in the states. You were a hero, never paid for a thing, and lived like a king.

But if you stunk it up and choked a few times in the clutch and lost them money and let them get to you, the boos and catcalls and insults and the garbage they threw at you, like rabid animals, they'd run you out of town, out of the league, have you on the first train home, like they did Dino Restelli, who came in with a big reputation but never got going. A lot of guys with big names quit and went home, because they couldn't take the fans, couldn't take the poor conditions of the ballparks, were scared they'd get lynched or shot, and they bitched about everything—the food, water, heat, humidity, language, the people, you name it.

I loved Mexico and I loved Cuba. First thing I did was make sure to learn the language, and if you tried hard to learn the words, well, these people bent over backwards to work with you, they would take you into their homes and hearts like you were family, because they were the warmest, most generous people...poor as they were they'd literally give you the shirt off their backs, or their last dish of black beans. I made good friends with my teammates and the people, associations I'd never forget and always cherish.

You can't imagine what places like Tampico and Mexico City and Havana were like in those days Havana was bursting with life, never went to sleep, it seemed. You could walk down the street and every cantina was full, the streets crowded, the trolleys running, the parks packed, and there were little bands everywhere, on street corners, in parks. The music never stopped, and the people loved to dance and sing, there was such happiness, like a festival that never stopped. A very romantic place for Rose and me.

I had one of my best years down there. I was still in my prime. I hit for power and average, led my team. Rose and I had the greatest time of our lives. We were

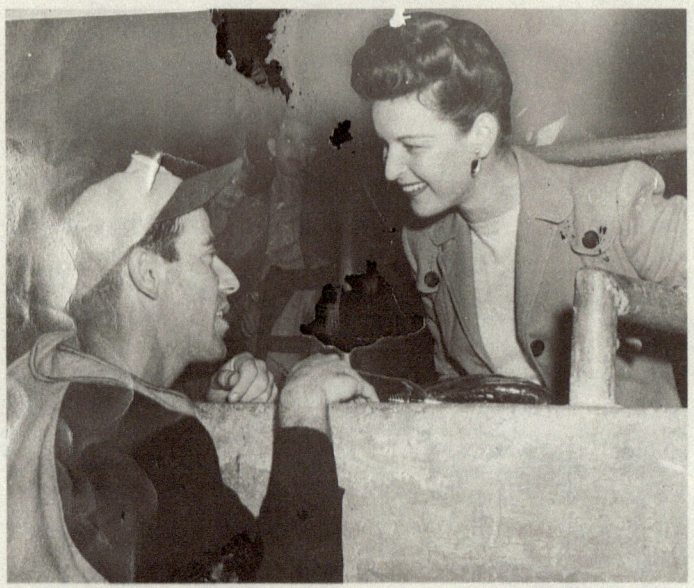

Mom and Dad in Cuba.

together again after being separated for two years in the war, and we really learned to appreciate and enjoy the little simple things, like sitting outside a café drinking a rum and coke and watching the people. It was probably the happiest time of our lives, and we both knew it, and milked every minute together.

There were some fine ballplayers, and some real characters down there. Minnie Minoso was just a great kid, always in a jubilant mood because he was playing a game he loved. Bobby Avila, who later won a batting championship with Cleveland, adopted a style of hitting I taught him and learned to make the double play as a second baseman when early on he was "spike shy." One of the best pitchers and hardest throwers was a mean Cuban with a missing front tooth replaced by a diamond. And there was this tall skinny kid with high pockets who hung around the ballpark in Havana, wanted to be a ballplayer in the worst way. His father was some kind of bigwig at the university and the kid was studying to be a lawyer, a very polite, bright kid, very eager to learn, followed me around like a puppy dog. I worked with him. He had a pretty good pair of hands, a decent glove, but he couldn't swing the bat, and you can't really teach that if the reflexes and hand-to-eye coordination and wrist action aren't there, and so the kid went on to bigger things, a kid by the name of Fidel Castro.

I don't know how long I would have stayed down there, because after all I am an American, wanted to come home at some point, and when the President of the league, Jorge Pasqual, a very rich man who bankrolled the league and paid us all our bonuses, died in a plane crash, the league fell apart. I had to get out of there anyway, because we played in tropical places like Tampico and Vera Cruz, and the malaria I caught in the South Pacific came back and nearly killed me. I lost 30 pounds, was weak as a kitten. So I went home, waited for my suspension to lift, and ended up with Hollywood in the PCL.

It's funny, but sometimes events in your life, and especially in baseball, take you to places you wouldn't dream of going to, and those places turn out to be the most pleasant surprises, the fondest, warmest memories. I think everything I learned down there, everything I experienced, made me a better, more thoughtful person, and helped prepare me for life after baseball.

The Beginning of a Soul

Vaguely, through the buzzing throb in my skull from the self-inflicted blows, I heard voices drawing closer as the lights went out in the stadium. Before me was a deep gully. I started the car, gunned the engine, and dipped over the edge, the car dropping and bouncing with a jolting thud, as if falling from a precipice. The shocks and springs cracked as my head smacked the ceiling. I sat there, dazed, finally got out and stumbled around. A voice shouted down at me from the lip of the gully. It was the first baseman, bundled in his warm-up jacket.

"What happened, man? How the hell'd you get down there?"

"Who the fuck cares?" My voice came from deep inside a well, strange to me. "Want this fuckin' car? You can have it."

"Hey, cool down, kid. It's just a game, you know. Don't go psycho on me. Everybody has bad games."

"Who gives a fuck? My life's a bad fucking game."

"Hey, get your ass up here, man. Right now."

I clambered up from the gully. He helped me over the lip, checked me out. "Man, you're all cut up and bleeding. What the fuck did you do to yourself?"

"I'm taking off. You can have the car."

"No, man. I don't want your car. I hate those bugs. I got my truck. Now settle down! You can't go anywhere the way you are."

"Hey, I don't give a fat fuck about nothin', so back off."

"Brother, you are off your gourd." He observed me staring back at him. He ordered me not to move. He pulled his truck over and backed it up to the lip of the gully, got out, withdrew a long chain from the bed. "Don't move now." He clambered down into the gully and hooked the chain to my rear bumper, clambered back up, and, after a bit of a struggle, a lot of noise and fumes, towed the VW up over the lip and settled it on flat ground. He got out of his truck and grinned at the car, which was sagging slightly. He smacked my shoulder playfully.

"It can't be that bad, man. It ain't the end of the world. You can't be throwing in the towel. I been where you're at and worse."

"No you haven't. Thanks for helping me out. I appreciate it."

He rolled up the chain, tossed it into the bed of the truck. "You weren't trying out there. In fact, it was like you were TRYING to fuck up. What's your problem?"

"Don't sweat it." My voice was a flat, distant monotone as I looked at his plump, easy-going face.

"I'm not sure you should be left alone. I don't like the look in your eye. You gonna be okay?"

"Yeh, thanks again for towing me out."

"Okay, I'm gonna get in my truck, and I'm gonna follow you out-a here, because I ain't pullin' you out-a that hole again. Okay?"

"Okay."

He followed me out of the parking lot and pulled alongside me on Wilshire, rolling down his window, gazing down at me. "You stay cool, guy. Don't do anything crazy. I don't wanna be reading about you tomorrow in the paper, okay?"

"Okay, thanks."

From time to time, cruising along Wilshire, I fought off the urge to gun the engine and slam head-on into a concrete light post. I wanted to drive and drive and never have to face anybody again, especially Dad, who would hear from Jules and be waiting for me—waiting for his son, who was nothing, while he, the Dad, was everything to everybody, while his son hated himself, deserved to hate himself. Fuck Dad. Fuck Lentini and Doc Bennett and Fido Murphy and Jules and Kincaid and the whole fucking baseball fraternity. Fuck Edwards, too, for trying to convince a callow pile of shit like myself that I had the talent and depth and internal stuffing to write about his fellow man. Fuck everybody. This is what it had come down to. Only the army would want me and take me, as they did all riffraff, washouts, losers, bums. Volunteer for infantry and combat, which was probably what I deserved and was destined for all along and just didn't realize it.

I got on Pacific Coast highway and headed north, with no idea where I was going. I considered driving nonstop until I went to sleep somewhere along the coast, but turned around near Santa Barbara and started back and ended up in Hermosa Beach, where I parked along the street and pushed my seat back and sat, unable to sleep in the wee, wee hours, fighting sleep and yet not fighting sleep, wanting to sleep, and finally out of exhaustion I nodded off until light crept through my window.

I walked down to the beach and found a bench along the strand. A soft pearl glow lightened the ocean like ballpark lights coming on in a twilight game. The eastern sun spread a dim light over the sand. I had no idea where I would go next or what I was to do, only that I was finished here. I had an eleven o'clock class with Mr. Edwards, the only class I'd ever cared about in all my years of schooling, and I'd let him know I was joining the army and refuse to let him talk me out of it.

As I sat, what had seized me at the ballpark miraculously drifted away, like a puff of smoke. No matter how tough the obstacles that lay ahead of me, I felt somehow released from a terrible burden that had filled me with such dread that I would never go near a baseball diamond or attend a professional baseball game for years. I suddenly felt strong and assured and determined, and for the first time in my life, ready for anything.

South Lake Tahoe

I was working the 3-to-12 evening shift at Harrah's Club as a barboy hoping to gain enough experience to become a bartender, so I could gain the inside track on getting laid, as I'd been in a drought since getting out of the army and was having no success during the height of the sexual revolution in California and all over America. In the army in Europe, at least I got laid by government-inspected prostitutes with good attitudes while on leave in places like Barcelona and Amsterdam.

After my discharge, I worked for my dad and lived in a cheap apartment in Long Beach and resumed my attempt at being a writer. Over an eight-month period I actually completed a novel I knew was mediocre but sent it anyway to a New York publisher and drove my old VW beetle to Lake Tahoe.

Since then, like my three years in the army and the time afterwards, I'd become a dedicated boozer, drinking beer and bourbon and vodka to quell the chaos still flitting through my mind and somehow getting me to sleep. At Harrah's Club, where I worked amiably with three great bartenders teaching me the trade, I pursued three girls: a recent college graduate from the university of Oklahoma who was a great sport but just 'wanted to be friends'; a plump blond graduate from Oregon State who loved talking literature and wanted to be an English teacher but just 'wanted to be friends'; and a luscious, sexy cocktail waitress from Memphis who was reportedly fucking just about any male with a cock and balls, but with me just 'wanted to be friends.'

Finally, after a couple months of this, I quit trying to write in my little one-bedroom duplex apartment and commenced gambling and drinking, ultimately sloshing myself into oblivion, losing all my money, gambling away my tips, having money for rent only because I won big one time and gave the winnings to my landlord. I hardly ate. I became bitter and angry and foul tempered. Only the dog next door had anything to do with me. Finally, in the Harrah's parking lot, my car went dead and at 6 in the morning after I'd gambled away my tips, I jumped on the hood, crushing it, and thumbed home.

I kept working. I hitchhiked to and from work, drinking prodigiously, still gambling away my tips and eating canned beans at the apartment. I was wasting away. I considered selling the VW and sticking my thumb out and hitchhiking across America, Jack Kerouac style, and whatever happened to me happened, and fuck it; at this point I had nothing to lose but my worthless failure of a life.

Finally, one evening around two in the morning as I thumbed home a car pulled over and when I got in I saw it was my dad.

"Who's the dog?" Dad wanted to know, looking me over. He looked worn and haggard, needed a shave. "I swung by your place looking for you and was greeted by a big dog."

"That's Duke, my new best friend. He's a Siberian husky."

We were driving along the lake on route 50, halfway between the clubs and motels and my apartment, which was eight miles away on the California side of the lake. He had flown to Reno, rented a car, found my apartment empty, and after asking the bartenders at the Keno bar in Harrah's where I might be, they told him they had no idea and so he searched the Sahara and Harvey's and was finally headed back to my place when he picked me up.

"He stuck that cold nose up my ass when I was looking in your window to see if you were alive and I thought it was a goddam bear."

Dad looked over at me, trying to size up my condition, explaining he'd come up after discovering I'd drained my bank account and quit writing mother, and chastising me for refusing to have a phone so I could stay in contact with them. Mother was worried sick about me. When we rolled up to the apartment he finally got a good look at me and almost gasped as he stepped close. There was a lot of moonlight.

"You look like you lost at least twenty pounds! You look like a goddam scarecrow and your nose sticks out like a goddam beacon."

He got his overnight bag from the car as Duke greeted us. "Jesus, great dog. Is he yours?"

"Lives across the street, but he's adopted me."

I opened the door and Dad came in and hit the light switch and asked, "Where's your goddam lights?"

"I gambled away my deposits. Gas and electric."

He cursed as I lit a candle. He peered around. "Jesus Christ, this place is the black hole of Calcutta. I'm almost glad I can't see anything, but I can smell it. What the hell's going on with you, Dell?"

I suggested we stretch our legs and walk Duke down to the lake, explaining this was a ritual. After the walk, he sat on a chair in the kitchen and said, "You have running water?"

"Yeh, it's cold. Tough shaving. Like the army."

"I thought the army might give you some direction, do you some good." He yawned. He looked beat. "Well, you get some sleep. I'll take the sofa. We'll hash things out in the morning."

I collapsed in my uniform. I needed a year of sleep. Somehow, having Dad with me allowed me to sleep and sleep and sleep, and when I walked into the kitchen around noon there was light, everything working, and the place had been cleaned, immaculate.

"Take a shower, dummy, it'll be a real luxury after the way you've been living." He stood, walked over. "What happened to your puss? You been fighting? Your eyes are piss-holes in the snow."

"You don't wanna know."

My statement bludgeoned Dad like a body blow. He sat down and placed his hand over his eyes and looked away and tried not to cry as I went to the shower and soaked up the soothing hot water and dressed in clean clothes and came out. Dad sat at the kitchen table holding the manuscript I'd sent to a publishing house in New York months back.

"I'm sorry," he said. "They rejected it. Hell of a birthday, huh?"

I realized yesterday had been my birthday. "Ah, don't worry about it, Dad. I expected it. I'm not ready. I just wanted to test the waters. It was a shot in the dark."

"You put a lot of effort into this, son, and I read it, and I think it's good."

"It stinks. It's amateurish gibberish." I walked over, snatched it from him, proceeded to tear it apart, and dropped it in the trash can. I sat back down. Dad stared at me, and his face was something I could not look at. I had made this man suffer, this man who was loved by all, who made decisions and built a business out of nothing to support his family and loved his family and was always there for his family and who had become involved with people in business and helped them out when things went bad and was admired and in some cases worshipped by them and whose teammates in the baseball world regarded him as the first guy they'd want to be with in a foxhole, this Jew, this Mensch, my father, crying, and why had I done this to him, why was I putting him through this?

"Dell," he said, looking up at me. "I think I probably screwed up pretty bad raising you…"

"No! You did the best you could, the only way you knew how. You always put me first, were always THERE for me. You were mostly right about a lot of things. I realized that in the army. It's me, Dad, I'm a different kettle of fish than you, or Mom, I just am, and it's got nothing to do with you, and I'm not trying to get back at you, hell, not at all, no, I'm just trying to grind my way through things, and it's gonna be the hard way, it's not gonna be an easy path I've chosen, and it has to be if I'm gonna be worth a shit as a writer. Look, I don't want you or mother worrying. I'm gonna be okay, Dad. Trust me."

The way Dad looked at me, I knew I must go to him, and I did, and we hugged, and he hugged me hard and told me he loved me more than anything on earth and respected me for the path I'd taken and wouldn't trade me for any son in the world, and I said I knew that, had always known that, and we disengaged and stood awkwardly, and then we sat down. Things calmed down and we sat drinking coffee, and Dad said, "We better go get your car running."

He was aghast when we reached the Harrah's parking lot and saw the heavily dented car. He got the VW towed to a garage, where a mechanic installed a new battery, while across the street at a diner he bought us bunkhouse breakfasts which, as always, tasted extraordinarily good.

We drove back to the apartment. He handed me a twenty. "This is to eat on. Don't gamble it."

"I won't. Gonna ask for extra shifts. No boozing."

"I don't want to see any more bruises on your face either, Dell."

"You won't."

We shook hands. He hugged Duke, got into the rental, beeped, and took off. I went to work and asked my supervisor for extra shifts and worked 30 straight shifts, some overtime on weekends, walked straight through the casino after work every shift, went home, cooked a steak for Duke and myself, took him on a walk, went to bed. I made back all I'd lost, paid back what I'd owed, and left in October, ready to hit the road like Jack Kerouac, and try and find out if I had what it took to be a writer.

I never gambled again, not even on a game, and nobody ever saw bruises on my face again unless I got in a good bar fight.

Big Moe had just established himself as a major leaguer when his career was interrupted for three years by World War II. He never made it back to the bigs.

Epilogue

When Dad died too young at 63, I had no choice but to take over his business. I had to collect money, pay bills, reassure customers of continued loyal service and special discounts, make deliveries, deal with worried salesmen who feared I'd stiff their suppliers and run down the inventory, maintain the stock and premises, and try and sell the kind of enterprise being squeezed out by major corporations in a town that had become a run-down dangerous ghetto.

At the time I was a carefree bartender in Manhattan Beach, 12 miles down the road, living the good life. Nobody expected me to succeed, except mother, but I managed to hold the business together for two years while working full time at the beach, then sell it and the building, turning the money over to mother, and getting the hell out of a situation I hated so I could go on with my life as a good-time Charlie and aspiring writer who was beginning to place articles in the local alternative weekly.

At Dad's funeral, a young rabbi urged me not to attempt the eulogy, explaining that "these things tend to be very difficult when one is too close to the deceased." His face was full of careful sympathy and understanding.

"You give the standard eulogy," I told him. "But I'm giving mine. I know him in a way nobody else does, because we both played baseball."

Me in 1978, by then publishing articles in local alternative papers.

The Jewish chapel at the cemetery was packed, every seat taken, people standing in aisles and in the back. Only three old baseball players attended—Chuck Stevens, representing baseball, and his two closest friends in the game, Tom Morgan and Jack Paepke. Besides relatives, the throng was made up mostly of shoemakers in their Sunday best and salesmen in their elegant suits.

I wanted to tell the throng about Jack Fessel, a kid who played on Dad's championship American Legion team back in 1955, but realized it would take too long. Fessel was a dead-end kid, wrong side of the tracks, already in trouble at school. Fessel, hearing Dad was coaching the team, showed up with his bulky body and ill-fitting uniform and wild blond spiky hair sprouting out from under his cap. He drove a dilapidated pick-up truck.

"Don't let him on the team," warned local coaches, and Dad's assistant, who'd booted Fessel off his junior high team years back. Fessel was an unorthodox, awkward player, but he threw accurately from the outfield, had a quick, level left-handed swing, and good judgment of fly balls. The team, composed mostly of reasonably straight-arrows considering this was Compton, and a few golden boys, and four kids who would go on to sign professional contracts, rolled their eyes when Fessel showed up.

Dad watched him hit in the cage. He made one adjustment—hold your bat lower on your shoulder and swing from there. Fessel hit ropes. He was stocky-strong. Dad encouraged him, smacked him on the ass after BP and then hit him every kind of fly ball and line drive in left field. Then he trotted out to left and talked to Fessel. He faced him, touched him occasionally on the shoulders. Showed him how to charge ground balls and get off his throws in one motion.

From this point on, Fessel was the first player to practice and the last to leave. He hustled like a madman. He was a smart baserunner. He was always looking over at Dad, wanting to please, and Dad clapped his hands, nodding, calling him "Big Fess," though he was only about 5'11." Big Fess turned out to be our best clutch hitter. He hit a ton. He dove after fly balls, threw people out. He became part of the fabric of the team, and the golden boys with nice cars and cheerleader girlfriends accepted Fessel, and Fessel, morose, kicked around like a dog with his tail between his legs when he first showed up, was happy. He was Dad's bobo.

Later, toward the end of our Anaheim tournament triumph, I asked Dad why he was so good to Fessel and so hard on everybody else.

"Dell," he said. "Always treat the underdogs with care, the black sheep, and they'll come back and pay dividends. You've got to give a kid like Fessel a lot of love, because a blind man can see he never got much at home, and everybody was down on him, kicking him while he was down. To see that kid blossom, it means more than winning. I don't know what will become of Fessel, he's a pretty scarred kid, but one thing he'll always have to lean on is that Murray Franklin, a big leaguer, liked him, believed in him, and he'll know he was a big part of winning a championship." He looked me straight in the eye. "Sometimes in life, things get tough, you feel like the world's got it in for you and you lose heart, and a kid like Fessel can look back at this summer, and, well, it might make a difference whether he sinks or swims."

* * *

Dad fought a virulent form of cancer. His 17-inch neck became a saggy beanpole, his blacksmith forearms, sticks. His voice reduced to a whisper. Before we ordered the doctor to with-draw life support systems, Dad asked me if he had any chance, and I told him he did not, and he nodded and whispered his thanks for my honesty and claimed he'd see me "down the line." I spent hours with him at his bedside. Even when he was totally incapacitated, he knew I was there, always reassuring him I'd take care of the business and mother.

So at the funeral I was long past tears. And in the eulogy I told the sea of mourners that the manner in which my father played the game of baseball was a reflection of his strong character, a quality he carried through life as a family man, veteran of war, businessman. More important than the surety that every ballplayer who'd ever played with and against Murray Frank-lin respected him, was the surety that every one of these men sought his respect. My father was incapable of letting a friend or even some helpless soul down, just as he was, as mother said, incapable of an indecent act.

When I stepped off the stage, the rabbi's eyes were strangely bright as he grabbed my arm and nodded solemnly. "You were right," he said. "You did well."

Goddam right.

There was a sort of wake. Friends and relatives drank and nib-bled appetizers at the house on the hill in San Pedro with the panoramic view of LA and the Pacific Ocean, Dad's dream house, in which he loved to entertain, and of which he was so proud. My girlfriend at the time, an artist/atheist/animal rights zealot with several cats, who felt close to Dad, repeatedly claimed to see a tiny light bobbing just over my shoulder, and she assured me this was my father watching over me, a guiding light. I believed her, and still do.

When all the guests were gone, mother, who had nursed, bathed, dressed and fed my father the last months of his life, and wit-nessed the day-to-day disintegration without once breaking down or losing her tenderness, or complaining, finally collapsed in grief. My sister Susie and my girlfriend tended to her. I wandered into the living room to finally inspect the numerous cards of Dad in his Detroit uniform that had been accumulating for weeks on the front table. They were from cities and small towns throughout the country, sent by fanatical baseball card collectors to be autographed. Enclosed in all the envelopes were five and ten dollar bills, as payment. Dad always signed the cards and added his best wishes to the names of all senders and returned them, via stamped and self-addressed envelopes, with the money included.

"I'll never take money from a kid for my autograph, Dell."

"Well, everybody's doing it, Dad. It's become a racket, a business, even an investment. Grownups are in on it, too. Lot of the old players didn't make much, so they're making up for it now. Like Feller, your old republican pal."

"I don't give a damn. It's horseshit. Your father never took anything out of the game he didn't deserve, and he's not starting now. I make enough money. Sure, I used my name to help get the business started, but that's different. I had associations with people. We were friends. I'll never take money for autographs. It desecrates the game and stinks of freeloading, and I've always hated freeloaders."

When Dad took his last breath in my arms, and the life went out of him, I removed from his finger the 1949 Hollywood Stars championship ring he had been trying to give me without success for 20 years and placed it on my finger. I felt an immediate surge of strength and hope. At the table I squeezed the ring and sat down and began answering the autograph seekers with small notes explaining my father was unable to sign their cards because he had died on March 16, 1978. I returned the cards and all cash, sealed the envelopes and walked down the street to mail them off.

I was a ballplayer's son, Murray Franklin's son, and this was the way we did things.

Murray "Big Moe" Franklin Career Batting Statistics

Year	Age	Tm	Lg	Lev	Aff	G	PA	AB	R	H	2B	3B	HR	RBI	SB	CS	BB	SO	BA	OBP	SLG	OPS	TB	GDP	HBP	SH	SF	IBB
1937	23	Beckley	MTNS	D	DET	51		187		49	10	3	6						.262		.444		83					
1938	24	Beckley	MTNS	D		94	435	385	91	169	31	13	26	110	13		38	17	.439	.497	.790	1.286	304		6	6		0
1939	25	Beaumont	TL	A1	DET	80		285		82	14	2	4						.288		.393		112					
1940	26	Beaumont	TL	A1	DET	146		538		156	30	6	5						.290		.396		213					
1941	27	Little Rock	SOUA	A1		95		374		109	18	12	3						.291		.428		160					
1941	27	DET	AL	Maj	DET	13	12	10	1	3	1	0	0	0	0	0	2	2	.300	.417	.400	.817	4	1	0	0		0
1942	28	DET	AL	Maj	DET	48	166	154	24	40	7	0	2	16	0	0	7	5	.260	.301	.344	.645	53	3	2	3		0
1943-45									MILITARY SERVICE																			
1946	32	Tampico	MEX	Ind																								
1947	33	Tampico	MEX	Ind																								
1949	35	Hollywood	PCL	AAA	BRO	38	90	82	12	26	6	0	3	16	0		6	6	.317	.364	.500	.864	41		0	2		
1950	36	Hollywood	PCL	AAA	BRO	151	563	507	56	132	20	1	8	59	2		38	28	.260	.313	.351	.664	178		1	17		
1951	37	Hollywood	PCL	AAA		110	364	311	37	80	11	2	13	49	1		39	21	.257	.346	.431	.777	134		3	11		
1952	38	San Diego	PCL	Opn		144	535	458	56	104	16	0	6	45	5		57	30	.227	.317	.301	.618	138		3	17		
1953	39	2 Teams	PCL	Opn	CHC	94	308	274	27	71	6	1	2	27	0		22	25					85	7	3	9		
1953	39	San Diego	PCL	Opn		49																						
1953	39	Los Angeles	PCL	Opn	CHC	45																						

Year		Tm	Lg	Lev		G	PA	AB	R	H	2B	3B	HR	RBI	SB	CS	BB	SO	BA	OBP	SLG	OPS	TB	GDP	HBP	SH	SF	IBB
		Majors (2 seasons)		Majors		61	178	164	25	43	8	0	2	16		0	9	7	.262	.309	.348	.656	57	4	2	3		0
		Minors (10 seasons)		Minors		1003	3371	3127	252	907	156	39	74	279	21	0	178	102					1363		13	53		
		Foreign (2 seasons)		Foreign																								
		All Levels (13 Seasons)				1064	3549	3291	277	950	164	39	76	295	21	0	187	109					1420		15	56		0

Statistics courtesy of Baseball-Reference.com.

www.ingramcontent.com/pod-product-compliance
Lightning Source LLC
Chambersburg PA
CBHW021612120626
46545CB00001B/187